FINISHING BUSINESS

FINISHING BUSINESS

Ten Steps To Defeat Global Terror

HARLAN ULLMAN

Foreword by Newt Gingrich
Afterword by Gen. Wesley Clark

Naval Institute Press
Annapolis, Maryland

Naval Institute Press
291 Wood Road
Annapolis, MD 21402

Library of Congress Cataloging-in-Publication Data

Ullman, Harlan.
    Finishing business : ten steps to defeat global terror / Harlan Ullman.
        p. cm.
    Includes index.
    ISBN 1-59114-906-1 (alk. paper)
    1. War on Terrorism, 2001- I. Title.
    HV6432.U42 2004
    973.931—dc22

                                            2004011821

Printed in the United States of America on acid-free paper ∞
11 10 09 08 07 06 05 04   9 8 7 6 5 4 3 2
First printing

—In preparation, caution
—In action, audacity
—In aftermath, humility

The United States will lead in bringing democracy and freedom to the greater Middle East . . .
President George W. Bush
November 6, 2003

There are no threats on our borders; however, there are no borders to our threats.
attributed to a French government spokesperson

Are we winning or losing the Global War on Terror?
Secretary of Defense Donald H. Rumsfeld
in a memo dated October 21, 2003

Contents

Foreword

arlan Ullman is doing for our generation what George Kennan, Paul Nitze, Herman Kahn, and Henry Kissinger did for the early Cold War generation. He is thinking widely, thinking boldly, and thinking critically. This kind of challenging book is exactly what we need if we are to come to grips with the life and death issues inherent in our national security situation.

It is precisely the kind of thinking Americans needed between 1945 and 1955. It is easy to forget, but there was a lot of confusion about the challenge to American interests posed by the Soviet Union. Was the Soviet Union an expansionist would-be world empire, or was it simply Russian national interests expressed in ideological language? Was the Soviet challenge a temporary phenomenon to be met with ad hoc temporary maneuvers, or was it a long-term threat requiring new alliances and new institutions?

Intellectual activists like Kennan, Nitze, Kahn, and Kissinger wrote, argued, and taught, and, as a result, the strategy of containment came into being, the Marshall Plan was launched, NATO was created, the Central Intelligence Agency and the Strategic Air Command were organized, and a forty-five-year plan of strategic containment was initiated.

Now we find ourselves in a similar period of uncertainty and ferment. Despite three years of speeches, two wars, and hundreds of billions of dollars in spending, there is still no clear understanding of the real threat or the necessary response.

Harlan Ullman sets out to change that in *Finishing Business*. He begins by correctly noting that the global war on terror is a misnomer. The real threat to America comes from an irreconcilable Islamist faction that has a coherent worldview and a very clear strategy.

Whether we have been inhibited by political correctness or by intellectual ignorance, it is a sad commentary on the American political system (and an even more bleak commentary on the willful avoidance of the European elites) that we continue to ignore or downplay the extraordinarily clear statements of Bin Laden and others.

Ullman draws the correct comparison between past generations ignoring Lenin, Hitler, and Mao when they were quite clear about their intentions. He returns again and again to the center of gravity being the Muslim world and the need for strategies that are based on winning the information war and the people-to-people efforts. These were skills we had in abundance during the Cold War, when the CIA's predecessor, the OSS, helped save Greece, Turkey, Italy, and France.

The CIA ran substantial foundations to sustain the anti-Communist left in Europe, and it collaborated with the Catholic Church to sustain solidarity in Poland in the 1980s and to distribute Korans in Soviet Central Asia as a part of a campaign to drive the Soviets out of Afghanistan.

The pathetic, virtually derisory, American information efforts since September 11, 2001, have been a major weakness and have crippled us in both Europe and the Middle East.

Ullman also understands that Iraq and Afghanistan are campaigns within a larger, longer war. *Finishing Business* ranges far beyond the immediate battlefields to identify possible nightmares that would make Iraq look simple.

I am particularly pleased with the recurrent theme of Pakistan's centrality as a danger. There has been far too little planning for the very real danger of an irreconcilable Islamist coup that would replace Musharraf with jihadist extremists willing to take enormous risks and already possessing over one hundred nuclear weapons.

Pakistan is the most dangerous country in the world today, and there is no comprehensive strategy to help the Pakistani people achieve the prosperity that would enable them to ignore the radicals and support a modernizing government.

Finishing Business also correctly focuses on Africa as a continent with great population growth (a lot of young males are available), combined with poverty, dysfunctional governments, and a rapid spread of both militant Islam and militant Christianity. The potential for Africa to become a vast breeding ground of violence across the "soft underbelly of Europe" (to use Churchill's World War II phrase) deserves far more attention than it currently gets. *Finishing Business* is helpful in highlighting the efforts of Gen. Jim Jones as the head of American forces in Europe to create a more sensible and systematic approach to Africa.

Finally, *Finishing Business* puts a spotlight on Congress, where it belongs. Neither the House nor the Senate is organized for national security or for homeland security. When Secretary of Homeland Security Tom Ridge has to report to eighty-five committees and subcommittees in the House and Senate, something is profoundly wrong with Congress.

Every person who cares about national security should insist that Congress clean up its own organization before investigating, posturing, and bemoaning the executive branch.

Congress will never reform itself until public pressure is irresistible. Hopefully, *Finishing Business* will help increase that pressure.

Anyone who cares about American survival will find this a remarkably thoughtful and wide-ranging book—a book worth recommending to their friends to begin a dialogue about rethinking the dangers we face and the strategies and structures we need to be safe.

Newt Gingrich

Author's Note

Two provocative arguments are central to understanding what must be done in securing the future safety and prosperity of the United States and its allies. First, while the term "global war on terror" (GWOT) is a powerful sound bite, it mischaracterizes the dangers and threats that lie ahead. The real danger is jihadist extremism.

"Jihadist extremism" is the perversion and hijacking of a great religion for political and selfish purposes. It includes what is meant by Islamic fundamentalism and radicalism but differentiates the revolutionary and political character of this movement beyond simply the use of terror. Hence, to avoid any confusion, the phrase "global war on terror" only refers to the policies of the Bush Administration. And, the task must be to defuse, contain, and eliminate the causes and consequences of what motivates jihadist extremism.

Second, the nature of the danger has been transformed from the Cold War threat of massive destruction in a thermonuclear war between East and West to one of massive disruption of society and all that it holds dear. Both of these arguments are expanded at length below.

After September 11, 2001, most Americans believed that Islamic terrorists, driven by intense hatred of us, our values and our free and open society, would strike again within the United States. But, as far as we know, Islamic terrorists have not carried out any further attacks on American soil. Yet sadly, as the world learned on March 11, 2004, with the killing of nearly two hundred people in Madrid, further attacks were inevitable. Despite that and other outrages abroad, support of President George W. Bush's global war against terror has eroded. Americans have not lost interest in what is happening in Iraq and Afghanistan, despite the near certainty that Saddam Hussein did not possess weapons of mass destruction (WMD), which was the administration's principal reason for a second Gulf war, nor as the peace in both lands became increasingly chaotic and violent.

In a democracy (as elsewhere), political debate often obscures reality. The dangers at hand go far beyond simplistic beliefs that hatred of America and its values are the principal motivating forces that explain why Islamic extremists have chosen to use terror against us. Instead, the appropriate phrase to use is JIHADIST EXTREMISM, reflecting political as well as ideological and theological motivations. As we will see, on a narrow basis, winning the global war on terror will be impossible. Regarding Iraq, the crucial point was not whether intelligence failed or was manipulated to provide sufficient evidence of Iraqi WMD to justify the case for war sooner rather than later, but rather whether the administration's judgment in attempting to bring democracy to that troubled region by force of arms would change the strategic landscape for the better and would prove correct or would be catastrophic for the United States, Iraq, and the world at large.

Tough cases making bad law is a legal aphorism. Likewise, tough questions can also make for bad politics. But, in the quest to protect America, tough questions must be asked and answered. The American political system prefers to deflect tough questions. Distorting the truth is not uncommon. Unfortunately, so are dissembling and prevaricating. Vietnam is a tragic example of how policies untempered by truth and candor prove catastrophic. Fortunately, Vietnam had no lasting strategic consequences.

The case for war in Iraq rested on the administration's certainty over Iraqi possession of WMD and the gravity of the danger posed by those weapons. In January 2004, Dr. David Kay, former head of the Iraqi Survey Group chartered to find Saddam's WMD, delivered his findings to Congress. Kay reported that, in his view, it was unlikely those weapons existed. In two sentences, the imminent threat argument vanished.

Immediately, allegations of intelligence failure captured headlines and sound bites. Embattled CIA Director George Tenet gave an impassioned defense of his agency at his alma mater, Georgetown University, on February 4, 2004—a day short of a year after Secretary of State Colin Powell went to the UN Security Council with "irrefutable" evidence of Iraqi WMD—and declared that at no time had the administration been warned the Iraqi threat was "imminent." Meanwhile the Bush administration began a long process of deflecting damning charges of failure to anticipate the magnitude of the difficulty that lay ahead in stabilizing postwar Iraq and Afghanistan and of excesses in waging the war against terrorism on the home front. Indeed many citizens and watchdog groups feared that the Patriot Act, passed with the nearly unanimous support of both houses of Congress, and other counterterror measures set in motion by the administration were on a collision course with individual freedoms and the image of America as a beacon for civil liberties. The revelations of former White House counterterror czar Richard A. Clarke—in his book *Against All Enemies*, his ubiquitous appearances on media shows, and his appearance before the National Commission on Preventing Terror Attacks Against the United States—have added gasoline to the already incendiary debate over Bush's policies with Clarke's charge that the administration ignored al Qaeda before September 11 and then embarked on an unnecessary war against Iraq at the expense of the global war on terror.

As America decides what must be done in waging the war on terror and in rebuilding Iraq and Afghanistan, it cannot shy away from hard questions. The Defense Department's policy regarding homosexual behavior termed "don't ask, don't tell" cannot be applied to the critical matter of making the nation safe and secure. The public must demand and get straight answers to a great deal of still unfinished business. Those answers must then direct the actions crucial to protecting the nation. That pursuit is a primary purpose of this book. And it begins with some of these probing questions.

We are told that the terrorist attacks of September 11, 2001, that provoked the global war on terror "changed everything." But what exactly have the deaths of three thousand innocent souls and the destruction of New York's Twin Towers and a wing of the Pentagon changed in America and the rest of world? And, if everything has changed, will America emerge safer, securer, and better for that experience and from the global war on terror subsequently declared by President Bush in response to those attacks?

Now that the nation is embarked on this global war against terror, Americans want to know if future September 11 attacks are likely or even inevitable and how much long-term danger the United States really faces from these groups and networks. As Secretary of Defense Donald H. Rumsfeld asked, "Is the United States winning or losing this global war on terror?"[1] In blunter terms, is such a war "winnable"; how do we know when we have won or lost it; what are the likely costs in blood, treasure, and infringements on individual liberties; and are there good metrics for answering these questions?

In the bluntest terms, given the strong likelihood that the United States will not find any large stockpiles of Iraqi WMD and indeed may have gone to war for what could be wrong or duplicitous reasons, how much political damage has been done by and to the Bush administration in its actions? And what has this damage done to American credibility and leadership in the quest to make the world and the nation safer and securer?

Regarding the breadth and extent of these dangers to America, are al Qaeda and other extremist groups, the avowed enemies in the global war on terror, the new Nazis and Bolsheviks of the twenty-first century—clear and present dangers with ambitions for power and control that threaten global safety, security, and stability and must be confronted? Or, will these extremists turn out to be passing storms that will soon dissipate or be dissipated by greater force?

Despite the powerful rhetoric proclaiming the justness of our cause and the danger at hand and irrespective of political party in power, can any U.S. administration make the nation safer and more secure and, as Rumsfeld asks, win this war on terror?

A refrain from a popular tune of the 1960s provides an important distinction— "the times they are a changin'." World Wars I and II and the Cold War were fought against clear and present dangers that threatened the United States. That clarity turned out to make winning them easier than we understood at the time. In those

---

1. See Rumsfeld's memo dated October 19, 2003, and reprinted in *USA Today*, October 21, 2003.

wars, the collective agreement on a common danger forged a "bipartisan" foreign policy that constrained many of the centrifugal political forces in a highly pluralistic nation and a system of divided government. Yet, yesterday's bipartisanship is absent today, along with clarity about the real consequences and full understanding of the danger.

The differences between the threats posed by the prospect of nuclear annihilation during the Cold War and today's Islamic terrorism are as profound as any in the nation's history. But full recognition and appreciation of these distinctions have not clarified yet. The result has been a focus on the symptoms, i.e., going after the terrorists, and not the causes that have produced these dangers. Hence, reactive and proactive strategies have been only partially effective. The current threats are far more diaphanous and borderless and cannot be defeated by military force alone. The survival of the nation is not at risk. Its way of life and standard of living are. The reason is the inherent vulnerability of a free and open society.

Virtually all nations are vulnerable to terrorism. Even in failed and failing states, disrupting commerce and society is easy to achieve. Iraq is a case in point. A relatively modest number of insurgents and terrorists have imposed a disproportionate impact through bombs and assassinations. It is impossible to defend an entire nation, even one as powerful as the United States, against a terrorist attack some, let alone all, of the time. Not only are national safety and well-being at risk, but also potentially intractable constitutional challenges are likely to be raised in fighting this war that extend well beyond past experiences of balancing freedom and security dating as far back as the Civil War.

In offering solutions and recommendations to deal with these dangers, this book has adopted a Dickensian flavor. On the one hand, it argues that this nation could be facing the greatest danger to its way of life since the Civil War, an assertion some will be disinclined to believe at first. If correct, the consequence is that the nation is vastly less safe or secure and may be for some time to come. The reasons for this assessment follow in the book. On the other hand, danger brings risk and risk brings opportunity.

The trick is ensuring that we are wise, bold, and courageous enough to seize this opportunity, a task complicated by our style of governance and a destructive quality to our politics. But, if applied with vision and skill, the huge political, human, intellectual, and physical resources that are going into waging the "global war on terror" can have great effect beyond this particular battle. Properly channeled, a strategic and economic renaissance could be generated. However, that goal will be as challenging as winning the fight against those who seek our defeat.

During World War II, America's leaders recognized that the folly following the World War I must not be repeated. President Woodrow Wilson failed to consult with a Republican Congress and thereby guaranteed that there would be no support of any peace treaty reached in Versailles during his long absence from America. World War II was profoundly different.

Postwar planning began in earnest in 1943. In 1944 Congress passed resolutions for the postwar period a full year before victory was won. Unless the foundations for a safe, secure, and prosperous community of nations were put in place, in the view that prevailed then, future world conflicts would become inevitable. At home, once the war ended the GI Bill and accessible federal home mortgages sent millions of Americans to college and made even more Americans homeowners. Government programs empowered a renaissance and were the seeds for future prosperity.

Abroad the Marshall or European Recovery Plan, the United Nations, the International Monetary Fund and World Bank and, as adversaries became allies and vice versa, NATO were created as mechanisms for securing the peace. The rebuilding and reconstruction of former enemies, probably the noblest as well as smartest of initiatives, turned Japan and Germany into peaceful democracies. Surely, as the United States looks to the future, it must be able to create initiatives that can have a similarly positive effect. This is the vision that is needed. But how is such a vision created and then implemented? That is a subtext of this book.

Visions are not guaranteed to work. Woodrow Wilson's idealism about the potential of the League of Nations failed. Within the current administration of George W. Bush, America's forty-third president, there clearly is a strategic vision. That vision was manifested in the decision to go to war in Iraq. With the stunningly quick military victory, some in the administration were thought wanting to move against Iran or Syria next. That has not happened.

The proponents of this vision, called neoconservatives for obscure reasons, reflected not merely power politics but Wilsonian idealism. Their notion was that military force could be used to bring peace, stability, and democracy to a region of instability, chaos, religious strife, and oil. These idealists, none of whom ever ventured in harm's way in war, have been challenged by a group known as realists.

Virtually all of these realists were casehardened in and by Vietnam and the war. Many were and are in military service. The conflict and differences between the idealists and realists are interwoven into the story that follows. And, as it turns out, the intellectual battles between realists and idealists, while in many ways as old as the founding fathers, had its current incarnation during the Kennedy-Johnson administrations. The present conflict between the two also raises the question of how well or badly the nation learns from its experiences.

All wars leave pieces of unfinished business. *Unfinished Business,* published in 2002, had the subtitle, "Defusing the Dangers That Threaten America's Security." This book extends that analyses and conclusions. Instead of identifying the business to be completed, this book provides a starting point for a new vision. In doing so, it will extol our most important resource—the people who will endeavor to make this a better and safer place to live.

Since September 11 I have spent a lot of time on the security issues of the day. At the level of the federal government, this has been frustrating. The inability to take decisive action because of the very nature of the political system that too often leads to bad choices, even for good reasons, would test the patience of Job. However, outside the Washington "Beltway," where daily life and duties of running towns and cities as well as the nation's military and security forces in the field leave no alternative except to act, one sees quite the reverse. Several of these "good news" stories are examples for Washington to see and perhaps even try to duplicate.

How New York and New Jersey are moving to protect their ports and places of ingress and how they are working to counter terror could be a very good story indeed. And they have application to homeland security. Internationally, how NATO is striving to make profound change, "transforming" itself to the challenges and dangers of this new world is a second example. Integral to these successes are the people who are doing the work. And, in both instances, these are early days with success still very much in doubt.

The Naval Institute Press does me the honor of publishing this book. Because of its audience many of the people and case studies that follow are in the naval service or engaged in things maritime. That focus does not diminish, however, the sweep of other agencies, institutions, and people who labor in those fields. I am grateful to the Smith-Richardson Foundation for a further grant and to the Center for Strategic and International Studies for placing the project under its auspices.

As noted in *Unfinished Business* and repeated, this book is not meant to be a comprehensive history. Selectivity is the rule. The intent is to use the various pieces of unfinished business as organizing themes around which relevant fact and record are assembled. In this work the case studies are provided as examples with relevance to enhancing and reinforcing our capacity to win not only the global war on terror but also the larger conflict against the causes, and not the symptoms, of what threatens us today.

Emerson wrote (as I used before), "In analyzing history, do not be too profound, for often the causes are quite superficial." That is this book's subtext. Any errors are my responsibility alone.

Harlan Ullman
Washington, D.C.
March 1, 2004

Acknowledgments

Far more people played a role in this book than space allows mention. I am indebted to the Naval Institute, the Smith-Richardson Foundation, and the Center for Strategic and International Studies (CSIS) for making this work possible. Many active and retired officers on both sides of the Atlantic provided important insights, especially Ian Forbes, Edmund Giambastiani, and James Jones. Gordon England, John Morgan, and Robert Earl offered wise counsel and support. Austin Carson and David Bill IV did yeoman work in research.

To former speaker of the House of Representatives Newt Gingrich and General Wesley Clark, I owe a special debt for lending their support and good names. Their presence underscores the need for a nonpartisan approach to security that is crucial if we are to succeed. Linda Earl served as my very able editor, and of course, Peter Rubie, my agent, was a source of strength. I would also like to acknowledge the men and women who serve this nation in and out of uniform and have shed their blood in our defense. Three who died recently had been particular mentors and friends.

Adm. R.L.J. "Bob" Long was among the wisest persons I ever knew. Adm. Huntington Hardisty was among the bravest. Both were former CinCPacs. And Adm. Thomas H. Moorer, former CNO and Chairman, allowed me to "room" with him for a considerable time, sharing both a suite at CSIS and his extraordinary advice and counsel.

Anthony McIvor offered a piece of vital criticism in setting forth the arguments and steps to defeat global terror at the very beginning of the book. I am grateful for that advice.

This list is purposely short. I apologize to any individuals who were important in writing this book and whose names do not appear. There is one exception: my wife, Julian. Since I am unable to do better than my praise for her in *Unfinished Business,* the operative term is "ditto," times ten.

Ten Steps To Defeat Global Terror

1. *Americans must recognize that the term "global war on terror" implies an aim of winning that is simply not achievable.* There is no way that "the global war on terror," like wars against crime, drugs, poverty, and disease, can ever bring total victory. Instead we must understand that the battle is against "jihadist extremism" and particularly those individuals who have captured and perverted a respected religion for political and revolutionary purposes and who use terror as a tool and a tactic to achieve political ends.

2. *Americans must recognize the extent of the real danger posed by jihadist extremism is political, in which terror is not an end in itself,* and the broader aims of these organizations and individuals are not significantly different from those of Lenin and the Bolsheviks one hundred years ago or Hitler and the National Socialist Party eighty years ago. The aim is to establish some form of regime or regimes steeped in the teachings of radical Islam with access to Saudi money and Pakistani nuclear weapons and with the broader intent of spreading their religion globally.

3. *Last, Americans must recognize the danger posed by jihadist extremism is not the massive destruction of society through thermonuclear war. The new danger is one of massive disruption through real or threatened terrorist attacks* aimed at dislocating and disrupting our lives, doing great harm to our economies and our perceptions of safety and security, and causing us to overreact in ways that advance the enemies' agenda by imposing penalties on our freedom and individual liberties.

4. *The current state of American governance is not up to the task of keeping the nation safe.* With an excessive fixation on campaigning for, winning, and keeping office rather than providing good governance as the sad outcome and with the profoundly negative partisan nature of politics today, we will fail in the task of keeping America safe, secure, and prosperous unless our government radically changes its priorities, policies, and organization.

5. *To prevail we must overhaul both our attitudes and machinery for securing the safety of the nation.* To that end the White House and Congress must be made to work more closely through major reform in organization and in the law that moves national security from its orientation in the Cold War and the last century to the challenges and demands of this century.

6. *To remove some of the dysfunctional aspects of government, disciplines for Congress and the executive branch must be instituted to ensure that the governing process is improved.* A proposed "Sarbanes-Oxley" law, passed in the wake of the corporate scandals to hold corporations, corporate leaders, and their accountants responsible, must be adopted for government.

7. *Fundamental changes in law enforcement and intelligence and in safeguards to protect individual liberties must be implemented at a time when security requires greater government imposition and intrusion.*

8. *America does not need a system for defense in the narrow sense but, more broadly, a system for ensuring security.* Defense is a subset of security with obvious implications for how we organize, train, equip, prepare, and educate our people for this task.

9. *In prevailing we must adopt comprehensive and not narrow solutions to the major problems facing us.* We must move to resolve the profoundly difficult conflicts between the Israelis and the Palestinians and between Indians and Pakistanis. This will require a global solution, with Arab recognition of Israel, and Israeli recognition and acceptance of a legitimate and viable Palestinian state. A modified Marshall Plan for the region with full international support is essential abroad as well.

10. *We must expand regional security arrangements more broadly. NATO is our first and most important relationship.* It must be transformed in keeping with the commitments made at the Prague Summit in November 2002. New relationships must be created. To that end a conference, such as the Conference on Cooperation and Security in Europe (CSCE) of the 1970s, regarding nuclear proliferation and elimination of nuclear weapons, along with the possibility of use, will be created among all known and suspected nuclear powers. Korea will be the first test case in showing how the nuclear genie can be returned to its bottle permanently.

FINISHING BUSINESS

Introduction
Contradictions, Imperatives, and Opportunities

One hundred years ago no one could have predicted that Lenin would lead a revolution that would turn Russia into the Soviet Union. Eighty years ago no one could have foreseen that a recently discharged corporal from the Kaiser's Army named Adolph Hitler would seize control of Germany. Bin Laden is neither a Lenin nor a Hitler. However, his call to arms wrapped in a theological perversion of Islam could be as seductive and appealing as Communism and Nazism once were. Furthermore, with over 1.3 billion Muslims to proselytize with a radical theology that could pose "the mother of all asymmetric threats" to peace-minded peoples around the globe, dismissing the more sinister possibilities would be foolhardy.

Riddles, enigmas, and contradictions, Winston Churchill believed, wonderfully described the Soviet Union. Churchill's prose, like the man, was brilliant, witty, and sometimes wide of the mark. However, the Cold War was still won against that superpower adversary, enigma or not. In large measure, victory was achieved because there was a common "clear and present danger" around which to rally and unify a powerful and enduring alliance, with the shared understanding that nuclear war would have catastrophic consequences and had to be prevented. Today Churchill's "riddles, enigmas, and contradictions" may be better descriptors of how the United States is waging the global war on terror and how it plans to bring "democracy and freedom" to the greater Middle East.

In plain English, the United States government and its citizens collectively do not comprehend the extent and insidious nature of the danger the nation potentially faces. The Bush administration casts this as a "global war on terror." However good the phrase, any shorthand slogan risks omitting or concealing the larger reality. That reality is more frightening. What we are facing is a long-term struggle against "jihadist extremism."

Despite the huge amounts of money spent and the new agencies created, as we will see, the United States is not fully or properly organized to deal with that danger or to win the global war on terror. Perhaps worse, the riddles, enigmas, and contradictions inherent in many of America's policies and politics in waging the war on terror are exacerbating the security challenges the nation must address. That the United States could dissipate the huge international good will and support following the September 11, 2001, attacks is a symptom of this condition and vulnerability.

These dangers reflect both older and newer pieces of unfinished business. The older pieces formed the basis of my last book of that title. The newer pieces, in part, emerged from the old and from events that have unfolded over the last two years. These events, in turn, created and then sharpened the major contradictions in our politics, policies, and plans for making the world safer and more secure. Consider perhaps the most perplexing and exquisite of these contradictions. At no time in its history has America been more powerful or wealthier in both relative and absolute measures. Yet, possibly at no time in the past 150 years has the United States been so vulnerable to external forces conspiring to do harm to its way and standard of life.

How the United States finds itself in such a diabolical predicament in which all its great economic wealth and military power are not sufficient to protect the nation from danger is the preamble. What can and must be done to defeat this grave and gathering danger is the basis for this book.

How the president and the nation fare in fighting this global war and eliminating the critical danger that threatens our friends and us may take years to determine. Shortly after World War II ended, General of the Army Dwight David Eisenhower predicted it could take fifty years to know whether the allies would succeed in making Germany a peaceful state. Today this book argues that it is not overstatement to observe that, if mishandled, the results may prove to pose the most dangerous challenge to America's future since the Civil War.

The reasons for this first contradiction and the inversion between power and security rest in what is the greatest strategic danger to the United States and its allies. No longer is the ultimate peril the specter of the destruction of society in a nuclear war. Clearly the Soviet Union and the United States possessed tens of thousands of nuclear weapons. But both East and West had a single common overriding strategic imperative—ensuring that those weapons were never used in anger. Aside from crises in Cuba over Soviet missiles in 1962 and the October War in the Middle East in 1973, the danger of nuclear war was mercifully small.

Today the strategic calculus has shifted from preventing the outright destruction of society to preventing its potential disruption. Nature demonstrates that every day. Terrorists too understand that terror can produce hugely disruptive effects. Unlike what turned out to be a very low probability of nuclear war during the Cold War, the chance of further al Qaeda attacks, from Iraq to Istanbul, is a certainty. They will occur. As President Bush profoundly worries, the use of nuclear, chemical, and biological weapons by terrorists is a real threat. The anthrax letter attacks shortly after September 11 engraved that fear indelibly on the White House.

Our enemies use the inherent vulnerability of all societies, intensified by the psychologically magnified effects of disruption wrought by terror, as their strategic and political focus. While intense storms, severe droughts, and the ravages of disease have always tested humanity, terror uses vulnerability as the irresistible point for attack. Incredibly, the United States stands at greater risk today in avoiding nuclear catastrophe than it did during the Cold War. Deterring disruption by terror attack, with or without the use of terror weapons, will prove to be a bigger test than averting nuclear world war.

There are other powerful contradictions. For a nation at war against global terror as President Bush constantly reminds us, America remains on a remarkable peacetime footing. There is no draft. No arsenal of democracy is busy churning out thousands of warplanes, tanks, and ships. There are no "Rosy the Riveters" hard at work in munitions factories and weapons assembly lines replacing men sent off to war.

There are no victory gardens, victory bonds, or ration cards. Gasoline is plentiful and, by world standards, cheap, even at $2 per gallon. Sacrifice has not been requested of the public and certainly not made a national priority.

Instead of "The Sands of Iwo Jima" and "They Were Expendable" playing on the big screen, or more likely DVDs, Americans are treated to "Saving Pvt. Jessica Lynch," the young American female soldier captured during the short Iraq war when her reserve unit took a wrong turn and stumbled into the Iraqi army. She was later saved in what was prominently billed at the time by the high command as a daring rescue from her hospital bed where she was recovering from her injuries and unguarded by Iraqi troops.

Through 2004 newspaper headlines and television sound bites carried reports and images of war as American service personnel, along with increasing numbers of Iraqi civilians, were attacked, killed, and wounded in action on and off battlefields far away in Iraq and Afghanistan. Those reports were filled largely with "bad news." E-mails, many originating inside the Coalition Provisional Authority (CPA) and from visitors sent to observe and report back, told grim tales of how efforts were going to establish democracy and, in the midst of an insurgency, rebuild a devastated country.

In response the White House and CPA argued that there was plenty of good news that the media failed to acknowledge and that the press was wrong in its pessimistic assessment of events in Iraq. Long lists of projects, kilowatt-hours of electricity returned to service, hospitals and schools repaired, and other measures of progress were routinely and often proudly announced. The move toward a national referendum to select a provisional government and hold elections in 2005 was seen as a very positive step. Yet as Secretary Rumsfeld asked about the war on terror, are we winning or losing the battle to democratize and rebuild Iraq?

The United States won overwhelming military victories in Afghanistan and then Iraq in 2002 and 2003. Those victories provoked a third contradiction. Waging modern war as Gen. Wesley Clark defines it is far easier than waging peace.

For reasons that will follow, waging war requires far fewer troops than winning the peace through bringing stability and democracy to Iraq. The last two are and have proven much harder objectives to achieve. And experienced observers such as Zbigniew Brzezinski, national security advisor to President Jimmy Carter, reject the notion that war can be waged against an ephemeral construct such as terror.

Beyond that, the nation also faces a perennial political challenge in governance. Can a political system created by the best minds of the eighteenth century survive the rigors of the twenty-first century? Government, as driven by the state of domestic politics, may simply not be capable of taking the necessary actions to contain this new danger in a timely, coherent, affordable, or effective manner. If this conclusion is sustained, that may be the most frightening news of all.

A further contradiction rests in governance and the tension between freedom and security. The greater the perceived danger, the more likely it will be that new laws and restrictions on individual liberty will be imposed to keep the nation safer. Hence, the threat of terrorist attack is also a threat to future liberty and individual freedom.

Current and future Patriot Acts, enacted for the common good, could make draconian changes, further disrupting what was once considered normal life. Terrorists fully appreciate that "it's the economy, stupid" and will conspire to hit us hard there. The prospect of disruption touches virtually all aspects of daily life. For the rest of our lives we will be removing shoes in airport security lines, a small reminder of how much life has been affected. Should a weapon of mass destruction be used, imagine what the backlash and consequences might be regarding future preventative laws.

There is a worrying corollary to this contradiction—freedom of worship in the United States and the pluralistic nature of Islam. While not an immediate issue, the two are in potential conflict. This is happening in Iraq. Debate over the degree to which religion can impose itself on the secular preferences (or demands) the United States has for the future government in Iraq will be difficult to resolve. In the Sharia (or Islamic law), for both Sunni and Shia there is the question of whether democracy is indeed compatible with Islam and whether Sharia requires a Muslim leader to be loyal to Islam. Furthermore, the role of women will be contested. Modernists obviously favor more or less equal rights. Traditionalists do not. Women who adapt the latter beliefs argue that their role is compatible with expanded women's rights. Yet those beliefs abut and can conflict with American values and traditions. Given the divisions across the various Islamic sects between modernists and traditionalists, this tension will not be easily resolved. That ultimately could produce a backlash in Europe and in the United States.

Islam is the largest growing religion in the United States. Many of its converts come from militant and activist backgrounds that know how to use the legal system to political advantage. In some sects the role of women is not in keeping with American values. All of these issues could form the basis for conflict over constitutional guarantees of freedom to worship. Add discomfort or distrust certain Americans now feel toward individuals of Arab or Islamic background since September 11, and all the ingredients are present for possibly unpleasant times ahead. They, of course, may never occur. September 11, the global war on terror, and the war in Iraq, however, have made the prospects more likely.

AN AMERICAN SAMSON?

Three years after September 11, after some stunning initial successes, the global war on terror seems to have bogged down. Terrorist attacks increased in intensity and scope beyond Iraq. Indeed, even before the United States launched military campaigns against the Taliban in Afghanistan, cynics wondered whether a global war on terror would have been declared by President Bush had al Qaeda struck London, Paris, Rome, Istanbul, Madrid, or any other foreign city instead of the Twin Towers and the Pentagon.

This grave and gathering danger took shape well before September 11 and extended far beyond Saddam Hussein and Iraq, although the Bush administration did not perceive this danger at the time. As the White House trained its gun sights on Baghdad and went to war to remove Saddam and eliminate his weapons of mass destruction, new problems were created. By declaring a global war on terror and, in November 2003 during the Muslim month-long celebration of Ramadan, broadening the mission to bring "democracy and freedom" to the greater Middle East, the president set the nation on a collision course with powerful and dangerous forces ranging from radical Islam to chronic regional conflicts, many of which may prove to be beyond anyone's control and ability to shape. Furthermore, by proposing a "forward strategy of freedom" later that same month and restating that aim in his trip to Britain, the president raised the stakes.

The last contradiction is perhaps the most telling. Presidential policies may succeed, fail, or have little visible impact. The political process must implement those policies. At a time when the nation is at great peril, the political process is floundering. Another September 11 may not be enough to unify the nation and constrain the centrifugal political forces that restrict or prevent action. The contradiction is clear: the political process, the basis for America's greatness, is now a source of weakness.

The actions of Osama bin Laden and other extremists will exploit this political condition. Initial evidence suggests that al Qaeda probably never anticipated the potential political leverage that could be generated through even the threat of attack. Over time, as the North Vietnamese learned in a different context, our enemies will more fully understand this weakness and exploit it. The remedy is tough, thoughtful, and highly coordinated actions to make the nation safer and securer. The government may not be capable of producing those actions, and adversaries are almost certainly going to capitalize on this weakness.

These contradictions reflect a broader reality. The security structure that served the nation well for a half century is, advertently or not, being dismantled. Taken to one logical extreme, the Biblical tale of Samson in the Philistine Temple is a chilling and plausible metaphor. The Bush administration is pushing, in some cases hard, on the pillars of American and Western security. The time may have come when the Cold War structure needs to be drastically overhauled. The danger is that such a major overhaul could lead to disarray that would diminish security. The question is whether the administration recognizes the collective impact of its specific policies and actions.

Virtually every Cold War foundation, from the strategy of containment and deterrence to an alliance- and consensus-based security system, is being challenged by the actions of the Bush administration. Charges of unilateralism, arrogance, and even naïveté have been hurled at the administration. Proponents counter that these policies are shrewd, bold, and essential political actions to confront the dangers of the greater Middle East. No matter who is correct, the pillars that have supported international security for decades are being shaken—inadvertently or not—by the Bush administration. Is Bush a metaphoric Samson and will the temple collapse? Or will a better structure be created? Those are the important questions. And there are others:

- How, as the most powerful and richest nation in history, did we arrive at this juncture?
- Why is the nation at such risk and why are the old foundations for security being displaced?
- Does Islam, either collectively or just the radical elements, present a new, great danger and why?
- What must be done to ensure the nation is secure?
- Why are the stakes so large and why are the dangers of miscalculation and failure so great?
- Can the United States win the global war on terror? How is winning defined and what will it take to win?

THE DANGER: DOMINOES, POLITICAL THEOCRACY, AND POLITICAL POWER

In blunt terms, the bulk of the danger—modern variants of the Soviet Union and Nazi Germany—that threatens this nation and much of the world emanates from radical Islam and the political realities and excesses that fuel it. Jihadist extremists have hijacked Islam. Osama bin Laden and others like him, reminiscent of the extremists and anarchists of the late nineteenth and early twentieth centuries, are using this perversion of Islam as a revolutionary ideology. Their purpose, like Lenin's and Trotsky's, is to seize power. Terror is the tactic. Its purpose is to terrorize. Furthermore, these extremists share a common geography—the crescent of crisis that runs from the eastern Mediterranean to the Bay of Bengal and then to the eastern tip of Indonesia.

The end state for bin Laden is some form of fundamentalist regime banked by Saudi oil money and armed with Pakistani nuclear weapons.[1] Whether this regime will require a host state as Bolshevism did or if it can be borderless is unclear. The appeal of this theocratic formula stretches across much of the Islamic world. However, Saudi Arabia and Pakistan are potential dominoes in this battle, as well as key targets for Islamic extremists.

September 11 and the subsequent defeat and elimination of Saddam in Iraq taught al Qaeda a great deal. There is the question whether, beforehand, bin Laden actually expected the Twin Towers to come crashing down. Nor did he comprehend the disruption and economic pain that would result from those tragedies. Also, he was most likely surprised by the quick and overpowering reaction by the United States in routing the Taliban in Afghanistan. These events were an expensive learning process. But learn al Qaeda did.

After September 11, al Qaeda took a horrible beating. Many of its leaders and cells were killed, captured, or dissipated. Unfortunately, bin Laden escaped and al Qaeda reconstituted itself. For a time, al Qaeda and other extremist groups concentrated on targets in the Arab and Muslim worlds and Iraq. That will change. Europe and the United States have not been forgotten or neglected.

The sum and substance of this is not a threat that will topple the democracies or defeat them militarily. Fortunately, the Nazis and Communists who tried are part of history's rubbish heap. The new threat is to our way of life and standard of living.

Disruption damages both. If we are careless and do not respond in time and with careful, appropriate actions, extremists will do major damage to our economies, cultures, and societies, using terror as the weapon of choice. One risk to democracy is overreacting with excessively strict antiterrorist laws and rules. Another is the psychological damage arising from allowing fear of the threat to affect us as much as, or more than, an actual terrorist attack. Franklin Roosevelt was correct when he told the nation that "the only thing we have to fear is fear itself."

Still another risk is seeing our standard of living erode and our lives becoming more difficult and unpleasant. Orwell's *1984* is not the future. However, the accumulated effects of disrupted economies, compounded by the interactions of "graying" populations, heavy demands on social security, and growing deficits, mean Americans would have to make do with less of everything. The unbridled optimism of the past would be throttled back. These negative psychological consequences, in turn, would be further damaged by a loss of influence and leadership around the world. Furthermore, if fundamentalism takes root, it will attempt to force America to retreat to its boundaries with the full weight of the terrorist tools it can bring to bear.

1. Refer to Chapter 3, "What a Global War on Terror," for further documentation.

UNFINISHED BUSINESS

Published nearly a year before Operation Iraqi Freedom was launched in March 2003, *Unfinished Business* analyzed the dangers and proposed remedial actions to protect the nation. Of eight chapters, seven "connected the dots" comprising the major and seemingly unrelated dangers to America's future safety in five pieces of "unfinished business." A single chapter proposed solutions to these challenges in terms of "three national security deficits." Although far-reaching and bold, the recommendations were purposely kept concise.

Of the five pieces of unfinished business that formed the challenges and dangers that lie ahead, "jihadist extremists" such as Osama bin Laden and those like him target the first piece—the very openness of American society. The freedom, lack of restrictions, and accessibility to society provide broad opportunities for al Qaeda to strike virtually anywhere in the United States. Any responses on our part could provoke consequences, intended or otherwise.

First, despite our unprecedented power, like Gulliver among the Lilliputians, we are extraordinarily vulnerable. The certainty of terrorist attack shifts the danger from massive destruction to massive disruption. Clearly, disruption could involve weapons of mass destruction.

At the same time, freedom and security are brought into conflict. Basic freedoms and our way of life are at risk as more power is assigned to government in order to safeguard the nation. An extremely vicious circle can be formed. The frequent issuing of domestic alerts against a possible terrorist attack and actual attacks abroad remind us that the danger is real. As fear grows, so too will support for strengthening the Patriot Act or, indeed, passing a Patriot Act II that grants government further powers for protecting the nation against terror. This fundamental tension between freedom and security is what extremists will exploit. Air travel provides one example. For the rest of our lives, after proceeding through security checkpoints we will often find flights suddenly canceled because of security alerts. Ironically, these consequences are unintended benefits that accrue to those wishing this nation ill.

Second, American society, that is, the networks of people, commerce, communications, finance, transport, energy, food, and emergency services, to name a few, is inherently vulnerable and susceptible to attack. Although a new cabinet office for Homeland Security was established in 2002, the fact is that open, advanced societies can never be fully safe and secure from terror.

Third, the United States government, still organized on the Cold War basis of the National Security Act of 1947, is, as the Hart-Rudman Commission reported in 2001, "dysfunctional." The vertical structure with stovepipes for defense, intelligence, law enforcement, diplomacy, and the like can not fully cope with the horizontal or cross-cutting dangers posed by extremism and terror.

The enormous difficulty in sorting out assignment of intelligence and law enforcement responsibilities and authorities is indicative.

Fourth, the crescent of crisis that extends from Israel and the eastern end of the Mediterranean to the Bay of Bengal is an incubator for terror and extremism from the white-hot Arab-Israeli-Palestinian and Indo-Pak conflicts to autocratic regimes and the impoverished. Recognition and articulation that this danger comes from one particular region and the perversion of one religion—Islam—were slow in coming.

Finally, the United States had to integrate more closely in its strategic framework its old adversaries and new partners, Russia and China. In addition, institutions from the UN to NATO had to be rejuvenated and redirected toward the realities of the twenty-first century. The United States had to understand what was happening and take comprehensive action to shore up those foundations if it and its friends were to be made safer and securer.

If that could not be done, then new structures and frameworks had to be invented. Indeed, the basic concepts of deterrence and containment that worked so well during the Cold War were not sufficient for the twenty-first century. Although the Bush administration advocated and demonstrated a preference for preemption in theory and practice, it did not produce a new strategic formulation. In a sense the United States remained trapped between the old and a still-undefined new security basis.

The major recommendations dealt with these five pieces in general terms. What made the largest difference from the past was that terror could no longer be isolated or contained in a single region and, as we learned, has and will hit here. Furthermore, weapons of mass destruction are present. If the causes and reasons for extremism that are unique to the crescent of crisis cannot be addressed and rectified, then the war on terror will never be won.

To defeat extremism, the most intractable problems from the Arab-Israeli conflict, the negative consequences of autocratic regimes in Saudi Arabia and Egypt, the potential for revolution in Pakistan, and other horrendous tasks that have proved so daunting in the past to defy solution had to be confronted. Part of the solution was the call for a new and broader version of the old Marshall Plan designed to deal with the full range of causes and symptoms that have sparked and nourished extremism. Plans for reinvigorating NATO and the United Nations, in addition to taking on the growing crisis of proliferation of nasty weapons and delivery systems, were proposed.

At home, recommendations to close the three most important domestic "deficits" were offered to address the political process and its inherent difficulty in making and sustaining decisions over complex and tough issues, fixing the nation's security "organization" and its dysfunctional character, and ensuring the means for attracting and retaining sufficient numbers of quality people to serve in positions that defend and protect the nation against all enemies foreign and domestic.

To these ends, revision of the National Security Act was essential to reflect the new dangers. This did not happen. Two of most important components of homeland security are intelligence and law enforcement. Both were omitted from the reorganization that created the new Homeland Security Department. The proposed amendment of the National Security Act would have corrected that deficiency as well as formed a joint congressional committee on homeland security and national defense. The purpose of this committee was to ensure that Congress could work more closely with the White House. New legislation to deal with the people deficit, that is, how to attract and retain the best and brightest in the protection of the nation, was also proposed to ensure that they would not be dissuaded from service.

Despite the events of September 11 that brought terror to American shores, the United States is still in the early stages of understanding how to wage the war on global terror and, more importantly, is still learning what must be done to keep the nation safe. In this battle the nation has not yet fully appreciated that the dangers have shifted from the potential threat of societal destruction (although biologically engineered disease could change that) to societal disruption.

Despite the soaring rhetoric and promises to win the war on terrorism, how is that fight going? Despite the huge additional sums appropriated for defense and homeland security since September 11, is the nation any safer? Despite the massive people and monetary resources going into rebuilding and democratizing Iraq, are we winning those battles? Despite the administration's interventions in the Israeli-Palestinian conflict, what are the prospects for any form of even partial respite in the violence? And what will the United States do vis à vis the surviving members of the Axis of Evil—Iran and North Korea? The answers are not reassuring.

Two issues capture the contradictions, dilemmas, and complexities of protecting America. The first deals with the global war on terror abroad with particular reference to Iraq and what the administration calls the central battleground in that war. The second pertains to the global war at home and how the United States is responding. More than a year has passed in which the United States has begun rebuilding and democratizing a defeated and occupied Iraq. That task was made vastly more difficult by what turned out to be a series of poor judgments. Prewar assumptions about the ease of winning the peace proved wildly optimistic. A new and democratic Iraqi government with legitimate and capable leadership did not emerge.

Internationalizing the reconstruction proved marginally successful, at least through mid-2004. About a third of the needed funding was raised at the donors' conference in Madrid in November 2003. Allies inside and out of NATO and the UN who opposed the war originally chose not to support the peace without a say in shaping that outcome. In retaliation the United States first excluded the major offenders—France, Germany, and Russia—from bidding on contracts for rebuilding Iraq. NATO, however, may still decide to deploy to Iraq as an alliance.

There were unmistakable signs that terror and violence were waxing, not the converse. Despite Saddam's capture in December 2003, Osama bin Laden appeared alive and well and continued to broadcast to the Iraqi people, usually through al Jazeera or al Arabiya, urging, among other things, suicide attacks to defend Islam. The pressures in the crescent of crisis are building, not retracting; the Bush administration's war on terror is fighting new and more plentiful converts; economies around the world continue to flag; and political and economic instability is spreading as far afield as South America and Indonesia and is rampant in Africa.

It would have been ironic if, in attacking Iraq to eliminate one nuclear threat, this had precipitated other threats. North Korea, Iran, and Libya have nuclear programs. For the moment these programs appear checked by diplomacy. Libya surprised many by voluntarily promising to abandon its WMD programs and permitting outside verification. Although there are grounds for optimism, they cannot be taken for granted. The war in Iraq and the war on terror also put great pressure on Pakistan. There is a real possibility that a radical regime could kill and displace President Pervez Musharraf.

The second issue is examining how the United States is waging the war on terror at home. This examination must cover all agencies of government, including law enforcement, intelligence, defense, and diplomacy, as well as the new Homeland Security Department. How the nation goes about this business is a perfect case study of the inherent difficulties in a democracy of making major bureaucratic reform. It also shows how the politically expedient response of settling on cures for symptoms and not the fundamental causes of these perplexing matters—namely, the divides between intelligence and law enforcement—will not finish the business at hand of making the nation more secure.

Beyond these issues, the transformation of the Department of Defense is a marvelous piece of unfinished business. That piece has now been expanded two ways. While the department has an unprecedented ability to wage and win major conventional war, as the postwar period in Iraq is showing, the so-called Phase Four stabilization and security operations to support reconstruction and democratization seemed to surprise the Department of Defense and the White House. Thus, transformation must be broadened to deal with peace across all pertinent agencies of government. As yet no one has satisfactorily defined how to apply transformation to this task.

Meanwhile, American anxiety about new rounds of terrorist attacks has been sharpened by the continuing security alerts, especially over Christmas 2003. The expectation that government must act decisively to reduce future dangers and put in place the means to cope with these and other threats to the nation has been temporarily replaced by fear of attack and anxiety over the competence of government to protect the nation. A perennial problem is that the nation tends to spend and not think its way clear of danger.

This preference is unlikely to work in a world in which threats are more diaphanous and arise as much from cultural animosity as strategic rivalry. We should not assume that the nation would have the resources it once had for security. Even if the economic recovery of late 2003 is sustained, the war in Iraq has already shown that, with a military force of 1.3 million, the military services' personnel are being stretched. Also, the federal debt and deficit are growing. Outside defense and homeland security, the federal budget deficeit grew by more than 20 percent in 2003. Resource constraints are a serious issue.

Meanwhile the danger has shifted from destruction to disruption. The threat that exploits this disruption is clear and present. It comes from one particular geographic region, and it is based on a perversion of Islam.

The causes and sources of the extremism and antagonism that underwrite this threat are varied. Yet they must all be dealt with if the United States is to be kept safe. Our enemies are actively seeking to and, given the chance, will re-attack us, our allies, and our friends, which the former Soviet Union was either reluctant to do or was deterred in doing. Because disruption of our society and way of life holds profoundly negative consequences, America is in jeopardy.

By any measure of power and wealth, from net asset value to advanced education to military force, the United States is perhaps the most advantaged nation in history. In sheer quantitative terms, it is the most powerful. However, in pursuing both the war on terror and the battle to disarm Iraq, the United States has, inadvertently perhaps, induced potentially tectonic shifts in the four principal pillars on which its security has rested for half a century. NATO Europe, extending to Russia, is in disarray and disagreement over the Gulf War and autocratic shifts by Moscow as well as by the war in Chechnya, the evolution of the European Union, and an integrated continent.

In Northeast Asia the bilateral relations with China, Japan, and South Korea were assaulted by North Korea and its nuclear ambitions. While some argue a nuclear Japan might be a good fallback, rearming Japan almost certainly will create more problems than such measures would resolve. The situation in the Middle East and the Persian Gulf is explosively unstable. Furthermore, the powerful economy, which provided the resources for winning the Cold War and for contributing to American greatness, is still recovering.

There are growing national security "deficits" that are conspiring to marginalize American power and influence further. As Osama bin Laden showed, the United States is a tempting and highly vulnerable target to those wishing to do this country ill. Two huge oceans no longer protect the United States from immediate danger and attack. Accessibility, while somewhat contained by border guards, immigration rules, and far closer scrutiny, is still relatively easy, if not in person, certainly electronically. American culture and its intrusive and often unwelcome presence reinforce those who do not view the United States in a favorable light or actively reject its values and authority derived from its great wealth and power.

Elsewhere the question of whether bin Laden was Pancho Villa and a one-time raid on the United States or Lenin and a seventy-year ideological struggle has been addressed. But what bin Laden offers to a more competent and capable successor is the way to gain political ends by attacking the vulnerability of the world's greatest power in ways that can never be fully defended. The matter is not whether the United States will be re-attacked. That barrier has been penetrated. The appropriate query is "when?" As to "who," the anthrax attacks of the fall of 2001 and later followed by a flurry of "pipe bombs" the next spring in the mid-West, suggest that perpetrators need not be foreigners. Americans are fully capable, too.

The administration has declared a war on terror. Yet that is a misnomer. As argued in *Unfinished Business,* the danger is jihadist extremism. Terror is a tool, tactic, and weapon. Unless the causes and sources of extremism are attacked and addressed, there will be no final victory except by accident or good fortune. Furthermore, by failing to educate and inform the public of the real nature of the threat and what to do about it, the government risks its credibility. This is precisely what happened in Vietnam.

The United States began increasing its commitment to Vietnam in the very early 1960s. By the time of the Gulf of Tonkin Incident in August 1964, it was ready and waiting to act decisively in ending the insurgency in the South. Eleven years and 58,000 dead Americans later, the United States evacuated its last personnel serving in country, ending its involvement and the war. Today is a far more dangerous time than then.

More than credibility of the government is at stake. Whether with malice aforethought or through inadvertence, the Bush administration has raised the stakes for the nation. The war goes well beyond Iraq, although we cannot "lose" in Iraq because we are committed to ensuring that some form of stable and enduring government under the rule of law is formed. Radical jihadists have a vision and a goal. The last thing the nation needs is to see that fight turn into a war against Islam.

A major danger to be avoided at virtually all costs is defeating the radicals and ending the breeding grounds that nourish them without sparking a war against Islam and the Arab world. This is not August 1914. However, as then, with a single assassination of the Arch Duke of Austro-Hungary, a catastrophic series of events quickly produced a world war. Terrorism, in whatever guise, cannot be allowed to repeat that disaster.

A final point: the war on terror and what it means irrespective of the efficacy of the phrase poses a direct and possibly overwhelming test for the U.S.

government. The government can be described as Air Force Chief of Staff Gen. John Jumper sees the past structure for national security—a collection of "stovepipes" and "ruts." What Jumper means is that the Soviet Union spoiled us. Government could be organized in "stovepipes." Policy could collect in "ruts." The relative constancy of the threat made this organization both possible and preferential, and it worked.

Because our borders are free of strategic threats and because threats no longer have borders, this Cold War structure does not fit today's reality. Worse, the political process that required compromise to limit the destructive effects of otherwise centrifugal forces finds difficulty in producing effective polices based on compromise. That intelligence and law enforcement could be untouched in the last security reorganization was inconceivable and understandable. The partisan excesses that further distort the political process are part of this dilemma. Although former Speaker of the House Newt Gingrich argues that American politics were always "hard ball" (and reminds us that not only was Alexander Hamilton killed in a duel by Aaron Burr but also both Hamilton and Jefferson purchased competing newspapers to challenge each other), that historical record is still no reason for partisanship to be allowed to harm the national well-being.

The danger requires sophisticated, disciplined, intelligent, and probably uncompromising solutions. There is the most fundamental question of whether the political process can respond in that manner short of a catastrophic act. September 11, no matter how traumatic, was not sufficient in that regard. Despite the international good will and support and the rallying of America to fight back, a great opportunity was lost. Enough was not achieved. Sadly, the strength of the United States, a representative government, may not be its salvation. It may, in fact, be the principal reason why the nation will not find itself safer and securer.

This is the single-most-important piece of unfinished business that must be fixed. The nation faces a situation in which it is increasingly probable that only an informed and vocal public can demand of its elected leaders responsible and bold actions to deal with the danger and threats we face.

1
From Destruction to Disruption
The First Contradiction

lbert Einstein remarked that the best answer to a complex problem should be made as simple as possible but no simpler. Achieving that economy in practice is not easy. Here is the heart of the strategic conundrum the United States faces: why is the most powerful and richest nation in history less safe and secure than perhaps anytime since the Civil War? The answers, to Einstein's regret, are not simple or reassuring.

First, some will respond that this premise is wrong. The United States is not less secure or less safe. This argument turns several basic facts into a fair and relevant question. Having survived an era with tens of thousands of nuclear weapons and the risks of their use made real by the Cold War, how is it possible that the United States is more vulnerable to harm today when that awesome threat is gone? Here are some answers.

Three broad sets of reasons are responsible for this first contradiction and the inversion between power and security. The first reason was that, during the two world wars of the last century and the Cold War, the dangers were clear, present, and ultimately could be defeated unconditionally. The new dangers are highly imprecise. Defeating them either unconditionally or sufficiently to prevent attack poses profound dilemmas and problems. Nor do the dangers of jihadist extremism always take the form of states and well-defined groups traditionally recognized by the international or any other body of law.

Second, a globalized and highly integrated and interconnected world purposely creates great access and networks. Without access or networks, the benefits of globalization could not be achieved or sustained. Globalization comes at a price. It has many downsides. One downside is that this access and networking induces potential fragility and vulnerability. To attack this interconnectivity, whether through computer hacking or with car bombs, would be simple, effective, and disruptive. Part of this vulnerability is psychological. Today American society tends to make Americans more risk adverse than in the past. Hence, even the threat of disruption takes a toll and often tends to be exaggerated in terms of possible consequences.

Third, unlike the Cold War when the chance of war between the superpowers turned out to be low, al Qaeda and other extremist groups have struck and will strike again. With a political agenda possibly no less ambitious than the Bolsheviks, like criminals, there will be repeat offenses. Unlike criminals the danger is not amenable only to law enforcement tools. Furthermore, the possibility of these groups obtaining and using chemical, nuclear, and, particularly, biological agents heightens the danger significantly.

The cumulative effects of these three factors are political, psychological, and cultural. The chief political consequences arise from the inherent checks and balances in American government that often impede taking fully rational and effective actions, from strongly held ideologies that empower or are central to each administration, and from the inherent difficulties any president must face in fighting terror that is global, uninhibited about using suicide, and intensely committed to its cause. The psychological consequences rest in the tension between the freedom to pursue life, liberty, and happiness and the growing likelihood that this freedom will be eroded or lost as terror waxes. The cultural consequences reflect the political and psychological reactions.

Several data points reinforce these conclusions. The political effects are examined in Chapter 3, What a Global War on Terror. One intractable dilemma, of course, is posed by the need to inform the public of a possible attack and the loss of credibility when attacks fail to materialize. Should a terrorist attack occur and the government withheld any warning, it would likely be crucified. Over time, as warnings accumulate and attacks do not, the public will grow cynical and dismissive. The government will be accused of overreacting, and advice and warnings will be ignored. In the summer of 2003, for example, citizens were advised to purchase duct tape and plastic to seal off rooms against biological or chemical attack. In addition to preventing airborne agents from entering the safe space, air would also have been sealed off—not a particularly sound piece of advice.

Ultimately, if, in order to defeat terrorism, the imposition of sufficient inconveniences exceeds a certain breaking point, public support will be lost. Only so much clothing can be removed in airports before the public reacts. Over time other restrictions, whether the showing of ID cards in office buildings or routine car searches in airports, will exact a political price. The analogy is not quite similar to the prohibition of alcohol in the 1920s that encouraged Americans to break the law. However, a political backlash and erosion of government credibility and competence will come as no surprise. September 11 caused hundreds of billions and even trillions of dollars of economic damage. The increased costs of future security will be measured in percentage points of GDP, considerable amounts for taxpayers to bear. The psychological and political effects of suicide bombers in Istanbul, Baghdad, Moscow, Bali, and elsewhere, carried live throughout the world instantaneously on television, are also real. The intent is to disrupt, divide, and isolate.

Over time the accumulated impact can be huge. It is too easy to imagine future attacks that have spectacularly damaging effect. Snipers and suicide bombers in American shopping malls are at the milder extremes of what could happen. Each of these factors can change culture and society, not always for the better.

The reasons for this contradiction between power and security can be placed in historical and political contexts reflecting the strength of particular ideological views held by presidents of both parties. Those contexts, are useful in understanding constraints and means to neutralize and defeat the current dangers, threats, and vulnerabilities. Context also reveals where and how the political process was good and bad in providing for the common defense. The recurring theme of intelligence failures in dealing with threats is not new and is a reminder of what can be learned from past experiences and errors—and usually is not—in allowing ideology to dominate intelligence and refusing to accept competing views. Establishing a national commission to assess why the administration misjudged the extent of Iraqi weapons of mass destruction (WMD) and how much of that was caused by a failure of intelligence reflects the most recent case.

After September 11, questions of intelligence and other related failures and, hence, responsibility for not preventing the attacks has fueled, but not necessarily informed, debate. Major inquiries and investigations were launched in both the United States and the United Kingdom to answer those questions and to try to place responsibility and accountability where they belonged. Whether those efforts will have long-term positive results is uncertain and probably unlikely.

The Hutton Commission, named for Law Lord Brian Hutton, was ordered in 2003 by Prime Minister Tony Blair to investigate the suicide of a senior civilian employee in the Ministry of Defence, Dr. David Kelly. BBC reporter Andrew Gilligan had revealed in a radio broadcast that the government had sexed up its intelligence on Saddam's weapons of mass destruction. An alleged forty-five-minute window in which Iraq could launch missiles presumably loaded with WMD became the cause célèbre. Kelly was the leaker and, in the aftermath, killed himself by slitting his wrists.

Lord Hutton issued his report in late January 2004, exonerating the government and holding the BBC responsible for poor journalism and an absence of editorial oversight. The chairman and executive director of the BBC resigned, and that pillar of British life was badly tarnished. There were cries of whitewash, and Mr. Blair survived a potentially crippling political debacle. Whether British intelligence will be affected, however, and whether any changes will be imposed on that structure seem unlikely.

Similar controversy was prevalent throughout much of the Cold War in assessing the intent of, and the danger posed by, the Soviet Union. Charges of bomber gaps, missile gaps, and misperceptions over actual Soviet aggressive intent were commonplace in the West and in Washington. Many accusations proved false.

Because politics and ideology ultimately controlled political decisions, at certain points the United States managed to distort Cold War realities for political purpose at times when its leadership should have known better. Similar distortions caused us to stumble into Vietnam and the tragic quagmire it became.

Clearly, Americans were profoundly worried by the threats and dangers that were real and had to be overcome or contained to win the struggles against Nazism and Communism. It was inevitable that our allies and we would win the two world wars, whether we realized that before the fact or not. Unfortunately, at the time, few observers imagined a victory as decisive as it turned out.

The Cold War pitted the West against an adversary that was doomed to fail because of profound internal contradictions and a political system based on concealing the truth. For better or worse, no one in the West fully understood the fatal flaws inside the Soviet Union and, of course, no one predicted its astonishing implosion in 1991. Mikhail Gorbachev, once president of the Soviet Union, described those realities in his books *Perestroika* and *A Time for Peace*. The Soviet Union was consigned to failure probably from its inception. The irrational system of government inserted political equivalents of carcinoma in the body politic. It would take time for these to metastasize.

Gorbachev tells us that the first sense of rot for his generation was hearing Khrushchev's Secret Speech delivered in November 1956. That speech revealed the excesses of Stalin and the murder and illegal incarceration and imprisonment of millions of Russians. Gorbachev and his fellow Communists were shaken by the revelations and accusations leveled against the regime. As idealists and fervent believers in Communism, there was disbelief that this could happen.

As Gorbachev worked his way up the hierarchy eventually to the Politburo, the Soviet Union's highest ruling body, the leadership had become antiquarian and brittle. Leonid Brezhnev took years to die. In his stead came a succession of the living dead, old men whose tenure was marked by illness and stagnation. As a result of this extraordinary turnover, the younger leadership in essence was exposed to the grave weaknesses that existed throughout the government, describing a system close to collapse.

When Gorbachev came to power in 1985, his plan was to correct these excesses and repair the Soviet Union. *Glasnost,* or openness, and *perestroika,* or reconstruction, were the tools to achieve this reform. The tools not only failed but they also managed to unleash a flood of chronic attempts to hide and cover up the true state of that nation. Confronted with the reality and incapable of responding, after taking down the Berlin wall and then giving the East European satellites independence, the Soviet Union imploded on Christmas Day 1989.

The lesson was clear. Marxism-Leninism and its dialectic were predicated on exploiting the contradictions in capitalism that would enable Communism to triumph in this struggle. Instead, the contradictions within the Soviet Union proved to be its undoing. Lenin's assertion that contradictions would destroy the West got it backward, a lesson not to be ignored. The Soviet Union ultimately imploded because it could not deal with the truth, and its attempts to cover up reality became fatal.

No matter how fierce America's rhetoric was about the nature of the Soviet Union, the fact was that the Russians were not ten feet tall ever. At best they were of modest stature, and not all of their vital organs were developed. In 1961 when the Kennedy-Johnson team assumed office, that understanding was, charitably, light years away. The best and the brightest, as David Halberstam told us in his book of that name, came to power with the spirit of can-do and Camelot. They were veterans of World War II and the Cold War. Most had been in uniform; many had seen action; and a few had been wounded in action.

JFK-LBJ: Misperceptions and Idealists

The first three years of the Kennedy, then Johnson, presidency are very informative in ways that eerily fit today's situation. JFK, young, ambitious, and energetic, defeated Dwight Eisenhower's vice president, Richard M. Nixon, in part by calling Ike soft on the Soviets. Kennedy, in essence, was the precursor idealist whose vision was hardheaded and tough in dealing with the adversary, much as many argued should have been the way to stop Hitler before he became a menace. The notion of a missile gap was invented and used to make the case against Ike and Nixon. Unfortunately, not only were the Soviets far behind the United States in nuclear armaments but also the decision had been made by Secretary-General Nikita S. Khrushchev by 1960 to decrease Soviet defense spending and reduce its military forces.

When the Cold War began in earnest in 1947 and 1948, notions such as deterrence and containment were just taking form. At that point nuclear weapons were generally regarded only as more destructive versions of conventional weapons. The United States had demobilized. America's military was less than two million strong, having demobilized after the war, and spending on new systems, readiness, and all the necessary items for maintaining military strength had been cut to the bone.

The Korean War changed all that. The United States was forced to rearm. Ike won the 1952 election promising to end the Korean War, which he did in 1953. The year before, the United States had tested the first super or hydrogen (H) bomb. The H-bomb had orders of magnitude more destructive power than did the atomic (A) bomb. An A-bomb's power was measured in kilotons or thousands of tons of TNT equivalent, while an H-bomb was measured in mega or millions of tons of TNT equivalent, ten orders of magnitude greater. A-bombs could destroy cities such as Hiroshima, Nagasaki, London, Washington, and Moscow. H-bombs implied the destruction of society.

Ike's national security strategy became one of massive retaliation. If the Soviet Union were foolish or miscalculating enough to launch an attack on the West, the United States and its allies would respond with nuclear and thermonuclear preponderance. As the Soviet Union did not explode an A-bomb until 1949, clearly, the technology balance was decisively in favor of the West. With Britain and France soon to obtain their own nuclear weapons, Moscow faced a triple threat.

By the time Khrushchev achieved preeminence in the Politburo in the mid-1950s, it was clear to the Soviets that a shortcut to circumventing America's nuclear superiority had to be found. Superiority in numbers of ground forces went only so far if Moscow and the rest of Russia were incinerated in a nuclear war. Sputnik was a tactical public relations victory in 1957. In fact later having the first man in space even for only a short time was a sufficient threat and challenge to arouse the United States. Soon space was a frontier that America would overtake the Soviet Union on, too.

During the 1950s despite major crises over Vietnam, Suez, and Hungary, and in the Taiwan Straits and the tiny islands of Matsu and Quemoy, nuclear weapons provided a form of strategic stability. Neither side had a clash of interests that inevitably would lead to war when that war could destroy society. Furthermore, neither side was prepared, except in the most extreme crisis, to provoke a confrontation that could lead to nuclear war and catastrophic consequences for both sides.

In essence Eisenhower's reliance on nuclear deterrence and the threat of massive retaliation was defense on the cheap. Expensive conventional forces need not be maintained in large numbers, nor did vast sums have to be spent on training, equipping, and preparing forces for conventional war. The military draft also helped in keeping costs down. Only a general with Eisenhower's experience in World War II and then waging the peace could have reached that conclusion and made it stick.

Slowly Khrushchev was drawn to the same logic. The Soviet leader knew that Russia's fiscal resources were strained. Regardless of huge deposits of oil, natural gas, and gold, much of it in inaccessible, distant, and frozen regions, the Soviet economy was in perpetual trouble. A large part was a figment of imagination with factory heads and managers routinely lying about production and capacity so that dishonesty and corruption became endemic.

The debate over future military strategy and capability was fierce among the general staff and the political leadership. The United States had unprecedented access to this fight. An extraordinary spy was in place—GRU (military intelligence) Col. Oleg Penkovsky. Penkovsky (furious with his leadership for not making promotion to general as Osama bin Laden was angered by the Saudi Royal family for not recognizing his contributions) turned over to his handler, British MI-6 agent cum journalist Greville Wynne, photographic copies of the most secret journal of the Soviet General Staff called *Voennya Mys'l,* or *Military Thought.* That document recorded the Soviet strategic debate for over two years from 1959 to late 1961. Second, the Soviet military was very efficient at informing its senior military on its decisions through books and journal articles that normally were published within a year or less after the debates concluded. The three editions of Marshall V. D. Sokolovskii's famous *Military Strategy,* published in 1962, 1963, and 1968, recorded which strategy decisions survived and which were changed during this debate.

As a source, Colonel Penkovsky's importance was downplayed because of CIA suspicion of disinformation on the part of Penkovsky and his documents. Another reason for downplaying this source was that knowledgeable analysts, who spent lifetimes doing content analysis of obscure Soviet military literature and who understood these debates, had little or no direct interaction with the nation's senior political leadership. Any reports of these strategic changes that Langley may have distributed to other government offices apparently had little impact. So when the Kennedy team and the new idealists assumed office promising to bear any burden and pay any price in the defense of freedom, hard-nosed assessments of restrained Soviet military decisions were not very likely to have any traction.

Many years after the Kennedy administration, I had separate discussions with Robert S. McNamara, secretary of defense from 1961 to 1967, and McGeorge Bundy, JFK's first national security advisor, about Penkovsky. Both made similar comments. Given Kennedy's attitude toward taking a tough stand against the Soviet Union, it would have been impossible to change the president's mind based on that limited evidence. Unfortunately the Bay of Pigs in April 1961 and the Berlin crisis prevented any form of dé tente and reconciliation for a decade. The Kennedy team was filled with idealists who saw military force as essential in confronting the Soviets and, to use a current phrase, transforming that strategic landscape. That thinking would also shape decisions on Vietnam. These were new Wilsonians when it came to American global ambitions.

Kennedy steamed into office in January 1961. On the defense side, the first priority was correcting the alleged strategic deficiencies of the Eisenhower defense programs. Immediately, supplemental defense bills were submitted to Congress. Kennedy also ordered a strategic reappraisal by the Pentagon.

Shortly before the Bay of Pigs fiasco in April, Kennedy had summoned his Joint Chiefs of Staff to the White House to discuss how much was enough, at least in regard to nuclear deterrence. The air force, under the pugnacious Gen. Curtis LeMay, who had directed the firebombing of Japan during World War II, called for doubling the number of strategic bombers and ballistic missiles. The navy, under its chief, Adm. Arleigh Burke, kept its counsel.

Kennedy, who had been a lieutenant junior grade in the Pacific while Burke had been a highly decorated and renowned wartime destroyer squadron commander in that theater, was an admirer of Burke's. He asked the admiral why the navy was not as aggressive as the air force in calling for more strategic nuclear weapons. Burke's answer still has relevance today.

Burke told the young president that, as a boy, he had the good fortune of growing up in Colorado. He was of an age that he could still remember cowboys. But, Burke told the president, rarely did he ever see a cowboy carrying three guns. "Two guns," he said to Kennedy, "were usually enough."

McNamara would later recall that, by encouraging the military to recommend increased forces, his challenge reverted to one of limiting the total number of nuclear weapons to levels that made strategic and fiscal sense. McNamara was led to invent the notion of assured destruction as the cornerstone for the new strategy. Assured destruction simply meant how much survivable nuclear firepower was needed to destroy the Soviet Union after a first strike had been delivered against and absorbed by the United States.

Ultimately that figure was arbitrarily set at 400 deliverable equivalent megatons (MT) of nuclear weapons, meaning any mix of bomber and missile warheads that would strike the Soviet Union with 400 MT of nuclear explosives. Using data from the elaborate nuclear testing program that went on in the Pacific after World War II, McNamara's team calculated that assured destruction of 400 MT would kill between one-quarter and one-third of the Soviet population and destroy about half of the Soviet Union's industrial capacity. In fact, because the military-industrial and societal-population target sets in the Soviet Union were largely collocated, far more Russians would likely have perished in a war.

The other side of assured destruction was flexible response. This concept was advanced by Gen. Maxwell Taylor, army chief of staff during the Eisenhower administration. Taylor questioned that, given the Soviet capability of challenging the United States at virtually all levels of conflict including revolutionary and guerrilla war, in order to deter attack, did the United States not require counterbalancing capability at each level? In other words, nuclear deterrence, it was reasoned—wrongly as it turned out—would extend only so far to prevent other forms of war. Conventional and unconventional force would be needed at these other levels. Furthermore, if the Soviet Union managed to reach nuclear parity, then a conventional military imbalance in favor of Moscow was also unacceptable.

Thus, at precisely the time the Soviet Union concluded it could reduce its military forces and improve ties to the United States, Washington was aggressively moving in precisely the opposite direction. With bad advice, Kennedy approved the Bay of Pigs invasion. Launched by Cuban exiles operating in the United States to end the regime of the Cuban Communist leader, Fidel Castro, and return democracy to the island nation, promised U.S. air support was withheld, and the invasion failed disastrously. Virtually all of the Cuban attacking force was killed or captured, and the fledgling Kennedy administration was handed its first foreign policy debacle.

To the Soviets the combination of a dramatic escalation in American military spending, a revised American strategy that increased both nuclear and conventional deterrence, and the Bay of Pigs led to a crisis in the Kremlin over Khrushchev's plans to reduce defenses. The aggressive thrust of the new American administration became a political nightmare for Khrushchev, who still wanted to divert funds from defense to civilian and economic needs beyond the military. Unfortunately the response generated a further supercrisis.

Khrushchev was seeking an end around these strategic challenges. How could he heed the warnings of his generals and preserve a budget that met civilian needs while the Americans were rearming? His conclusion seemed brilliantly simple. Why not bypass building more long-range ballistic missiles and rely instead on short-range weapons based in Cuba to deter the Americans.

The United States was strategically outflanked by Soviet nuclear bases in Cuba, making American new missile programs obsolete, as well as a waste of money, had Washington chosen to build them. For Khrushchev this strategic gambit would allow him to have his cake and eat it, too. A strong American response to Soviet missiles in Cuba could be neutralized in advance by secretly putting the weapons in place beforehand and only then announcing their presence. Khrushchev believed the young president would accept the *fait accompli* much as he had buckled over Berlin in the spring of 1961 when the two leaders met face to face.

Kennedy, of course, did not buckle. The United States, relying on U-2 reconnaissance aircraft, detected the missile sites as they were being constructed. For thirteen days the world held its breath as the United States imposed a naval blockade around Cuba to keep Soviet ships from delivering the missiles. The standoff ended. In the subsequent agreement Khrushchev withdrew and would not return Soviet missiles to Cuba provided the United States would not re-invade. However, the bargain was never widely reported in the West nor taken seriously, and Kennedy was touted for winning a great victory.

Unfortunately the missile crisis was pyrrhic for both sides. After the setback in Cuba the Soviet Union reversed Khrushchev's plans (and in late 1964 kicked him out of office) and increased defense spending to match or surpass the United States in military capacity. If not an arms race certainly an arms crawl was on. The opportunity for any form of rapprochement was lost for a decade. The United States, for its sins, would find itself enmeshed in the quagmire that was Vietnam, and Khrushchev was out of a job.

LEGACIES OF VIETNAM

The current violence in Iraq, especially as resistance continues, has been compared with Vietnam. The differences outweigh any similarities, at least in one crucial way. Vietnam was a war over uniting that country, not establishing a democracy. Ho Chi Minh after all had gone to Versailles in 1919 to seek his country's independence from France.

Vietnam was also a civil war in the South between the ruling classes and the Viet Cong. It was a struggle for power between the North and its allies in the South. Even if Iraq should disintegrate, that division would not be similar to the situation in Vietnam. Furthermore, China and the Soviet Union were engaged on the North's side, and the North had a vast army, much of which would be deployed to the South to fight a conventional war. Still there are parallels. In America intelligence had been manipulated both to support greater engagement in Vietnam and then to justify expansion and escalation. In August 1964 the destroyer USS *Maddox* was attacked in international waters off the North Vietnamese coast by North Vietnamese patrol boats acting under the orders of a local commander. As it turned out the commander had thought the warship was part of a separate coastal raid being carried out by South Vietnamese special forces and the CIA.

When the Maddox was later ordered back on station off the North Vietnamese *coast* and in international waters with the destroyer USS Turner Joy as consort, the naval unit commander flashed news of a second attack, mistaking sonar contacts for patrol boats and white caps for torpedo wakes. No attacks had taken place and, from electronic intercepts of North Vietnamese communications, the White House knew at the time that the report lacked credibility.

LBJ, however, ordered retaliatory air strikes. The war escalated to a new level. It would take eleven years and fifty-eight thousand American lives before it was over. But Johnson believed that if the United States did not act in Vietnam, its credibility with the Soviets would be tarnished. LBJ, too, was an idealist who believed that military power could change the strategic balance in Southeast Asia. He also believed, or at least purported to, that left unchecked, a Communist victory in Vietnam would cause other regional states to collapse like dominoes, a theory that first gained prominence in the 1950s.

Today there is great controversy over allegations of intelligence failures in Iraq. These charges will be examined in later chapters. But the fact is that administrations have always used intelligence to support policies for which the evidence may not have been entirely present. Indeed, Franklin Roosevelt was the master. In the late 1930s he promised to stay clear of war in Europe while deftly maneuvering the United States into a de facto alliance with Britain. Of course FDR was proven correct. Whether he felt that way on December 7, 1941, when, after Japan's surprise attack on Pearl Harbor sunk the American battle fleet at anchor, we found ourselves at war with the wrong enemy in the wrong ocean, will never be known.

The second parallel is dominoes. At this writing Saudi Arabia and Pakistan are still very much in al Qaeda's gun sights. The task is to ensure that neither becomes a domino and falls to an extremist or revolutionary regime as did South Vietnam.

From Assured Destruction: Defending the Realm

Defense of the homeland, although that phrase had not been invented then, had always been central to the strategic debate, even in the Eisenhower years of massive retaliation. In the 1950s air defenses had been established around the United States consisting of both fighters and missiles to shoot down Soviet bombers. In fact, George W. Bush's service in the Air National Guard was in an air defense fighter squadron.

As technology advanced, in part because of the space program, defense against enemy ballistic missiles became potentially feasible. At first nuclear warheads were deployed in defense missiles so that inaccuracy could be countered with a kill zone large enough to destroy the incoming enemy missile. Later, hit-to-kill technologies would replace the nuclear tips as accuracies improved. However, warhead lethality was always an issue. During the first Gulf War the failure of Patriot air defense missiles to hit any Iraqi Scud ballistic missiles revived criticism of ABM capabilities.

The Kennedy administration took missile defense very seriously, but it came to the conclusion that successfully defending against an incoming nuclear attack was ultimately infeasible and too costly. Even a few warheads could cause catastrophic damage. However, defense still had an important role—to defend U.S. missiles.

The strategic logic was that if the United States could guarantee the survival of sufficient nuclear systems to assure the destruction of the Soviet Union in a follow-on strike, deterrence would be maintained. Hence, missile defenses would assure survival of land-based systems rather than the protection of cities and populations. Secretary of Defense Robert McNamara announced this policy in 1962 at Ann Arbor, Michigan, in what became known as the no cities speech.

As both sides developed antiballistic missile systems throughout the 1960s and moved to deploy accurate ICBMs with counterforce (wrongly named first strike) capabilities to destroy enemy missiles in their silos, the fear of an uncontrolled arms race was real. Leaders in Washington and the Kremlin recognized the peril of allowing the arms competition to escalate. But only Moscow understood how far its technology lagged the West, giving the United States a huge advantage.

Hence, America and Russia shared a common interest in applying reasonable limits to the quality and quantity of strategic nuclear forces. This debate over deterrence and defense persisted through the LBJ and first Nixon terms, culminating in the landmark Anti-Ballistic Missile (ABM) treaty and separate strategic arms limitations agreements. By limiting ABMs and numbers of nuclear strike systems, neither side could gain the strategic upper hand. Called mutual assured destruction or MAD by critics, restraints on strategic arms were put in place. These agreements became the cornerstones of security throughout the remainder of the Cold War and the first decade thereafter.

MAD and the realities of assured destruction did not satisfy everyone. Massive destruction in nuclear war that killed millions of Americans, Europeans, and Russians would be catastrophic and, in that view, was a bankrupt moral policy. President Ronald W. Reagan was the most vocal and active supporter of defenses. In March 1983 he announced his Strategic Defense Initiative (SDI), designed to make nuclear weapons impotent and obsolete by destroying them after launch and before attacking the United States. Although a research and development program, at some stage SDI would abut against the limits of the ABM Treaty regarding testing and deployment of new systems. However, it would take nearly twenty years for that to happen. SDI offered no defense against bombers and cruise missiles.

In the 2000 presidential campaign, candidate Bush promised to transform the U.S. military for the twenty-first century and develop missile defense at the cost of abrogating the ABM Treaty. In 2001 and the first months of his administration the president kept his promise. Despite political predictions that abandoning the ABM treaty after thirty years would lead to instability and provoke the Russians, American withdrawal did not have these effects. Indeed, the relative absence of a backlash surprised many critics.

In September 2002 the Bush administration published its National Security Strategy. In it was a paragraph that cited the policy of preemption. The rationale was that in the post–September 11 world, knowledge of a pending attack was sufficient grounds to prevent that attack by striking first. That policy evoked enormous controversy and still does. It will be examined more closely in the next chapter. However, the end of containment and deterrence as they had been known for nearly sixty years was imminent. The dilemma was that no suitable replacement construct had yet been found.

From Mass Destruction to Mass Disruption

This explains why the first contradiction is so striking. With the end of the Soviet Union and the strength of the American economy, the United States entered the new century with unprecedented and unchallenged strength. The term sole remaining superpower was used freely to describe this unrivaled ascent. But, as with other slogans and fancy phrases, it sounded more impressive than it really was. The absence of a competing superpower would not make the United States safer or securer.

The new threat, termed asymmetric by the Pentagon, in fact is far more complicated. Asymmetric actually means that the enemy will not fight according to our rules or necessarily with like forces. Goliath was perhaps the first victim of asymmetric war when he was slain by a rock slung by the young David. The North Vietnamese won victory not in battle in the South. That war was waged in living rooms, college dorms, and the halls of Congress on TV screens and in newspapers.

The North Vietnamese used their forces in strictly Clausewitzian terms to win the political as opposed to the military conflict of wills. Clearly terror is used for leverage and psychological impact, and it fits the asymmetric definition because its target is not the conventional might of the armed forces but the will and perception of the people.

The U.S. military, surely in Desert Storm, in Enduring Freedom in Afghanistan in 2002, and in Iraqi Freedom in 2003, relied on its advantages in asymmetric warfare. Its capabilities, effects-based targeting (about which more will be said), and extraordinarily trained and dedicated personnel maintained so much superiority over the adversaries that those conflicts were asymmetric. However, jihadist extremism and extremists occupy a different space in the spectrum of asymmetric enemies.

Unlike the Nazis and Communists, the new enemy is faceless, difficult to identify and track down, does not rely on like conventional forces, goes after hard and soft targets and military and civilian personnel with equal vigor, and is often prepared to die in the process. The current weapon of choice is the bomb, very reminiscent of the late-nineteenth and early-twentieth-century extremists and anarchists who chose similar tools, along with assassination of national leaders. Terror is the tool, the tactic, and the outcome. The purpose is to terrorize, intimidate, disrupt, divide, isolate, and ultimately to achieve some political end point.

In the greater Middle East for bin Laden, that outcome is revolution and regime change in Saudi Arabia and Pakistan to Islamic fundamentalists (or fellow travelers). The current reign of terror in Saudi Arabia is designed to weaken the government. Elsewhere as in Turkey, the intent is to divide and isolate the government from its citizens and to drive a wedge into Turkey's alliance with the United States, Britain, and NATO. In Iraq the aim is to force out the American occupiers by making the costs of occupation too expensive in human, resource, and political terms.

Practically, jihadist extremists have exploited globalization, the second reason why the danger is so great. Globalization has integrated markets and cultures with positive and negative results. The linkage and interdependence of financial, trade, electronic, communications, and other markets and networks clearly have created vulnerabilities and fragilities. Disruption of these networks has powerful consequences, measurable in billions and even trillions of dollars. September 11 proved that. Hence, one attack point for jihadist extremists is these networks and products of globalization.

Finally, unlike the Cold War when the probability of nuclear war turned out to be minimal, al Qaeda and other terrorist groups will strike. The questions are when and where will the next September 11 take place, not whether. Furthermore, as all American presidents have recognized since the Cold War ended, jihadist extremists and terrorists cannot be excluded from obtaining and using chemical, nuclear, and perhaps most likely biological agents in future attacks, although there are grounds to believe this danger may be exaggerated.

That the United States and indeed virtually all states are vulnerable to disruption is hardly news. Every single U.S. commission and study on vulnerability in at least the past decade makes this point. The Hart-Rudman National Security Strategy/21st Century Commission predicted in February 2001 that within twenty-five years a terror attack against the United States would use weapons of mass destruction. Later that year came anthrax letters mailed through the post to Congress and a number of media offices.

The Commission was twenty-four and a half years prescient. Subsequent studies and congressional hearings continue to reveal how vulnerable the United States and its infrastructure remain to potential disruption and attack. Creation of the Homeland Security Department and the fusion of many agencies of government into counterterrorist task forces, working groups, and interagency committees were meant to deal with these vulnerabilities. However, as Churchill remarked early in the World War II, this marks more the end of the beginning than the beginning of the end.

In the first place, because of their inherent openness, democratic societies are fundamentally vulnerable to disruption. The greater the danger, the more likely that stricter laws and rules will be enacted to protect the public good, further inhibiting basic individual freedoms. Such infringements are additional dividends for those out to inflict terror on these societies. Gaming the system with disinformation and deception, such as threatening to hijack aircraft or attack specific cites merely to force a reaction, is probably something that terrorists are increasingly prone to do. A cell phone becomes a major weapon in any disinformation program, with the expectation that the purposely deceptive conversations will be intercepted.

Americans generally recognize this condition of vulnerability. However, it is very difficult to maintain a high level of concern and alert without either more attacks to shock and scare or convincing proof of attacks that were thwarted. The latter is made more difficult by secrecy and concern about whether release of such information will literally kill human intelligence sources or disclose sensitive material to the enemy. Unfortunately there is no easy answer to this quandary.

Americans have also adopted a risk-free approach to life, given the high standard of living most enjoy, certainly in comparison with the rest of the world, along with the opportunity to gain great material and financial success and, despite all the political squabbles over who pays for medical treatment, an extraordinary breadth of health care facilities. As a result American life expectancies are now in the late seventies and early eighties. More to the point, American expectations about life style are generally high.

During the first century of the nation's life, all was not so risk free. Families were usually large in order that a few children would survive. Mortality was greater because of disease, privation, and the risks of moving West and enduring the hardships that were part of Manifest Destiny, including Indians that were inclined to resist the settlers from the East. Taking risks was part of life then. Today risk aversion is understandable and widespread.

The consequence is that, psychologically, terrorist attacks play on this risk aversion mentality, magnifying the impact. When the Homeland Security Department advised the nation to stock up on duct tape and airtight plastic covering material as a defense against biological attack, not everyone took the warning as excessive. Many were truly frightened. The fact is, however, that attacks will occur and Americans will be hurt and killed. Accepting that reality is difficult. Yet public attitudes must change, and the risk of terrorist attacks must be accepted as a part of life.

That America and its colossal infrastructure are inherently vulnerable comes as no surprise. Living in Georgetown in the nation's capital reveals that vulnerability nearly every day. Storms, summer heat, and an ancient electric grid mean that power is disrupted with surprising frequency. For a time, exploding manhole covers were a problem. Even the phone systems were lost for about ten days when a utility worker inadvertently cut a major cable and failed to report it to the phone company. Those, in retrospect, were humorous anecdotes. But suppose the loss of power in August 2003 to fifty million Americans and Canadians in the Northeast had been caused not by human error but by premeditated terrorist attack. What would have been the reaction?

Hollywood, television, and fiction writers have all anticipated the range of possible terrorist attacks, from large ships plowing into crowded city waterfronts and then detonating explosive cargoes aboard to smallpox-infected suicide bombers promiscuously spreading the infectious disease before succumbing to the deadly virus. No doubt Americans and potential terrorist attackers have different perceptions about which targets are preferable and have higher value. Al Qaeda would probably prefer to stage an even bigger September 11.

Hence, the notion of al Qaeda dispatching teams of snipers to shut down a number of cities as happened in the Washington corridor in 2002 or dozens of suicide bombers to blow themselves up in shopping malls is probably outside their preferred set of targets. That reasoning may not apply to every extremist group. However, it is prudent to assume that terrorists are as likely to be clever and imaginative in choosing targets and attacks as not.

From all of the vulnerability studies available on the Internet or from the Government Printing Office, it is not difficult to conjure up a list of potential targets that would bring the United States or any other state literally to its knees. Three examples make the point.

The United States, in an age of electronic and paperless communications, is still entirely dependent on paper. Newspapers, letters, money, magazines, and stamps all use one form of paper or another. Suppose the paper supply were infected with a chemical or poisonous residue that could be absorbed by a single contact with human skin. Even the threat or a rumor of such an attack would have profound consequences. Who would pick up the morning newspaper or handle cash if there were a chance that the paper was the carrier of a deadly toxin? The impact would be devastating.

A second vulnerability is food. Nearly twenty years ago an individual premeditatively inserted cyanide into Tylenol bottles that were readily available in food and drugstores. The effect was nationwide and instantaneous. Every container of Tylenol was taken off the shelves and tamper-resistant bottle caps would become the order of the day. However, suppose the milk or other major food supply were contaminated by terrorists. Consider the consequences. The single case of Mad Cow disease that was discovered in late 2003 in Washington State is a further reminder and warning of how an infected food supply can affect us.

The third example is the unleashing of a flood of illegal aliens crossing the Mexican border into the United States. Sheer numbers would overwhelm border and other guards. In essence this could be an invasion by another name. Also, it could be precipitated by terrorist groups imposing havoc in Mexico, perhaps by shutting down the power grid or indeed poisoning the food or water supplies, or simply by claiming to have done so. The result would be a huge influx of refugees across the border. The United States would be faced with an extraordinary humanitarian and legal problem. Surely disruption would be severe and rumors no doubt would heighten public fears. Recall how difficult it was dealing with the thousands of Cuban boat people forced by Castro to flee to Florida in the 1970s.

The point is that even if the United States were able to protect its infrastructure from terrorist attacks, it still needs to be concerned with occurrences in countries adjacent to or near it—Mexico and Canada in particular. In a short example that follows, port and border security, with six million shipborne containers entering the United States along with a hundred million or so visitors, presents a daunting task in defending against very likely sources of terrorist attacks from anywhere on the planet.

A FINAL WARNING

Deterrence and a complete understanding of the political and geostrategic consequences of nuclear weapons did not occur overnight. It took at least half a decade or more for that understanding to take hold. Similarly, resolving the great paradox in which extraordinary power is insufficient to keep the nation safe will not occur quickly. The United States and its friends are still groping their way along this perilous and often opaque path.

That we are less safe than when we were threatened with massive nuclear destruction is not a statement that is easy to accept at first. However, to jihadist extremists, who are unhindered by our logic and way of thinking, the psychological and physical vulnerability of the United States and its citizens (or, for that matter, any state of interest) is the prime target for attack.

The aim is to disrupt. A fundamental problem is deriving a metric to express in quantitative terms what the threat of disruption implies. There is no assured destruction or equivalent megaton chart to suggest the amount of damage or a means to measure what terrorist-imposed disruption can do to any society. Qualitative measures derived from the costs of the Great Depression, the Spanish Flu epidemic of 1919, and natural disasters can provide approximate data as to what future September 11s could mean for casualties. Then, of course, there is the price of what would happen should al Qaeda and other jihadist extremist groups succeed in overthrowing regimes in Saudi Arabia and Pakistan.

Suppose that some form of extremist state were created in the greater Middle East. Further suppose that this regime, predicated on an interpretation of Islam in a most radical and extreme form, had access to large amounts of Saudi oil revenues, perhaps directly or as bribes, along with Pakistani nuclear weapons. Under those circumstances the entire greater Middle East and most of the world would be turned upside down.

Within the region the moderate states would feel directly threatened. Iran, if it disagreed with the new regime, particularly if it were Wahabi and not Shia in character, would look to acquiring nuclear weapons if it had not already done so. Israel would see itself under grave and immediate threat. Turkey might be forced to re-examine its long-term policy of choosing a secular over a religious rule. Certainly Russia and the bordering "stans" would be challenged. The United States could find itself isolated. Strategic options and new coalitions to counterbalance or contain this new regime would be sought.

As with revolutions that did not go our way, such as China in 1949 and Iran in 1979, there are no guarantees that American responses would be in keeping with changed conditions. "Who lost Pakistan or Saudi Arabia?" would be a question that would resonate throughout Washington and the media. Reverberations would be felt in Europe, and further divisions could be driven into NATO, especially over the one item surely to dominate the agenda: oil.

The developed world has always had unfettered access to relatively inexpensive oil. Clearly, a fundamentalist jihadist regime would understand that. If it needed large amounts of money, then Saudi and Gulf oil would flow. If, however, the new regime were truly fundamentalist, then control of oil could have other political uses. The West could choose to intervene. But the presence of nuclear weapons and the uncertainty of whether they had fallen into the wrong hands would prove to be an interesting and inconvenient question to ponder.

Western Europe is entirely dependent on importing oil and gas, much of it through two pipelines that cross Eurasia. If those pipelines were cut, economic chaos would reign. Europe would lack fuel to power its economic needs. The effects would ripple outward with powerful force. Huge economic tremors would be generated and felt instantly around the world. An economic catastrophe could be created. Although August 1914 brought the world to war, disruption of energy supplies to Europe could produce an economically equivalent impact.

These concerns can be dismissed as overly pessimistic and unrealistic. Yet Lenin and the Communists were dismissed a hundred years ago as minor problems, and eighty years ago no one worried about Hitler and his Black Shirts. Still, given the aspirations of bin Laden, it is far from inconceivable that such a vision is not within his ambition. There is another factor—1.3 billion Muslims.

The causes for radicalism are many and need not be elaborated beyond basic factors. Poverty, exclusion, disenfranchisement, humiliation, and zealotry top the list. If 99.9 percent of all Muslims reject bin Laden and extremism, the remaining .1 percent is a very big number and potential pool of converts—about 1.3 million, the size of America's active duty military. As events in Iraq show daily, from a population of about 25 million, even a small number of dedicated insurgents pose huge security problems. Conversations with several intelligence officials and former senior members of Congress revealed unofficial estimates of a potential Muslim population base for recruiting terrorists between 35 and 50 million.[1]

Americans need to be concerned about this. We also need to be informed. The ultimate danger is not the overthrow of democracy or an enemy who can decisively defeat us on the field of battle and therefore hold the nation hostage. The danger is to our way of life, culture, and society.

Disruption simply will make living more difficult. Standards will decline, and Americans will have to make do with less. With an aging population and huge and growing liabilities in health care, retirement and social security accounts, the impact of terrorism could be to turn each of those into bankruptcy or insolvency by crippling and impairing the economy. That is not a direct attack on the sovereignty of the United States. However, the results would be politically disastrous. That linkage is crucial in understanding why and how mass disruption is so potentially dangerous.

Finally, in understanding the implications of the change in strategic threat from mass destruction to mass disruption, the interplay of politics, ideology and intelligence is a recurring theme. Presidents enter office, if not with visions, certainly with strongly held views, correct or incorrect. John Kennedy was prepared to ignore any estimate of Soviet intent that did not conform to the notion that the United States was behind and needed to catch up. Uninformed by reality, the United States proceeded to increase its defense spending and its nuclear capabili-

1. Conversations with several intelligence officials and former senior members of Congress.

ties substantially. That occurred as the Soviets, under Khrushchev, were reducing their own forces.

Decisions over American involvement in Vietnam were based less on ignorance of the facts at the beginning and more on the conviction that the United States had to take a stand in Southeast Asia to demonstrate to Moscow and Beijing resolution in opposing Communism and to prevent other dominoes from falling. Of course the only dominoes that fell were in Saigon and Lyndon Johnson's White House.

The current Bush administration came into office with an extraordinarily experienced national security team and a president who, by his own admission, was unseasoned in foreign and defense policy. Bush's avowed national security intentions were to transform the U.S. military for the twenty-first century; put in place missile defenses to defend against North Korea and other states who might, in the future, develop nuclear weapons and long-range means to deliver them; and avoid the trap of nation-building and peacekeeping that had haunted the Clinton administration. To many, particularly outside the United States, Bush's unilateralism and hint of isolationism ran counter to the dangers that required American leadership and engagement, the latter a bad word since it was Clinton's, to maintain stability and peace throughout an increasingly chaotic and troubled globe.

Surely, September 11 forced the president to change his thinking and his objectives dramatically. Yet change must be accompanied by complete understanding of what needs to be changed and what can or cannot be accomplished. Failure to have that understanding was the critical flaw of the Kennedy years.

As will be shown, the Bush ideology was reflected throughout his administration and in the decisions that were made. Iraq became an opportunity to change the strategic landscape of the greater Middle East. The means was through imposing democracy and freedom. A stunningly brief war was fought. Saddam Hussein was defeated. Eight months after Baghdad fell, American forces finally apprehended Saddam. However, pacifying and democratizing Iraq turned out to be far more perplexing matters than routing the Iraqi army. Here the administration's assumptions about the ease of occupation and of finding an Iraqi leader to mobilize the country proved hollow. Yet strategy and policy were based on those assumptions and the ideology underpinning both.

A FINAL PLEA

Because they are not entirely clear and present and require no state or formal boundaries, the dangers that lie ahead must be carefully measured and understood. Understanding requires objectivity and a certain cool-headedness from which ideology and preconceptions must be notably absent or contained. If that level of objectivity in understanding cannot be met, the new dangers could be far worse than an avoidable arms race with the Soviet Union that still ended in our favor and a war in Vietnam that misperceptions and failure to accept the truth caused us to lose. As we will see, the battle is being joined by twenty-first century versions of idealists and realists.

There are no ironclad laws that mandate perpetual economic growth. Despite America's preference and optimism over its system of government, there are no absolute guarantees that it is able to deal adequately with all problems. Although Osama bin Laden may resemble more a caricature of a tall, rangy, will-o'-the-wisp rather than a dedicated and proven revolutionary, Americans cannot be deceived by looks or presumptions about how technological superiority will inevitably defeat terrorists hiding in caves and dependent on foot or donkey for transportation.

Arrogance is indeed a deadly sin. Among the approximate 1.3 billion practitioners of Islam, as noted, even a fraction of a single percentage point of that community who are converted to extremism is a huge number. Given that al Qaeda probably numbered in the hundreds, that its trainees were in the tens of thousands, and that fellow travelers were perhaps a hundred thousand, the potential reservoir for future jihadist extremists is strikingly large.

Because all societies are perpetually and irreversibly vulnerable to disruption and attack, the magnitude of the danger cannot be dismissed. As the global war on terror has unfolded, a number of natural disasters have come to pass. Enormous forest fires raged across much of California during the summer of 2003. Droughts and floods simultaneously struck different regions in America. That same summer, a faulty transformer and personnel errors in dealing with the power failure ended up depriving fifty million North Americans of electrical power. Furthermore, at the end of 2003, BSE or Mad Cow Disease hit the United States for the first time.

If any of these disasters had been the result of terrorist attacks, the political response would have been extraordinary. For better or worse, each had natural or accidental causes.

The conclusion is obvious. All states and persons are at the mercy of natural disasters from floods and fire to disease. In late 2003 an earthquake demolished the Iranian city of Bam killing an estimated forty thousand souls. These natural disasters, tragic as they may be, are accepted parts of life.

One role of government has been to minimize the effects of these events, or in today's jargon, to have the capacity for consequence management. Consequence management has the advantage of dealing with both forms of vulnerability to natural and manmade actions. This vulnerability is inherent and is the target for terrorists, one they will exploit and magnify as surely as they intend to terrorize.

The battle against the global war on terror must have (in addition to a new name) as its larger and, so far, unstated goal ensuring that bin Laden, al Qaeda, and the theocratic-political aim of creating an extremism regime are defeated. For that to happen, the war must strike against more than symptoms. Terrorists are symptoms. Killing or capturing them only works in ending the danger when aspirants and recruits no longer seek to join that cause. Hence, the causes of jihadist extremism and its attraction must be eliminated or remedied.

The contradiction that despite its power the United States may never have been so vulnerable complicates the ability to attack the causes, not only the symptoms, of the dangers that threaten the nation and its friends and allies. A seemingly weak and largely invisible force that shares a radical theology in which surrendering one's life for the greater good has religious appeal is not a new phenomenon.

Many freedom movements, even in the first days of this republic, had common traits. But it is the perverted and entirely ruthless aspects of this brand of jihadist extremism that make it so dangerous. Neither al Qaeda nor other theological extremists have the capacity to destroy American society in a thermonuclear holocaust as did the Soviet Union. The danger is more pernicious, however. The threat to our standard of living, our values, and our expectations is real. It is also probably quite large, far larger than most people can conceive.

Terror, because its explicit purpose is to terrorize, intensifies the political and psychological reactions to it, both before any acts take place and surely after terror has struck. For many Americans this is a new form of vulnerability. Unfortunately, the vulnerability has always been present. This is the first time in decades and possibly centuries that this vulnerability now poses the greatest challenge to the nation's security.

The government's first responsibility is to protect its citizens. Here the nature of America's political system has created both a danger and a salvation. Only government possesses the responsibility, authority, and resources to protect the nation. Contracting out that function, despite the spate of private firms now engaged in all aspects of the security business, from hiring Ghurkas to guard facilities in Iraq to renting police to protect people of wealth or position, is not an option. Government must be made to work.

Unfortunately, especially in years divisible by four, when presidential elections exert powerful gravitational effects on politics, government often fails the common sense test. That failing is not restricted to either the White House or Congress. One telling example makes this point. The nation spends billions to screen passengers in airport security points searching for bombs and weapons that could be used to hijack or destroy an airliner. Yet similar controls regulating cargo and noncommercial aircraft that could be commandeered by terrorists are not in place. Why?

An enormous challenge, in an era when the danger is not mass destruction but mass disruption, is how to make government more responsive. As it turned out in the Cold War, there was (unexpected) enormous margin for error. What happens when or if those margins are no longer broad? What happens when government must respond sensibly, effectively, and affordably?

In the wake of Enron and a spate of other corporate misdeeds and scandals, Congress passed HR-3763, the Sarbanes-Oxley Act of 2002. Sarbanes-Oxley was meant to correct these ills by imposing greater visibility and accountability on publicly traded companies. Three provisions are relevant in improving the ability of government to conduct its business.

In that law chief executives were required to certify that information in required financial reports did not contain any "untrue statement . . . or omit" material facts in "fairly presenting" the firm's financial condition. Boards of directors were enjoined to impose greater scrutiny. Assignment to the audit committee, to which the firm's auditors would now report, would become a second full-time job. Last, the Public Company Accounting Oversight Board was created, ending the era of self-regulation for the accounting industry.

If these virtues are as important to good government as to a healthy private sector, then a Sarbanes-Oxley Act for government is a reasonable idea to consider. Of course any White House would rightly claim executive privilege and resist the need for transparency and scrutiny. Turnover of people, as well as size of government, is a huge constraint to fixing accountability.

How might these three provisions of Sarbanes-Oxley—certification of reports, audits, and oversight—be applied to government and would they have much chance of success? To start, every time the president sent a budget or fiscal request to Congress, he, or, given the size of his branch of government, the responsible executive, would provide the same certifications required of corporate management. If those certifications proved wrong or misleading, some consequence would follow.

That the Medicare Prescription Drug Bill of 2004 proved to understate the costs by about one hundred fifty billion dollars when that was known beforehand is a glaring example of why this provision is needed. So, too, was the purposeful omission of some eighty billion dollars in additional spending for the war in Iraq from the $521 billion deficit projection for 2004. Other accounting shorthand is commonly used to disguise the real costs and financial conditions.

Although reorganizational chemotherapy may be a surer cure for Congress, how could Sarbanes-Oxley be applied on Capitol Hill? Consider the coins of the realm in Congress: the bills that are debated and passed. Many are unread and some provisions unwritten at the time of the vote.

There are good and bad reasons for this. Bills, such as Defense, would take hours or days to read. Sarbanes-Oxley was sixty-six pages long, and the prose is not easy to digest. The current trend of massive omnibus bills stuffed with so many provisions that not even the staff may fully understand them is a further step in the wrong direction.

As corporate executives must certify their reports, why not require members of Congress to certify reading and understanding the legislation on which they are voting beforehand? For complex bills, or situations when revision or completion is necessary after the vote, any of those provisions would be redlined for all to see. Also, for every individual spending bill, ceilings could be set that, once broken because of unanticipated or wrongly estimated cost growth, would be automatically subject to legislative review.

Understanding, assimilating, and reacting to these dangers could well be the greatest challenge the nation has faced since the Civil War. Each of these actions is necessary but not sufficient. All must happen if the nation is to be safe and secure.

2
Operation Iraqi Freedom
Good Intentions, Bad Judgments—Idealists and Realists

hy did the Bush administration elect to go to war in Iraq? Is America safer or securer as a result? Has the war put in place the foundations for a new and, from the West's perspective, more favorable strategic landscape in the greater Middle East? Or has the war provoked an intractable and unstable situation in Iraq, exacerbated the confrontation with radical Islam, and put in place forces that will make the strategic landscape more hostile and dangerous?

What should be learned from the conduct of the war; the assumptions that went into those decisions and how they shaped or were shaped by intelligence; and how the administration made its strategic, political, and operational choices regarding allies and the scope of international support on which to draw? Perhaps most important, what should be learned from the postwar conduct of the peace?

The short 2003 war in Iraq has already had surprisingly unintended consequences. The war itself was a brilliant example of how competent, well-led, highly trained, and extraordinarily equipped forces can win a decisive, indeed overwhelming military victory, occupying a state the size of California and with a population of about twenty-five million in less than four weeks. In the process an army of four hundred thousand was driven from the field. Those who stood and fought were literally blown away, as were many of the prewar critics who complained that the United States and its partners had too few forces for the job and thus the attack would bog down. Planning for the subsequent peace and the intelligence and judgments that provoked the war were not treated as kindly.

Just months after an ebullient President Bush landed aboard the navy aircraft carrier USS *Lincoln* and declared an end to hostilities, the occupation and process of rebuilding and democratizing Iraq began to disintegrate. Winning the peace was proving to be far harder and harsher than fighting the war. Despite the reluctance of the Bush administration to acknowledge it, winning wars, at least this one, required less manpower than waging the peace.

More people were needed in the occupation. Admittedly the shape of that extra manpower was less directed for fighting wars and more for enforcing and imposing peace and security—a combination of military, law enforcement, and civil administration capabilities. The unanswerable question is whether a Desert Storm strategy of overwhelming force with far more troops and probably a much slower advance to Baghdad would have eased the trauma of postwar occupation by virtue of having more "boots on the ground."

Containing the mounting insurgency inevitably resulted in more aggressive use of military force by the United States. Three types of risk grew from these robust counterinsurgency operations that more and more resembled the search and destroy missions of the Vietnam War. Their aggressive and intrusive nature provoked some and could provoke possibly many Iraqis who otherwise might have remained friendly or neutral into resisting or opposing American occupation. The broader danger is a popular backlash that could spread the insurgency to the Shia and Kurdish regions or could induce the Shia to form an Islamic Republic in the south.

Second, more intense operations risk provoking stronger retaliation. The insurgents used the intensified counterinsurgency operations as the bloody reason for enticing recruits to join the resistance, escalating the violence and subsequent casualties to insurgents and civilians who were killed or wounded. The American strategy was based on the proposition that a limited number of insurgents will ultimately be defeated—reversing the war plan that called for speed and maneuver and replacing it with the old and familiar strategy of attrition. Attrition, however, brings nasty baggage.

As in Vietnam, if the death toll on both sides reaches a certain, still undefined level, the horrible body count syndrome will inevitably resurface, either as a metric to show how the war is progressing or as a propaganda tool to use against the United States. Casualties have direct political consequences. Although the American public accepts the current level of dead and wounded as tragic but necessary, at some point domestic support will erode as blood continues to flow.

Last is the physical and psychological risk to American and coalition forces of intensified operations and fighting. No matter how well force protection is achieved, i.e., defending against enemy attacks, more intense counterinsurgency operations will bring more casualties. Casualties are a risk of war. But unless there are signs of progress, eventually morale must be adversely affected.

A Sisyphean Labor

Imposing democracy is a difficult (and could prove to be unworkable) task politically, physically, culturally, and intellectually, particularly in a state such as Iraq without any history of pluralism. The majority Shia unsurprisingly favored direct elections. There were also signs that the Shia were preparing to impose an Islamic republic in the south once political authority was returned to Iraqis. Regardless, given the demographics, elections would put the Shia in power for the first time in decades.

The minority Sunni wished to preserve their power and resisted full-blown elections. Traditionalist Muslims argued for a religious as opposed to a completely secular state. In some cases traditionalists resisted the idea of a democracy as violating the Sharia and the requirement to have a practicing Muslim in charge of any Islamic state. Whenever elections were held, sufficient security had to be assured to prevent violence and terror from impeding the vote, thereby delaying the process until the insurgency was finally put down or posed a lesser threat.

As a result, the United States was trapped between good intentions and the promise of democracy and the contradictions over the meaning and means for making Iraq into a more pluralistic state under the rule of law. Progress was also hindered, in retrospect, by the initial decision not to share any political authority with the United Nations in the reconstruction. The Iraqi Governing Council, selected by the Coalition Provisional Authority, reflected these conflicting perspectives. No single leader emerged with authority or legitimacy to serve as the head of the new government. As the postwar violence continued, the Bush administration reluctantly sought to obtain UN cooperation. With eighteen NATO states engaged with the International Division in southern Iraq, it seems possible that NATO might take over those responsibilities by the end of 2004.

The contrast with Afghanistan was instructive. After driving the Taliban out of power in Afghanistan, the Bonn Conference brought together key Afghan leaders. Under the leadership of Colin Powell and others, Hamid Karzai was chosen as the legitimate first president of Afghanistan by a traditional tribal council of elders, called the loya jirga. Outside the Defense Department's preference for Ahmed Chalabi, an Iraqi Karzai has yet to be found.

The extent of these difficulties was reflected in the frequent shifting of American policy as it attempted to keep pace with the Augean task of changing the political landscape of Iraq. Following the removal of retired Army Lt. Gen. Jay Garner as the first U.S. official to lead the reconstruction, his successor, Ambassador L. Paul Bremer announced that the U.S. intent was to draft a constitution before elections and defer transitioning political authority to an Iraqi government. That plan broke down. The next plan was to hold modified elections in the form of eighteen regional caucuses and to move authority to that government by June 30, 2004. Meanwhile the White House resisted sharing any political control with other partners, deferring any real chance for internationalizing the peace and bringing more states into Iraq to help stabilize that country. The aim remained to turn power and sovereignty over to a government by June 30 and, no matter the promises of the president to stay the course, reduce American presence as quickly as possible.

In dealing with the increasingly deadly security problems, a profound split between the American doctrine of escalating the use of military force to put the insurgency down and the British doctrine of peace support with less intense use of military force developed. The incompatibility of doctrinal views prevented the United States from drawing more heavily on British capabilities and also continued, as in Vietnam, the practice of physically separating operating areas because of this lack of interoperability. These distinctions were relevant to understand other differences that arose from and in spite of the successful military campaign in Iraq.

With the First Marine Division's return to Iraq in the spring of 2004, along with a different doctrinal approach to ending the insurgency that relied less on overwhelming force and more on winning hearts and minds, a better idea of which was the more effective approach will be determined. The army predicted that the violence permeating the Sunni Triangle would cause the marines to change their doctrine and rely more heavily on applying military force as both deterrent and punishment. By the end of 2004 one would expect a resolution to this doctrinal division.

It may take historians decades to determine which reasons and factors best explain why the Bush administration went to war in Iraq. It will also take time to understand why the Bush administration failed to mobilize the powerful international support it gained after the September 11 attacks. As German Army General and former chairman of the NATO Military Committee Klaus Naumann asked after NATO members took the unprecedented action of invoking Article V of the treaty that an attack against one was an attack against all, why had the Bush team failed to draw on NATO for more support?

After September 11 the administration was embarked on a course of action with two fixed conclusions: inevitability of war in Iraq and retention of complete political control of the war, whenever it started, and the subsequent peace. The United Nations would not be allowed to share political control, at least not until an Iraqi government was in place. Subsequently, a coalition of the willing that ultimately would include some eighteen NATO states would be assembled for Iraq. That the Afghanistan campaign went so well reinforced the administration's intent to keep tight political control of the war and peace in Iraq.

In fairness to the Bush policy, unexpected opposition to an early start of any military campaign against Iraq arose from Germany and France. Germany's opposition was based on election year politics. Gerhard Schroeder was fighting a tough reelection campaign. The great majority of Germans were opposed to war. Schroeder therefore took an antiwar and anti-Bush stance. He won. However, relations with the United States were understandably strained. Germany's advocacy of an independent military force under the European Union and outside NATO further deteriorated relations.

France was more problematic. France actively opposed the war before all options to find a peaceful solution had been exhausted. French Foreign Minister Dominique Villepin actively lobbied members of the UN Security Council to vote against the second resolution that would have reaffirmed the authority to use force to compel Iraqi compliance with previous UN orders and been the mandate Prime Minister Tony Blair needed to counter political opposition at home.

In a strategic sense, French President Jacques Chirac had legitimate concerns based on first-hand experience. Fifty years earlier he had served as a young officer in the Algerian Civil War, where he was wounded in action. He believed that by rushing to war the United States was repeating the mistakes of France and would bear the bitter fruit as the French had in Algeria. Further, Chirac worried that the United States could inadvertently be provoking a wider conflict with jihadist extremism.

The bitter split with France, despite a meeting between the two presidents in September 2003, had not healed. The Defense Department, in particular, following the lead of its Secretary, remained openly hostile to the French. A reported phone intercept of the French President's conversation revealed the active intent to prevent the United States from going to war. Details are said to be "damning in the extreme."

One consequence was that French companies, along with Russian and German, were prohibited from bidding on any of the U.S. contracts for reconstructing and rebuilding Iraq, clearly punishment for their opposition to the war and to American policy. That prohibition will doubtlessly change. However, the atmosphere was bitter and acrimonious.

A decade earlier the Clinton administration chose to avoid using major military options, believing that, beyond retaliatory strikes, terror was better handled as a law enforcement and intelligence matter. Of course September 11 occurred after his watch, although an attempt to bomb the Twin Towers in 1993 had literally fizzled. The Clinton policy was most likely not the result of a single, carefully made decision to avoid a major confrontation but rather a cautious (and some argue excessively so) approach to using force. Bush was far more decisive and aggressive regarding force. Which approach will be proven the better in making America safer and securer is relevant. After the terrorist attacks, had Al Gore been president, it is unlikely that he would have had little option except to go after al Qaeda in Afghanistan.

How the United States found itself in Iraq and how it determined its courses of action rest in a Churchillian brew of riddles, enigmas, and contradictions arising from noble intentions and judgments that grew suspect if not flawed.

THE CASE FOR WAR NOW OR WAR LATER

Churchill's potion was made more volatile by highly publicized and bipartisan demands for ending Saddam's regime and his programs for weapons of mass destruction, in large part because of alleged links to terror and terrorist groups and a past and unequivocal record of using chemical and biological agents against his enemies. Unfortunately, at first neither Saddam nor his weapons had been found, although Saddam has since been captured. While the United States has probably reduced the population of Arabs six foot three inches or taller in the hunt for bin Laden, he remains at large, still unfinished business.

In the summer of 2003 the Joint Intelligence Committee of Congress released a fairly scathing report assessing the shortcomings of the intelligence community and their failure to anticipate September 11. By late 2003, triggered by revelations of intelligence failures in the United States and Britain, debate, criticism, and controversy over the war and the occupation shifted back to intelligence and why and how it produced many incorrect and flawed findings that drove policy. A national commission on September 11, investigations and hearings by Congress, and an inquiry in London under Lord Justice Brian Hutton examined this particular issue in detail. What will come of these efforts is uncertain and, if history repeats, probably not of much use. Indeed, that is what happened when the Hutton Report was issued in late January 2004, exonerating the British government.

Unfortunately the 2004 presidential campaign will distort and probably not clarify better understanding of how all of this unfolded. Republicans will defend the president and his decisions. Democrats, even those who voted for the war, will find ways of avoiding that responsibility and chastise the president for diminishing the war on terror by pursuit of the war against Saddam. Intelligence failures rather than the validity of political judgment will dominate debate. There was overwhelming bipartisan support for removing Saddam Hussein and denying Iraq "the capacity to develop weapons of mass destruction and the missiles to deliver them," a promise made by President Bill Clinton and repeated not only by the most senior members of his administration but also by both parties in Congress.

More important, before September 11, neither the Clinton administration nor Congress proposed war or U.S. military force to end Saddam's regime. The Iraqi Liberation Act passed unanimously by Congress in late 1998 was a paper tiger because the use of force was not authorized, a little cited fact. The Clinton administration has been rightly blamed for understanding the larger menace of terror but taking insufficient preventive and punitive actions to contain it.[1] That reinforced the question of whether the Clinton administration's policy of regarding terror as a law enforcement and intelligence matter rather than a military matter, by accident or intent, would have proved less damaging than Bush's far more aggressive actions in advancing American security.

There was no dispute over the evil nature of Saddam and his regime. His egregious record of human rights abuses and blatant disregard of sixteen UN resolutions calling for WMD disarmament were unarguable. His military aggression

---

1. These arguments were made in *Unfinished Business: Afghanistan, the Middle East and Beyond: Defusing the Dangers That Threaten America's Security* (Citadel Press: New York, 2002), 288.

against two neighbor states and his use of WMD were further ammunition against his continued rule. The debate over war would revolve around these issues: the two key aims of regime change and WMD disarmament and the role of intelligence in providing policymakers with sufficient, accurate, and verifiable material on which to make proper decisions and take appropriate and effective action. The less visible theme was the degree to which ideology and preconceived political agendas drove intelligence and the conclusions on which it was based.

A CLASH OF VISIONS: IDEALISTS AND REALISTS

After the attacks of September 11 and President Bush's declaration of a war on global terror, it was inevitable that Iraq would become the major target for American military might. The stunningly swift military campaign in Afghanistan, code named Enduring Freedom, which drove the Taliban from power and routed al Qaeda, gave powerful proof to the administration that profound change could be successful when engineered by force. The naysayers who predicted Afghanistan would be as disastrous for the Americans as it was for the Soviets two decades earlier hardly had time to make their critiques before the campaign ended. A very small mix of ground, special, and air forces, operating with the Afghan Northern Alliance and using precision fire, overwhelmed and collapsed a vastly larger force—this was more than a confirmation of military transformation and the unmatched combat power of America. The victory created an aura of American military invincibility.

To an administration that had been foundering from the first days in office, Enduring Freedom was more than a new lease on life for President Bush. It permitted the idealists with ambitious and, some would say, highly exaggerated intentions to change the strategic map of the greater Middle East, unprecedented opportunity. The combination of that vision along with the president's compelling sense of mission to make America safer and securer would lead to a highly controversial and risky plan of action to protect the United States and its friends from future terrorist attacks. To critics the president's personality played a very important consideration in this.

George W. Bush has proven to be a surprisingly polarizing figure. To supporters, his determination to win the global war on terror is among his most admired qualities. He is not overly fixated on detail, is willing to delegate, and is able to focus on a few major agenda items. His stand on matters of principle and import to conservatives and his gregarious personality are also highly regarded. Bush is also physically attractive and very good with people. His surprise visit to U.S. forces in Baghdad on Thanksgiving 2003 offered visual images of how well he related with the some six hundred soldiers on hand to share a turkey meal.

To his detractors at home and abroad, Bush is the "toxic Texan," playing to the high and mighty who, in the light of Enron, Arthur Anderson, the mutual fund scandals, and other egregious cases of business misdeeds, were the leaders of a very corrupt corporate world. Vice President Dick Cheney's past chairmanship of Halliburton, one of two large American energy and construction companies (the other is Bechtel) contracted to do billions of dollars worth of business in rebuilding Iraq, was commonly cited as further complicity with corporate America (unfortunately a gross oversimplification that lies outside the scope of this book but a topic that needs balanced review). The Bush administration's withdrawl from the Kyoto environmental and climatic treaty, ABM—a centerpiece of U.S. nuclear strategy for decades—and the International Criminal Court and then his announcement in the war on terror that "you are either with us or against us," a favorite warning of Lenin's, produced accusations of arrogance, unilateralism, and naïveté by Bush's critics.

Perhaps it was also inevitable that American politics would descend to the current degree of mutual hostility between the two parties. Whatever the level of Republican visceral animosity toward President Bill Clinton may have been, Democratic opposition to Bush is at least as fierce and in many ways less rational. There is no hard data to demonstrate this deterioration.

A great Supreme Court associate justice remarked about pornography, "I know it when I see it"—the same consideration applies here. Politics have turned far nastier and bitter, a further complication for the nation in dealing with the threat of mass disruption in the shadow of weapons of mass destruction, a war on terror that is hard to wage and to win, and an economy that may be recovering but running up trillions of dollars of future debt in that process. The 2004 presidential election campaign will continue these trends with probably even more bitter partisanship.

In fashioning the global war on terror the president relied on a number of close advisors, in and out of government, described as neoconservatives, a term going back decades and ascribed to the well-known conservative Irving Kristol. Vice President Cheney and Deputy Secretary of Defense Paul Wolfowitz are described as the best-known neos. Secretary of Defense Donald Rumsfeld is often lumped into this group. In reality the hard-driving former businessman now in his second tour as defense secretary is too pragmatic to fit easy categorization. However, Rumsfeld was certainly amenable to the neo's general propositions.

In common with the best and brightest of the Kennedy administration, neoconservatives are, at bottom, idealists. Their belief is that American power can and should be brought to bear to change strategic conditions for the better. A cynic might add that neos are willing to pay any price and bear not every burden as a more commonsense way of defining this outlook.

Virtually all of the neos are veterans of the Reagan and first Bush administrations. During those twelve years the world was transformed and the Soviet Union defeated. The carry-forward reasoning was that if a threat as formidable as the Soviet Union could be overcome, then terrorism and the dangers emanating from the Middle East could be countered by an imaginative and aggressive strategic plan.

For an administration looking at the greater Middle East, from the seemingly permanently intractable Israeli-Palestinian conflict to the Indo-Pakistani standoff and with Egypt, Saudi Arabia, Syria, Jordan, the Gulf States, and Iran in between, the easiest and indeed perhaps only feasible overarching strategic approach went through Iraq. Labeled by the president in his first State of the Union address as a charter member of the axis of evil, along with Iran and North Korea, Iraq was perceived as the strategic lever for transforming the entire region, or so the logic went.

Displacing Saddam and replacing his rule with a democratic regime would have profound strategic value and consequence. At the least, Iraq would be removed from the list of enemy states and, as a democracy, would presumably become friendly. In a friendly state, the danger of weapons of mass destruction could be ended by fiat once the weapons were found and destroyed. However, beyond Iraq, democratization would have salutary effect within the region and beyond.

Autocratic regimes in Saudi Arabia and Egypt would take careful note and would be encouraged to move more quickly to reform. Iran's religious leaders would find their authority diminished as democratic elements would be encouraged to transform that country to secular rule. Syria would understand that it might be next on America's regime change list and become more reasonable in limiting support to Hamas and Hezbollah in Lebanon. Ultimately the security of Israel would be ensured, and steps taken to resolve the conflict with the Palestinians would be made easier by a friendly Iraq.

In other words, changing the regime in Iraq was "one stop" strategic shopping at its best. Going to war to end Saddam's rule and replace it with some form of democracy was an unprecedented opportunity and the most urgent policy imperative in the minds of these idealists. Hence, the issue was never whether to go to war against Iraq. The issue was to go to war as quickly as the political process would permit so that this strategic opportunity would not be lost.

Removing Saddam also would conveniently put to rest any nagging criticisms for not doing so in the first Gulf War, a prospect then that was politically impossible, as the coalition and UN support would have disintegrated. In 1991 in responding to critics who urged the first Bush administration to continue the march to Baghdad and eliminate Saddam permanently, then–Secretary of Defense Dick Cheney gave an eloquent explanation of why that was a bad idea. Cheney predicted that had we invaded and occupied Iraq, the United States would find itself trapped in a country likely to be torn by religious and ethnic conflict, possibly leading to a civil war.

Clearly the vice president saw things differently in 2003 and argued that circumstances had changed dramatically. As he said, Iraq could not be allowed to continue its WMD programs. And of course retribution for Saddam's attempt to assassinate the elder President Bush, an understandable human reaction, was present but probably only on the margins.

President Bush probably did not share the same explicit strategic vision as the idealists in his administration, certainly not before September 11. After those attacks and the anthrax-filled letters that followed, by all accounts Bush came to the conclusion that his overriding and probably historic mission was to protect the nation from future terror, attacks that he correctly understood were inevitable. To use the pop-art term, this was a life-changing experience for the president.

By his own account Bush had two earlier life-changing experiences. In other eras some might have considered these events epiphanies. According to his autobiography, *A Charge to Keep,* the morning after his fortieth birthday celebration at the Broadmoor Hotel complex in Colorado Springs, Bush awoke having had too much to drink and decided then and there to give up alcohol, an extraordinary feat of will power. There are other accounts that dramatize the circumstances. The point is that Bush realized he had a problem and corrected it. To this day he remains a teetotaler.

The second life-changing event was returning to Christianity, or in the vernacular, to be born again. This renewal was largely attributed to the help of the Rev. Billy Graham, a family friend and one of America's most famous religious leaders. To his credit the president has largely kept his faith to himself and to his family and close friends and not permitted his religious beliefs to impinge publicly on his presidency. Critics, of course, disagree and cite "faith-based initiatives" and courting of the far religious right as excessive examples of the president not fully separating church and state.

Those experiences forever changed the president. The third experience was September 11. Compulsion may be too strong a word to describe his motivations. However, his single most important, self-imposed mission became winning the war on terror. If press reports were accurate, Bush told his closest advisors that the task of winning the war on terror was far more important than winning a second term.

Bush's focus on the war on terror and the strategic opportunity seen by the idealists in his administration converged on Iraq. The exact date that war with Iraq became inevitable and when the president ultimately took that decision will no doubt be revealed. July or August 2002 is the best estimate. However, the coincidence of Bush's conversion and the neo's view of Iraq as a unique strategic opportunity catalyzed, making the case for removing Saddam. To achieve that goal, however, Saddam had to be seen as a clear and present danger and his weapons of mass destruction as a source of immediate threat, either from him or from those he might provide with these agents.

Not all of Bush's cabinet and advisors were idealists, nor did everyone share the opinion of how to transform the strategic landscape of the Middle East. Realists, inside and out of government, were profoundly troubled by what they generally agreed was a rush to war that was neither justified nor urgent. Realists had also served in the Reagan and first Bush administrations.

Realists held no book for Saddam Hussein. Under the proper circumstances, ridding the world of Saddam was a good, just, and necessary thing. For the realists, the crucial questions of why, when, and how and what to do about the consequences of another war in the Gulf were not fully answered by the idealists. After all, going to war was meant to improve and not worsen the strategic condition. The end state and outcome were unclear, and the idealists were accused of having overly optimist visions about both.

Secretary of State Colin Powell shared many of these realists' views. Former national security advisor to Presidents Ford and Bush 41, retired Air Force Lt. Gen. Brent Scrowcroft was another. Very likely, former secretary of state James Baker, close friend and advisor to the senior Bush, would not have dissociated himself from these cautions. Further, a large number of retired and active duty senior military were realists, almost all having served in Vietnam.

Two former commanders in chief of central command, retired Marine Generals Joseph Hoar and Anthony C. Zinni, were respectfully critical of the idealists' intentions toward Iraq. Zinni, with reference to Kennedy's debacle at the Bay of Pigs, warned pointedly of the dangers of launching a "Bay of Goats" operation with obvious reference to the Middle East. As war plans progressed, a number of senior officers in the Pentagon warned of negative consequences for the postwar as well as planning stages, which, in the view of former army chief of staff Gen. Eric Shinseki and his former secretary of the army Thomas White, simply proposed using too few ground troops.

It is interesting that in Congress, while there was a silent majority to echo Richard Nixon's famous phrase decades earlier who were worried by the rush to war, few were actively critical. Sens. John McCain and Chuck Hagel, both decorated veterans of Vietnam, reflected the views of the realists. However, as it would turn out there was little debate in Congress over the whether and also over the why and when reasons for war.

Elimination of the Regime or Its Weapons of Mass Destruction?

The original case the administration began to make over Iraq was over the urgency in removing Saddam. The White House contended that Saddam was a real threat—later a grave and gathering one—and the only prudent alternative was to end his regime as quickly as possible. Regime change became the order of the day at least as 2002 progressed, and there were many good reasons to see Saddam go.

He was in violation of sixteen UN resolutions in clear defiance of international law. He had attacked two of his neighbors, launching wars of aggression against Iran in 1979 and Kuwait in 1990. He had used chemical and probably biological weapons against Iran and his own people, admittedly years before. He was a monster, and his abuses of human rights were unconscionable. Each of these points was unarguable and required no verification or proof from the intelligence community.

But the political reality was "So what?" The world was full of bad people and rulers who deserved to be removed. Generally, there was reluctance on the part of the international community to resort to force in order to deal with despots and villains who abused their power and authority. The crisis in the former Yugoslavia and the mass genocide that was described by the less brutal-sounding synonym of ethnic cleansing was not finally addressed until 1999 by NATO and the seventy-eight-day bombing campaign that forced Slobodan Milosevic to retreat from Kosovo. There was reluctance on the part of the allies to act even then.

More important, the UN Security Council and most of the international community did not agree with the argument for urgency in using force to remove Saddam. Sanctions, no-fly zones, and authorization to fire back in self-defense were deemed sufficient to punish and to contain the Iraqi dictator. Opinion was greatly divided as to how much of a threat Saddam posed and the amount of weapons of mass destruction he actually possessed.

UN weapons inspectors and the International Atomic Energy Agency (IAEA), who Saddam reluctantly allowed back into Iraq in late 2002, were unable to uncover any smoking guns. Even Iraqi obstructions that blocked the inspections and created the perception that there was something to hide were not sufficient to change international attitudes for war. Hence, no matter the rhetoric, if the Bush administration were to gain international support, regime change was not a powerful enough argument to win that case, at least in the United Nations and the international community.

By late summer of 2002, the White House signaled that, should it decide to forcibly remove Saddam, neither UN supporting resolutions nor congressional approval was necessary. The signals were so strong that British Prime Minister Tony Blair chose to send his Minister of Defence Geoff Hoon to Washington shortly before Labor Day. Hoon's task was to slow the administration down while international support could be gathered.

At a small dinner at the British Embassy in Washington hosted by Ambassador Sir Christopher Meyer, Hoon met with a handful of senior Americans with extensive experience in foreign affairs, divided between private citizens and those serving either officially or unofficially in the administration. Two senior senators representing the more conservative wings of the Republican and Democratic parties were also present.

Hoon laid out a forceful case for dealing with Iraq. However, there was no sense of urgency in having to move to war at that point. Saddam was not, in the British view, a clear and present danger even though he was surely a prime candidate for military action if he continued to defy UN resolutions requiring Iraq to end its pursuit and destroy all of its weapons of mass destruction programs. That was the message Hoon delivered to the administration.

Britain would stand with the United States. Blair's reasoning was that Britain had to remain America's senior "junior" partner. Abandoning America, Blair further reasoned, would isolate Washington from Europe. Hence, there was a clear strategic-political case for joining the United States. However, in the British view all other reasonable means had to be exhausted in dealing with Saddam first before the war option could be taken up. Public opinion in Britain was running strongly against war. To most Britons Saddam had been successfully contained, and the threat he posed to the world at large did not require war. This was no Hitler, in the British view. Also the British public did not hold President Bush in particularly high regard. The term "toxic Texan" was frequently used in the press to describe him.

The political consequence for Blair was the pressing need to obtain a UN resolution unambiguously authorizing force to compel Iraqi compliance with the prior UN resolutions. Blair, a lawyer, felt strongly that such defiance of international law was a *casus belli* once it was clear the offending party would not submit to UN mandates. In that regard Blair's closest ally was Colin Powell.

Powell was caught in the middle of a difficult situation. He knew that it was imperative to win UN and congressional support before going to war. That was a lesson he had learned during the first Gulf War when he was Bush 41's chairman of the Joint Chiefs of Staff. However, there were powerful voices in the administration, probably led by the vice president, who argued that as commander in chief, the president had enough authority to send forces into action. What went by the board was the argument for war based on regime change. Eliminating Saddam sooner rather than later meant that the case for urgency was essential. That rested on weapons of mass destruction, the immediate danger it posed, if at all, and the intelligence to support or refute either case.

Powell had two tasks. First, he had to convince the administration that UN and congressional support were essential. Second, he had to shift the grounds for war from regime change, an argument that would not win the needed support in the United Nations, to the more urgent threat of weapons of mass destruction.

Privately, Powell concluded that if Saddam did disarm and it could be verified, this would constitute a regime change and eliminate the need for war. Powell also recognized the thinness of that logic. However, with a White House that seemed determined to go to war and a vice president who was one of the most active advocates for that course of action, slowing down the administration was far from a done deal.

During the fall of 2002, the president's National Security Strategy was released, drafted we are told by the NSC staff under national security advisor Condoleezza Rice. Preemption was explicit as part of the options available to the nation. Although that phrase evoked and continues to evoke controversy, especially given uncertainty over the veracity of intelligence, the important debate shifted to Saddam's weapons of mass destruction and arguments for why those programs constituted a clear and present danger.

The administration tried to establish that linkage on the basis of shadowy intelligence reports, including an alleged meeting between one of the September 11 hijackers, Mohammed Atta, and Iraqi intelligence agents in Europe. The conclusion was that Baghdad had been working with al Qaeda and that it was possible, if not likely, Saddam would share his weapons of mass destruction with these jihadist extremists. Why Saddam, a secular Sunni, would ally with radical Sunnis out to topple his own regime was a question that was overlooked or ignored.

The logic that Saddam possessed WMD and used them to kill thousands was critical in the judgment to go to war. On this basis of past conduct most objective observers would conclude that Iraq still possessed and would use weapons of mass destruction again. That Saddam had refused full cooperation with UN and IAEA weapons inspectors was confirmation. Otherwise why would Iraq take such a position unless it still possessed these weapons?

As pressure mounted on Saddam, UN weapons inspectors under Hans Blix and the IAEA under Mohamed el-Baredi were permitted by Iraq to recommence inspections but without complete freedom for surprise and random visits to sites suspected of housing WMD. Saddam had thrown the inspectors out in December 1998. The new round of inspections would uncover no hard evidence of WMD, no smoking guns, and were largely derided and dismissed by a White House confident that WMD would be discovered once Saddam was gone.

Meanwhile American and British forces began pouring into Saudi Arabia, Kuwait, and surrounding states. Those forces were needed as diplomatic leverage to coerce Saddam to accept the UN resolutions or suffer the consequences. The forces were also a double-edged sword. They could not be kept on station indefinitely. Moreover, as the spring and hot weather approached, from a military perspective, it was far better to attack in cooler conditions. The decision, many felt, had been made. Bush was simply waiting for the right moment. To the idealists negotiations were neither desirable nor necessary.

While the White House was pressing its case for war, it was joked at the time that the *New York Times* wanted Powell to resign in protest, while the more conservative leaning *Washington Times* wanted him fired for not toeing the party line. But Powell and Blair persevered. The president finally chose to go to Congress for a resolution to use force. There he won overwhelming support. He had been given a blank check.

Later many Democrats, several who were candidates for their party's presidential nomination, would regret voting approval. In December the UN Security Council approved Resolution 1441. That resolution, at least as far as the Bush team was concerned, was sufficient authority to use force against Iraq. Other Security Council members disagreed, seeing the resolution as the last chance for Saddam that, if he did not accept, would lead the United Nations to authorize the use of force.

Blair was under great pressure at home. For reasons not entirely clear, in August 2002, when Hoon was dispatched to America, Blair ordered a dossier be prepared to document the evidence and make the case to disprove Saddam's denials of having any weapons of mass destruction. Blair understood that the majority of Britons did not favor war at that point either to remove or disarm Saddam. Furthermore, public opinion in Europe was far more negative in opposing war. Hard intelligence was critical to persuading skeptical publics of the ultimate and, as it turned out, urgent need for war.

Bush understood his chief ally's political predicament. A second UN resolution was proposed as an ultimatum to Saddam to disarm and give inspectors full and complete access or face the use of force. After heated debate and a final try by Powell, who held forth for nearly two hours on February 5, 2003, to convince his colleagues in the Security Council of Saddam's deceit and continuing possession of WMD (with CIA director George Tenet seated directly behind to give visible support for the veracity of the material being provided), the UN Security Council, led by strong French opposition, voted the resolution down. A year later less a day, Director Tenet gave his spirited defense of the CIA speech to Georgetown. Contrasted with Powell's UN statement before the war, one could wonder whether the two had served in the same administration. The United States and Britain, supported by Australia and New Zealand, were unperturbed by the absence of further UN authorization and would make war on Saddam. The idealists had won. That victory was based less on regime change and eliminating weapons of mass destruction than on the broader vision of changing the strategic landscape of the Middle East. That vision and the perceived opportunity were the principal reasons for going to war. Military forces were in place. Saddam had not yielded to UN demands. War was certain.

One other argument that supported the administration's decision for war was Saddam's actions regarding WMD. It seemed inconceivable that if these weapons had been destroyed or eliminated by the United Nations, there was no rational reason for Saddam not to comply with the United Nations and permit unhindered inspections to prove he was telling the truth. Also, it seemed to make little sense for Saddam to forego billions of dollars in oil revenues imposed by the embargo if he did not possess weapons of mass destruction.

This sidebar controversy sheds light on why ideology, policy, and intelligence do not always mix or fit the state or issue involved. Saddam probably believed that even the hint that he had WMD would work in his favor. The weapons gave his regime legitimacy and convinced his people he had stood up to the Americans and did not give in. Further, ambiguity over these weapons offered some measure of deterrence vis à vis Israel and Iran. In fact, the oil embargo served to strengthen Saddam's political control because he completely controlled the distribution of food and medicines to his people as he alone saw fit.

As it turned out, while his country suffered greatly, Saddam was not pinched by lack of oil money. Dozens of obscenely expensive palaces sprung up, and the family owned other luxury items from a stable of cars to the finest wine. There were two other possibilities.

Saddam may well have believed that an American attack was inevitable regardless of whatever actions he took. Evidence suggests that Saddam may have been advised by the French and the Russians that they could get war deferred in the Security Council. In either case, his behavior, which convinced many that Iraq did possess weapons of mass destruction, was possibly a rear guard action to slow down the Bush administration's rush to war.

The fact is that intelligence failed to provide the National Security Council and the president with accurate assessments as to the extent of Iraqi weapons of mass destruction and WMD programs, and Saddam's links with terror. Forecasts of what the postwar situation would be like, if accurate, seemed to have been ignored. Were the intelligence reports manipulated to fit the case for war, however subtly? Or were these reports simply wrong?

Given the nuance of National Intelligence Estimates and the reluctance of intelligence professionals to make firm and fixed predictions in categorical terms, it is very possible that the accurate information and data were there but were not seen or presented properly. On the other hand, it is also possible that the administration's preference for war was so obvious that the intelligence community knew what was expected of it, not a new phenomenon and reminiscent of the Kennedy administration.

OPERATION IRAQI FREEDOM: SHOCK AND AWE OR OVERPOWERING FORCE?

The war began nearly two days earlier than planned, in part because the March date was the earliest British forces would be in place. The firefighters' strike and the outbreak of foot and mouth disease in Britain were contained with the substantial help of the British military. However, filling those responsibilities meant they couldn't be sent to the Gulf. H-hour for Operation Iraqi Freedom was set for 2100 on March 20, the last day before spring.

H-hour was advanced on the basis of hard information on Saddam's location. That imposed considerable challenges for the planners, who had to move up the entire operation, no mean feat. Two F-117 Stealth fighters and forty Tomahawk cruise missiles were targeted to hit a house in Baghdad where Saddam and his sons had been sighted entering. That the time from the go order in the White House to ordnance on target was two hours was a remarkable example of coordination. Some of the cruise missiles had a time of flight of over an hour and a half. The first of four two-thousand-pound Joint Direct Attack Munitions (JDAMs) hit their target on March 20 at 5:35 A.M. Baghdad time.

The strategic bombing campaign began shortly thereafter. "Shock and awe," a term I coauthored five years ago, fell on Baghdad. At approximately 2100 on March 20, a multi-pronged ground attack, led by the First Marine Division, Third Infantry Division, the 101st and 82nd Air mobile divisions, the 173rd Airborne Brigade, and special forces, drove into Iraq.

The advance to Baghdad was extraordinarily swift. On March 25, a sandstorm halted the attack. The media began broadcasting stories of breakdown and bogdown. When irregular forces called Saddam's fedayeen began attacking the long supply lines, the reporting became more pessimistic. Those critics who called for more forces seemed to be right. They were not.

The fedayeen were more a tactical nuisance then a strategic threat to the entire campaign, although those American soldiers and marines who had to deal with them would not share that view. During the sandstorm U.S. air forces had no difficulty penetrating the dense atmosphere with radar, infrared, and other sensors. The Medinah division was rendered hors d'combat by this extraordinary technology and was shocked and awed by the fires that easily penetrated the swirling sands with devastating effect on Iraqi forces.

Twenty-eight days into the campaign, Baghdad fell. Weapons of mass destruction had not been used. Nor had there been the much feared city resistance, accompanied by thousands of civilian casualties. Less than two months after the war started, in a very public display of victory aboard USS *Abraham Lincoln* as she was just returning from her role in winning the war, President Bush declared that hostilities were over.

A word of disclosure before returning to the prosecution of that war: As in the first Gulf War, I spent a great of time in television studios as a contributor for Fox News, the BBC, and other international networks. Most of that time was simply waiting and watching more or less simultaneously some ten or twelve different monitors covering the major broadcast and cable networks. Because of the policy of embedding reporting with frontline troops, television provided instant snapshots of many isolated parts of the large battlefield extending over much of Iraq. Unlike any previous war in history, the amount of visual and aural reporting was overwhelming. To anyone experienced in combat and military operations, this was a treasure trove of material for instant analysis.

Second, in January while the buildup was massing for the attack, CBS Pentagon correspondent David Martin called me to enquire about the Pentagon's war plan. Martin's question began "Well, the Pentagon has adopted shock and awe as its strategy. What do you think about that?"

My response was not printable. While I had been co-chairman of the group that invented the strategy of Rapid Dominance and indeed had derived the phrase "shock and awe," this was the first indication that the Defense Department (DoD) was using any or all of the doctrine. Even though Secretary Rumsfeld had been a "rump" member of the group and, along with three other former secretaries of defense, had recommended to then secretary William S. Cohen that the concept be further explored (two members of the original team sat on DoD's Defense Policy and Defense Science Boards), there was no lack of awareness of the concept. This was the first public notice I had received.

As soon as the war started, however, the phrase, originally scripted as a sound bite for consumption only inside the Pentagon, became shorthand for a strategic bombing campaign of death and destruction—which was never the intent of shock and awe nor the way the attack plan was designed or carried out. The front page of London's *Daily Telegraph* underscored the public relations disaster: "Baghdad Blitz" read the huge headline, under which a color photo graphically showed an enormous explosion enveloping a building in the middle of the city. The phrase quickly sunk with little trace. However, the number of hate e-mails sent to me was quite extraordinary.

The original intent of shock and awe was to "affect, influence and control the will and perception of the adversary" for the very sensible purposes of doing whatever it was that we wanted or stop doing what we did not, as quickly, decisively and in as least costly manner as possible. The philosophy was as old as war, but technology had provided the capabilities to achieve this aim. Not quite immaculate war, the notion was that, by combining near perfect knowledge, rapidity, brilliance in execution, and control of the environment, we could decisively and swiftly defeat an enemy with as few casualties as possible.

To make that point in 1995 when the first document was written, eight examples of employing shock and awe were provided. At one end was the Royal Canadian Mounted Police's unofficial motto of "never send a man where you can send a bullet." The implication was that selective targeting could bring great strategic and political leverage in affecting will and perception. At the other end of the scale, the report made reference to Hiroshima and Nagasaki. Clearly the reference had a carefully written caveat.

Japan had chosen to use suicidal resistance. Kamikazes routinely crashed into U.S. Navy ships causing enormous damage. In the invasion of Saipan virtually all of the Japanese forces either were killed or killed themselves. Civilians too jumped off cliffs, opting to commit suicide rather than surrender. The home islands had been choked off by blockade. Japanese were starving. Fire bombings of Tokyo, Haruna, and other major cities killed hundreds of thousands in night-long raids. Still the Japanese fought on. The allies estimated that invading Japan would cost a million or more friendly casualties and probably depopulate most of the civilian population who might choose suicide.

After the bomb destroyed Hiroshima, the War Cabinet voted to continue the war. A few days later, after Nagasaki was incinerated, the cabinet was deadlocked, and the Emperor chose to surrender unconditionally. The key question was what made Japan quit? After all, the atom bombs, terrifying and destructive as they were, killed no more people than did the firebomb raids. The answer was shock and awe.

The Japanese could understand the effects of thousands of B-29s dropping tons of ordnance on cities in which tens of thousands perished. Some of the raids were so massive and the flight corridors so narrow that they went on for hours at a time. However, one bomb dropped and one city destroyed was inconceivable as far as the Japanese psyche was concerned. Not knowing how many more weapons the United States had, the Japanese surrendered.

Shock and awe, in this case, defeated suicidal resistance. In concrete terms, there was little more damage that the allies could inflict on Japan using conventional weapons. This was the ultimate example of affecting will and perception. The question was whether similar effects could be achieved using minimum amounts of force. Unfortunately, however, the linkage with nuclear weapons induced the wrong conclusions, particularly on the part of individuals who opposed this or any war. Hence, shock and awe was taken out of context.

As it turned out in the final briefing to the president before the war, Gen. Tommy Franks referred to a campaign based on shock and awe. But the battle plan was fashioned more along the lines of transformation of the military, promised by candidate Bush and the central priority of Rumsfeld's tenure at the Defense Department. The original war plan proposed by Central Command could be characterized as an updated and modernized version of Desert Storm, relying on overwhelming force. To Rumsfeld, however, because of huge improvements in capability and fighting power, the half million troops in Desert Storm were not needed. The war could be won quickly and decisively with far fewer people. Rumsfeld prevailed. As it turned out, he was quite correct in what it took to win the war. Peace was another matter.

Historians will uncover the details of how the planning proceeded. The result, however, was a relatively small force of fewer than one hundred seventy thousand. The strategy was to race to Baghdad, destroy all of the Iraqi army that resisted en route, protect the oil wells and other infrastructure from destruction by Saddam, and collapse the regime as quickly as possible. From the south the Third Infantry Division and First Marine Division formed twin spearheads, supported by the 82nd and 101st Air Assault Divisions, 173rd Airborne Brigade, Special Forces, and other maneuver units that were inserted into Iraq. From the west, the army's most modern and digitized division, the Fourth, was to charge in from Turkey, creating a pincers movement from at least three directions.

In the end the Turks demurred. The Fourth Division, having to move from the Mediterranean to the Persian Gulf, did not get into the fight until well after Baghdad fell. All the time some eighteen hundred coalition combat aircraft were in direct fire support missions of the advancing forces and striking strategic and tactical Iraqi targets throughout Iraq. Eight hundred and two Tomahawk cruise missiles would also be fired during the war.

The Joint Chiefs of Staff were uncomfortable with the lower force levels Rumsfeld approved to fight the war. The military inherently took a more cautious and conservative position toward risk. More force was generally better than less.

The Joint Chiefs' concern was based on preference for overwhelming force that General Powell had so strongly advocated and the understanding that the postwar period would need more "boots on the ground" than winning the war would require. Indeed, Army Chief of Staff Gen. Eric Shinseki testified to Congress before the war that at least two hundred thousand troops were needed. Senior civilian defense officials called the comment "widely off the mark."

What Rumsfeld had done was change the military's traditional and conservative assessment of risk in planning, an extraordinary feat considering how long that mindset had prevailed. He was proven correct. A good lesson was learned. But the peace raised challenges that were not fully considered. Although the administration argued there were enough forces on the ground to cope with the occupation, more were needed. As a result Iraqis would be called into service well after the fact and on a crash basis to fill these security roles.

WHY THE WAR WENT SO WELL

The details of the war have been covered extensively elsewhere. The crucial questions are why the military victory was so swift and decisive, what can be learned from that experience, including the planning process and the assumptions it used, and what were the major shortcomings and deficiencies in the use of these forces that contributed or exacerbated the postwar occupation and reconstruction. Beyond the military component, other lessons for other departments and agencies of government are drawn in subsequent chapters, particularly Chapter 5, "The Crescent of Crisis."

The decisive reasons that dictated the military results spanned tactics and planning that were largely effects based; extraordinary technology and capability; training and readiness; superior professionalism; and an enemy that was weakened by twelve years of embargoes and incompetent leadership and was outclassed by a far more capable adversary. For most of history warfare was attrition based. It was force on force: army versus army and navy versus navy. The side that killed or eliminated more enemies in combat usually won. As Clausewitz wrote, a principal aim of war was to disarm the adversary.

Of course guile, surprise, and maneuver, as well as brilliant generalship, changed battles and outcomes. Still, disarming the enemy of the means to resist was the principal object. Effects-based operations are directed not at destroying individual enemy forces but at obtaining specific outcomes through the use of force. An example from World War II makes this point.

The allies attacked dozens if not hundreds of German power plants, often with dozens if not hundreds of bombers and thousands of tons of bombs. The aim was to flatten the plant. Given the lack of accuracy of so-called dumb bombs, a great deal of collateral damage to adjacent areas, many of them civilian residences, was routine. However, the plant or target eventually would be eviscerated and power production halted.

The effect of eliminating the electric production, however, was not critical in considering how to accomplish that task since only total destruction was sought. If the power plant had been carefully examined, obtaining the same outcome could have been accomplished by destroying a key junction box, power line or distribution point, leaving much of the plant undamaged. What physically prevented this effects-based outcome was lack of precision.

Throughout history, until literally a decade or so ago, war had one common characteristic. Virtually every rock, arrow, spear, bullet, and projectile fired, launched, and hurled missed. Technology had radically transformed this historical condition. The opposite is the case today. Not only is the probability high that a target will be hit on the first shot but also the high probability that the target will be destroyed with the first round. Today targets can be engaged simultaneously.

Returning to the German power plant, many bombers were needed to destroy it. Today a single aircraft with a single weapon can incapacitate the same target while engaging other targets at the same time. The metric is no longer sorties per target but targets per sortie. This mixture of effects-based targeting, new tactics, and technology has created extraordinary military capability.

Combined with this capability are highly trained and ready forces. Staffed with highly professional officers and enlisted personnel and using new tactics and technology, the United States has the most capable military in history, at least in terms of being able to fight and to win wars. No matter how well prepared the Iraqi army was, it had no chance of resisting this irresistible force.

Along with embedded journalists, a number of civilian observers went along for the ride, driving a captured Iraqi general's bright yellow SUV. Two who were with the 1st Marine Division were F. J. "Bing" West, a former assistant secretary of defense in the Reagan administration and marine Vietnam veteran, and retired Maj. Gen. Ray Smith, one of the Marine Corps' most highly decorated officers in that war. When asked what their strongest impressions of the brief conflict were, Smith talked about the extraordinary accuracy of the fires. From M-16s with laser sights to 2,000-pound JDAMs with GPS guidance, virtually every round hit its mark.

Smith recalled that when Iraqis were foolish enough to attack in pick-up trucks and SUVs, drivers would be routinely killed by multiple gunshots that generally left holes in the windshield no larger than a grapefruit. To Smith and West, with Vietnam experiences in which rarely was accuracy so good, this precision left a strong impression on how much war had changed. The same results were repeated throughout the entire theater and across each of the army, marine, navy, and air force units that fought and won the war. Indeed, former army vice chief of staff Jack Keane described one battle in which an army armored unit destroyed two dozen Iraqi tanks, armored personnel carriers, and other vehicles in a matter of seconds, their firepower and accuracy being so overwhelming.

Fuller discussion of the lessons and observations about the war that are most relevant to the Department of Defense and what should be done in continuing the transformation of America's defenses fall in Chapter 6. A few broad takeaways set the context not only for the actual fighting of the war but also for understanding the strengths and weaknesses of the planning process, the role of and oversight by Congress, and the vital need to expand transformation to other departments and agencies of government so that the next time the nation goes to war, it will be better prepared for the aftermath.

A Cold, Hard Look at the War

During this war, as in 1990 and 1991, I spent much of my time in television studios waiting for the occasional one- or two-minute hit and the chance to make the appropriate sound bite. As each of the networks was in keen competition for ratings, clearly the emphasis was as much on punchy and electric commentary as on clarity and gravity in presenting observations about the fighting. There was another interesting aspect, however.

With so much dead time and as many as ten monitors televising different channels and embedded journalists, the war could be observed through many separate "soda straws" simultaneously. On one hand, there were extraordinary images. On the other, unless the viewer had substantial military experience, there was no way to extract any tactical and strategic appraisal of how well or how badly the war was going. To complicate yet focus my observations of the war, I had been asked to write what turned out to be daily columns for the *New York Post* and the *Australian*, along with my responsibilities for the *Washington Times*.

The results were good and bad. Samuel Johnson observed that the prospect of hanging clears the mind. Two daily deadlines came close to that. However, the discipline required both a hardheaded assessment and at least a few minutes to reflect on what had been broadcast on many screens. As it turned out, there was at least one glaring misperception. Fortunately it was not reported on the air.

During Desert Storm the performance of the U.S. Marine Corps under the command of then Lt. Gen. Walter C. Boomer was extremely impressive. The marines had been assigned what was thought to be the most difficult mission of the war—attacking the Saddam line that guarded the southeastern portion of Kuwait. Indeed, the commander in chief of Central Command, Army Gen. Norman Schwarzkopf, had planned the assault on the presumption that the Iraqi reserve would move south to oppose the marine assault, giving VII Corps under the command of then Lt. Gen. Fred C. Franks enough time to carry out its famous left hook and trap the Iraqi army in Kuwait. (Freddie and Tommy Franks are not related.)

Boomer's plan was perfectly executed. The marines cut through the Saddam line without a casualty in the initial assault. The next day units occupied Kuwait City. The marine attack had been so stunning and brilliantly carried out that Iraq's reserves simply didn't have time to move south.

When Franks shut the door, sealing off exit routes north back into Iraq, few Iraqis were home. The reserve couldn't move quickly enough and was spared. The same level of performance, at the time of Iraqi Freedom, seemed to shift from the marines to the Third Infantry Division. The reason was interesting.

Given the coincidence of timing, most of the channels I watched during the war featured high visibility journalists such as Ted Koppel and David Bloom, who suffered a fatal embolism and died of natural causes during the battle. Most of these celebrity journalists were embedded with the army. The army, as with the other forces, performed extremely well. It was not until after the war ended that I raised the comparison of the marines with Desert Storm with some senior marine generals. Their sage advice was to take a closer look. That look was revealing.

There were two different styles of war that were fought by the Third Infantry Division and the 1st Marine Division (actually the U.S. Army's V Corps and the III Marine Expeditionary Force). The Marine Corps had always been expeditionary in character. It was lighter, more mobile, and in some ways less lethal than its army counterparts. However, every marine was trained as a rifleman. That meant there were more infantry troops per unit available to the marines.

Because of its expeditionary nature, its logistics were more closely integrated. Further, close air support from marine and navy aviation units was part of the organization and had been integrated since before World War II. As the current Commandant of the Marine Corps, Gen. Mike Hagee, argues, "Marines win battles, not wars." In his and other marines' views, it is up to the larger, heavier, and more powerfully equipped army to win the wars.

The Third Infantry Division was designed to fight and win wars against the Soviet Army that was largely but not entirely a similarly configured force with tanks, armored personnel vehicles, huge artillery formations, and, of course, supporting aviation units. It was also designed so that much of the firepower and other capabilities such as aviation were at the next higher echelon called the corps. To get an army division into action, therefore, required a heavier slice, making it purposely less mobile and deployable than the marines. In addition to attack helicopters that were part of army formations, the air force had the responsibility for providing close-air support. Since the Air Force became a separate service, close-air support has been the topic of debate, discussion, and dissension.

After Desert Storm the army and the air force took strong steps to ensure the closer integration of the two services, reconciling some of the problems that had plagued the linking of air and ground power for decades. The Marine Corps, with its airpower fully integrated and under its command, has the advantage over the other services. There has always been a great controversy with the navy over the years on air support, as well as a further distinction between the army and marines.

After the Vietnam War the army under Gen. Creighton Abrams convinced the civilian leadership that to prevent future Vietnams and to rally domestic support for any war, a substantial part of army combat support and combat service support—everything from logistics to MPs to Civil Affairs—should be shifted to the national guard and army reserve components.

By taking that step the intent was to mandate domestic support before going to war. Without that support mobilizing reserves and guard forces was believed to be difficult. Hence, a structural inhibition was placed on politicians in declaring or waging a major war by the design of the army and its complete dependence on guard and reserve forces. Because the marines were much smaller in size, they were not quite so affected.

For planning purposes the war was organized around four phases: initial deployments, buildup and preparation, execution, and postwar. The tactical planning reflected that of Secretary Rumsfeld to get the job done with as few troops as possible but no fewer. Rumsfeld also was rightly constrained by what he called industrial age planning systems in an information era. DoD planning is deliberate and purposely so, a reflection of the Cold War.

In the event of war with the Soviets, forces would be deployed through the time-phased force deployment (TYPFD) and the time-phased force deployment logistics plan (TYPFDL.) Plans were excruciatingly and carefully crafted to ensure that the hundreds of thousands of troops and millions of things that went with them would be closely coordinated, coming together at the right place at the right time, from tanks and bullets to mobile showers and Xerox machines. Push the button and a huge bureaucracy would spring into action to produce the greatest flow of forces and equipment since World War II.

But as Rumsfeld knew, this was not World War II. During Desert Storm it took six months to get the forces in place. For this operation it was not clear that a similar period of time might be available. Rumsfeld abhors waste and inefficiency and was appalled by the cumbersome nature of the deployment system that greatly restricted flexibility in moving forces. He changed the process at the same time the nation was sending forces to war. The Department of Defense needed a modern information-based process to replace the relic of the past industrial age. It got one.

Deployment was conducted under his direct supervision. Orders went out in line with Central Command's requests once the secretary or the president had approved them. The old process was discarded. Because many officers and civilians had key roles in the old process, it was obvious that discontent and criticism would surface. But Rumsfeld was right. In the future there must be information age means to move forces.

WHY THE PEACE WENT SO BADLY

Strategic planning for the postwar period did not go so well. For reasons that still are unclear, Phase IV, planning for the postwar period, was simply not up to the task. Planning authority was placed in the Pentagon, which it actively sought to control. For whatever reasons, the National Security Council (NSC) did not wish to take charge. Further, there was dissent, rivalry, and distrust between the Defense Department and the State Department.

Before the war the State Department undertook a massive planning effort called Project Iraqi Future, as did the CIA in a different form. State's final document was some six hundred pages, and it reportedly was painstakingly thorough in detail. Many of the problems and obstacles were predicted with some prescience. State also offered some twenty-four nominees to join the reconstruction effort. By late January 2003 Rumsfeld had selected retired Army Lt. Gen. Jay Garner to head the reconstruction effort. Garner had gained great experience and praise for his handling of Operation Provide Comfort in northern Iraq in 1991 after the first Gulf War.

Defense rejected summarily State Department's plan, as well as a number of its nominees, as being "too Arabist." That allegation meant these individuals were either opposed to Ahmed Chalabi or to DoD's view of postwar management of Iraq. Hence, in bureaucratic terms, the proposed State Department officials were not in full agreement with DoD's policies regarding reconstructing and democratizing Iraq, a prospect that, if correct, no defense secretary could accept.

Clearly the neoconservatives believed that coalition forces would be welcomed as liberators. Overjoyed with the overthrow of Saddam, in this view, Iraqis would willingly support the transition to a democratic government. The handover could move swiftly, and American military forces could be withdrawn with relative speed.

No doubt much of the optimism was a result of the influence of the Iraqi National Congress (INC) and its leader Ahmed Chalabi. Chalabi, a Shia, fled Iraq with his family in 1960. Educated at MIT and then the University of Chicago, where he was awarded a PhD in mathematics, Chalabi cultivated many members of the Bush administration long before Bush took office.

Deputy Secretary Paul Wolfowitz, former chairman of DoD's Defense Policy Board, Richard Perle, and others were taken with Chalabi. During the Clinton administration Congress appropriated one hundred million dollars for the overthrow of Saddam using the INC. The plan did not work. Very little of the money was transferred to the INC and, in the process, State and the CIA became convinced that Chalabi was untrustworthy.

The planning that was done was focused more on coping with humanitarian issues: outbreaks of disease, huge refugee flows, oil wells set ablaze, and starvation caused by lack of food and water. These contingencies and others like them were the basis for DoD's rebuilding plan. Unfortunately other secondary tasks that would prove crucial included preparations to deal with looting; quickly appointing a legitimate government; bringing together key Iraqi leaders; determining whether to demobilize the Iraqi army; putting in place economic plans to cope with unemployment; speedy reconstructing of vital infrastructure; and securing Iraq's vast weapons stores and internationalizing the occupation, which meant sharing power and authority with others (presumably the United Nations).

Fortunately disease, starvation, and refugee crises did not arise. Seizure of oil wells early in the war by Special Forces prevented wholesale destruction. However, regarding the primary matter of reconstruction and what to do politically, economically, socially, and culturally, planning was lacking or nonexistent. Garner was sent over with virtually no say in the matter. He lasted only a few months until Ambassador Bremer replaced him.

At this stage dissecting what went wrong and why serves little purpose beyond the obvious conclusion that post-conflict planning must have far greater prominence in future contingencies. The organizational scheme in which Central Command and the Coalition Provisional Authority (CPA) existed as two separate and equal organizations under the Secretary of Defense seemed to violate basic command principles. Who was in charge of Iraq was not immediately answerable. The greatest failure was that Defense's planning emphasized the conduct of war and not the waging of the peace. Who in government has that responsibility?

At present, outside the White House, there is no agency or department chartered by law with the responsibility and authority for postwar planning. The Department of Defense under Title X of the U.S. Code is directed to conduct prompt and sustained military operations incident to combat on land, sea or in the air. Post-conflict, peace support is not a primary or even an explicit secondary role.

Hence, an obvious requirement is ensuring that government has the capability to conduct this type of planning and that specific assignment and delegation of authority is made under the law to the office or department charged with this responsibility. Such a step will require a change in the National Security Act and possibly in congressional organization and oversight for this mission, as no single or joint committee has been assigned that jurisdiction.

The conclusions and lessons from this war are clear on the tactical and operational levels. Lessons at the strategic and political levels are more blurred, vague, and even opaque. Given huge advantages in effects-based planning; the superb training, readiness, and equipage of the force; the superiority of American military systems and technology in accuracy and lethality, among others; and the great leadership it possesses, U.S. military power in a conventional battle will remain superior. Significant improvements in organization, use of the guard and reserve, and doctrine as well as integration of airpower should be made. These will be covered later.

The weaknesses at the strategic and political levels and in the judgments that guided planning, however, were profound. The optimism that Iraqis would welcome the occupation force as liberators and quickly assume responsibility for governing themselves was immediately dissipated. No acceptable or legitimate leader emerged. Disputes between Shias, Sunnis, and Kurds and traditionalists and modernists arose. Security became an increasing problem.

None of these issues or other roadblocks that confounded the occupation should have been surprises. During the war virtually all of these potential problems and hard points were raised by knowledgeable experts and the usual media commentators. Inexplicably, the administration ignored or dismissed them. Members of Rumsfeld's Defense Policy Board said privately that when specifically queried about the post-war planning and its difficulties, senior Defense officials reassured them that all of these considerations had been taken into account.

Concerned with the state of the occupation and the growing insurgency, chairman of the Joint Chiefs of Staff, Gen. Richard Myers, and chief of Central Command, Gen. John Abizaid, were invited to London for a special briefing by a combined MOD and intelligence briefing in early November. Reports of that briefing varied. One senior civilian told a journalist that the British presented a harsh and highly pessimistic assessment of the American handling of the occupation.

Minister of Defence Geoff Hoon and chief of the UK Defence Staff Gen. Sir Michael Walker challenged that version. Both noted that there were substantive differences between the British doctrine of peace support and the United States' more aggressive use of force to put down the insurgency. Both went on to say that Britain's assignment of the southern part of Iraq was far easier because the Shia were anti-Saddam and the United States had to operate in a much more difficult area. However, with diplomatic nicety, perhaps their view is that both would "end up at the same place."

A more cynical reading would conclude that such an unusual briefing could not have been accidental. In private conversations with senior British officials there clearly was fear that the occupation was not going well. A former senior ambassador to the region believed that the United States had stumbled into a quagmire. Despite the good intentions, the planning deficiencies and failure to anticipate predictable problems had put the United States on a collision course with the challenge of not just imposing a democracy but also moving toward an inevitable battle with much of Islam.

3

What a Global War on Terror

Are we winning or losing the global war on terror?
Secretary of Defense Donald H. Rumsfeld

In mid-2004 the answer to Secretary Rumsfeld's question is not reassuring, and there is no guarantee that a better answer will be found for some time to come. The task of bringing democracy to Iraq or, for that matter, anywhere is daunting enough. Trying to create a society that is whole and free after decades of destructive rule under Saddam, in which political power rested in repressing, brutalizing, and keeping Iraqis purposely divided, may prove even a more difficult task.

The Bush administration is completely committed to winning this global war against jihadist extremism. It has promised repeatedly "to stay the course." No signs of declaring early victory and going home or making radical changes to its strategy to win the war have surfaced. But dealing with Iraq once power and sovereignty are returned to the Iraqis and the vagaries and unhappy surprises in the run-up to the November presidential election could cause dramatic shifts in policy.

Along with two extraordinary military victories in Afghanistan and Iraq, a rising torrent of criticism flooded the White House, matched by a vigorous defense of the administration's policies. While Osama bin Laden remains at large, or so it seems, the capture of Saddam Hussein in December 2003 was a temporary boost to the Bush administration and was used as powerful evidence in citing progress in the battle against jihadist extremism. Furthermore, Libya's remarkable declaration to eliminate all of its weapons of mass destruction and intent to rejoin the family of respectable nations were vindications and evidence of the wisdom of the Bush administration to its supporters.

Yet for all of these tactical victories, there is considerable worry that the United States is not winning the battle against global terror. In fact, it may be losing if ambiguity is the measure of success. This pessimistic assessment rests in the administration's strategies, priorities, and declarations for waging this war. Former White House counterterror chief Richard A. Clarke's allegations against the Bush administration noted earlier escalated this debate several levels.

The Bush strategy in the war against jihadist extremism is offensive—to attack the terrorists and their networks at home and abroad rather than waiting to fight them on U.S. soil. In this war the principal effort has been placed on neutralizing the terrorists wherever they may be found rather than on mitigating the conditions that produced them. To quote the White House progress report on the war, "we are on the offensive . . . our efforts . . . have disrupted terrorist plots and incapacitated terrorists."

The chief flaws in this strategy rest in targeting the symptoms and not the root causes of terrorism, along with failure to recognize that terror is a political tool to achieve political ends and not an end in itself. Until the causes of this extremism are remedied, unless there are only a limited number of terrorists, it will make no difference how many are killed or captured because more will take their place.

Furthermore, by repeatedly casting this battle as a "war," the net result may have been the inadvertent creation of a goal—winning—that is unachievable by any means. Given the zero-sum nature of American politics, once committed to winning a war, no White House can back down or easily change course. The promise of delivering a victory may lead to distortions or ignorance of truth and fact.

As in Vietnam this "war" may be without strategic consequence. The Cold War was not jeopardized and the United States was not at risk of having its sovereignty, freedom, or security diminished, even as we were thrown out of Vietnam. The war on terror may not prove that benign regardless of whether or not the strategic landscape in the Middle East is transformed.

THE GLOBAL WAR ON TERROR

On September 12, 2001, President George W. Bush declared a global war on terror. Only Congress, of course, has that power. Given the events of the previous day, few members of that body or the public at large dissented with Bush's rhetoric.

For the president the destruction and death in New York, Washington, and western Pennsylvania were twenty-first century equivalents of Pearl Harbor. In his view, supported by many Americans, the nation could no longer avoid confronting the terrorists. Three thousand innocent lives lost in those attacks demanded a strong and indeed overpowering response. In making the war on terror the nation's most important mission, the Bush administration would find a new lease on life. The confusion and ineptness of the first months of office would be swept aside. Virtually all of the resources of the United States would be brought to bear in fighting this war, and the president would emerge as a strong and uncompromising leader in this fight.

The phrase was both a good sound bite and powerful political slogan. In an economy of words and in the heat of anger, the term "war on terror" seemed to encapsulate the dangers facing the United States. But this declaration also included, like an iceberg, a great deal of unseen substructure. There were semantic and strategic deficiencies beyond the simplicity of the pronouncement. A declaration of war left no alternative outcome except to "win" that war. As General of the Army Douglas McArthur had put it, "there is no substitute for victory."

Yet in this war how would or could victory be defined? How would anyone know when or if we had won and indeed who the real enemy was. And as with all wars Clausewitz' marvelous reference to the "fog of war" applies.

The fog of war hides the dangerous, volatile, and unpredictable path of armed conflict. The global war on terror, while not fought between like armies or forces, suffered from similar uncertainties and unknowns. Understandably, the great majority of Americans supported the president and his intent to deal with the perpetrators of this terror. His popularity ratings soared. Yet Pandora's box had been opened.

In committing the United States to hunt down and "root out" the evil ones, the president was embarking on a course that could prove to be one of the most dangerous the nation faced since the Civil War tore the United States apart. At the time no one could have guessed how difficult the global war on terror would prove to be or what the consequences could be. Furthermore, the term "war" may prove to have been an unfortunate one.

"War": Semantic and Strategic Shortcomings

Oddly enough, although the U.S. Congress declared war only once in the last hundred years (U.S. entry into World War I was the result of a congressional resolution), the United States has been at war considerably more than that. Korea, Vietnam, and the 1991 Gulf Wars notwithstanding, the United States has been engaged in other wars. Notably, presidents have declared wars against crime, drugs, poverty, racial intolerance, disease, and other social ills with similar outcomes. Not one of those wars was definitely won. Indeed, each is still a work in progress, much as resolving all human problems is a goal that can never be attained.

The strategic and tactical focus for the Bush administration is taking the war to the enemy—that is, killing or capturing terrorists outside the United States and punishing those who support them through aggressive, offensive military, law enforcement, and intelligence operations. Obviously, preventing terrorists from entering the United States is very much part of the administration's strategy. Also, reorganizing the government has been a necessary step in taking on this enemy.

Clearly, fighting a war beyond the U.S. borders is wise. But this intense concentration on finding and neutralizing individual terrorists and their cells and their state sponsors and supporters only works when there is a finite number of them, and accessions and recruits are killed and captured as well. As long as the causes persist, more extremists are likely to be recruited than are killed or captured. Until extremists recognize the futility of their cause, something that the reward of eternal afterlife would seem to reject, no war can be fully won until the last terrorist is dispatched.

Third, in fighting a war on terror there are very real distinctions between and among "terrorists." Members of the IRA, Red Brigades, Basque Separatists, Chechens, and Tamil Tigers, to name a few, are terrorists. But the United States did not declare war against them. The reason was that this terror was not international and rarely crossed borders. Some would argue that this definition is a distinction without a difference. The significant difference was that none of these terrorist organizations had directly targeted America.[1]

To slice through the "fog" of this particular war on terror and the danger the United States actually faces it is essential to understand the motivations behind September 11 and the other terrorist attacks carried out around the world. The bulk of the danger emanates from a radicalized strain of Islam, largely Wahabi in outlook. The intent is to fashion a regime that adheres to the Sharia in the strictest sense and the means include all methods, fair or foul, along with a willingness to die in the process, ensuring a trip to paradise. The best phrase to describe this ideology is "jihadist extremism."

THIS STUFF IS REAL AND SCARY

On November 24, 2002, the full text of what was reported as Osama bin Laden's "letter to America" was published in the London *Observer*. Although the letter's author cannot be authenticated, Islamic fundamentalists thought it reflected the thinking of al Qaeda and bin Laden. Rather like the collected works of Lenin and Hitler's *Mein Kampf*, the letter conveyed a chilling philosophy, a scathing list of grievances and a plan of action. Especially for Muslims who felt ostracized from power in Saudi Arabia, out of work in Egypt, in abject poverty in Pakistan, or desperate for other reasons, the letter offered a theological, moral, and political call to arms. For many that call will be compelling. For those who disagree or are skeptical, a rereading of Lenin and Hitler and the polemics on Communism and Fascism is informing.

The letter asks and answers two fundamental questions. Why are we (the fundamentalists) fighting and opposing you? What are we calling you to do and what do we want from you?

The first answer is very simple. The letter asserts "you attacked us and continue to attack us . . . (and) . . . you attacked Palestine." The embrace of the Palestinian cause is new. Earlier bin Laden demanded the withdrawal of infidels, meaning Americans, from Saudi Arabia. Israel was not a *casus belli*. But as al Qaeda matured, seizing the Israeli-Palestinian conflict as grounds for advancing

---

1. President Bush declared that in this war, "you are either with us or against us"; had Britain used the same standard in battling the IRA, it would have forced a confrontation with America—the source of strong financial and political support for the IRA.

its revolutionary call was sensible and powerful. Those arguments are well known and are not repeated.

As to the first question, the letter claims that the West attacked "us in Somalia; supported the Russian atrocities against us in Chechnya; the Indian oppression against Kashmir and the Jewish aggression against us in Lebanon."

"Us" presumably is the world of Islam and not the radical fringes.

The litany of further charges is a clever mixture of the critiques of the far left and right and of the more strident anti-American groups in general. These allegations have enough grains of truth to attract the unsophisticated, the embittered, and those looking for a cause. The overarching grievance rests with the West's prevention of the establishment of the Islamic Sharia with "violence and lies," a potential and, to some, a plausible call to arms.

The parallels with Marxism-Leninism and capitalism's exploitation of the proletariat or Hitler's racist condemnation of the Jews as the basis of evil are stark. It is the West, largely the United States and Israel, who are, like capitalism and the Jews, held responsible for these outrages and for whom Jihad (holy war) is the only justified response. The letter then accuses the West and nonbelievers of specific acts to "steal our oil wealth at paltry prices . . . planning to destroy the Al-Aqsa mosque (in Jerusalem) . . . occupy our countries . . . starved the Muslims of Iraq . . . and are only a few examples . . . of your oppression and aggression."

The argument is then directed largely against the United States. To understand the thrust, part of the letter is quoted in full.

> You may then dispute that all of the above, i.e., the grievances, does not justify aggression against civilians, for crimes they did not commit and offenses in which they did not partake.
>
> This argument contradicts your continuous repetition that America is the land of freedom, and its leaders in this world. Therefore the American people are the ones who choose their government of their own free will; a choice that stems from their agreement to its policies. Thus, the American people have chosen, consented to, and affirmed their support for the Israeli oppression of the Palestinians, the occupation and usurpation of their land, and its continuous killing, torture, punishment, and expulsion of the Palestinians. The American people have the ability and choice to refuse the policies of their government and even to change it if they want.
>
> The American people are the ones who pay the taxes which fund the planes that bomb us in Afghanistan, the tanks that strike and destroy our homes in Palestine, the armies which occupy our lands in the Arabian Gulf and the fleets that ensure the blockade of Iraq. These tax dollars are given to Israel for it to continue to attack us and penetrate our lands. So the American people are the ones who the attacks

against us, and they are the ones who oversee the expenditure of these monies the way they wish through their elected candidates.

The American army is part of the American people. It is helping the very same people who are shamelessly helping the Jews fight against us. The American people are the ones who employ both their men and women in the American forces that attack us.

That is why the American people cannot be innocent of the crimes committed by the Americans and Jews against us.

These charges are familiar. They also must be taken seriously. To many Arabs and Muslims, especially those disenfranchised, ill educated, out of work, or in poverty and despair, the arguments are carefully worded and powerful propaganda. To dismiss them would be a serious mistake. That was also true of Mao and Ho Chi Minh, lessons we learned at great expense.

What should America do, according to this letter? The first answer is come to Islam and benefit from the sereneness and goodness of the "seal of all the previous religions" that guarantees, by the way, "total equality between all people without regard to color, sex, or language." The second answer is "to stop your oppression, lies, immorality, and debauchery that has spread among you. We call you to be a people of manners, principles, honor, and purity and to reject the immoral acts of fornication, homosexuality, intoxicants, gambling, and trading with interest, i.e., usury."

What follows is a harsh critique of American society and morality, as well as its hypocrisy and dual standards. These arguments, factoring out references to Islam and Allah, strike a common and familiar chord with the far left and right in broadly attacking America across many fronts, from destroying nature with industrial wastes, to promoting law of the rich, to using force to destroy more of mankind than any other nation in history, to disrespecting international law and human rights and to creating AIDS.

President Clinton, mentioned for his immoral acts in the Oval Office, and the failure to bring him to account are examples of the absence of decency in the United States. For those who argue for gender equality, the letter notes:

> You are a nation that exploits women like consumer products or advertising tools calling customers to purchase them. You use women to serve passengers, visitors, and strangers to increase your profit margins. You then rant and rave that you support the liberation of women. You are a nation that practices the sex trade in all its forms, directly and indirectly. Giant corporations are established under the name of art, entertainment, tourism, and freedom and other deceptive names you attribute to it.

To complete the flavor and the bile in this letter, America is condemned for its record on Human Rights and for the hypocrisy of issuing annual human rights reports.

You captured thousands of Muslims and Arabs, took them into custody with neither reason, court trial nor even disclosing their names. You issued newer, harsher laws.

What happens in Guantanamo is a historical embarrassment to America and its values, and it screams in your faces—you hypocrites, "what is the value of your signature on any agreement or treaty?"

It is easy to dismiss this letter and others like it as nonsense, forgeries, or propaganda, although there are more than occasional bits of truths scattered throughout with which many Americans would agree and which both political parties would use to attack the other, such as abandoning Kyoto or impeaching but not convicting President Clinton of high crimes and misdemeanors.[2] But in a world torn by powerful hatreds, wracked by violence, filled with poverty and despair, and propagandized by many competing factions, the letter is a rallying point. It will attract converts.

A JIHADIST'S VISION AND ORGANIZATION

The aim of jihadist extremists is not simply to become terrorists, committing suicide in order to reach paradise. Nor, as President Bush has repeatedly argued, do they practice terror because of an overarching hatred of democracy and freedom. The vision and rationale are far broader and better conceived than the rather simple explanation of hate-induced terror.

First and foremost the radicals are, in the classic meaning of the term, "true believers." Islam, in the most conservative reading of the Koran and understanding of Sharia, is the foundation and basis for their actions and intentions. From the Sharia comes legitimacy and the sanction of morality. Hence, as with Leninism and Nazism, ideology is crucial to recruit and rally the converts, even though this ideology is better labeled as theology. Regarding Islamic extremists such as al Qaeda as only terrorists and not in the broader context is a sure way to lose that war.

Second, these true believers should not be confused with many of the insurgents currently operating in Iraq. The number of foreign jihadists fighting in Iraq has been exaggerated if U.S. Army reports are correct. So-called former regime loyalists including Saddam Fedayeen, Baathists, and criminals whose services can

---

2. On November 11, 2001, Veteran's Day in America, a document written by Mahfuyz ibn-al-Walid, a close aide to bin Laden, called "A Legal and Factual View on the Consequences of the Attacks on the United States" was discovered in an al Qaeda safe house in northern Afghanistan. The letter, reproduced by the Jamestown Foundation in December 2003, may or may not prove authentic. However, the arguments it makes are quite similar to bin Laden's Open Letter and are representative of the theology of these extremists and the cause they advocate. In particular al-Walid is quoted as warning,

> America has not succeeded in toppling the Taliban and so far the movement has maintained its cohesion and has become more flexible in its political positions. . . . Terrorism is a divine commandment . . . the Muslim has two choices . . . either he believes . . . or he denies these verses and (becomes) an infidel.

be bought are the principal insurgents. Iraqi Sunni Wahabis are representative of fundamentalist extremists and probably are relatively few in number.

Third, the aim is to establish some form of a rigid Fundamentalist regime, with or without borders, ultimately with access or control of Saudi oil money and Pakistani nuclear weapons. While there is no absolute proof of this conclusion, careful reading of statements attributed to Osama bin Laden and radical clerics provides the best evidence of their objective. Clearly, provoking revolution in the two domino states is part of this plan. Furthermore, with the closer embrace between Indian and Pakistan in early 2004, the prospect of closing that rift will make Pakistan's President Pervez Musharraf an even more tempting target for assassination by extremists committed to toppling the regime. Some claim that reinstating the ancient "caliphate," when Islam ruled much of the world, is a fair assessment of the broader aims of these fundamentalist extremists.

Fourth, humiliating the United States and defeating it by forcing it out of the region is important. No doubt the extremists have taken careful note of Vietnam, Beirut in 1983, and Somalia in 1993 as examples to replicate. The logic is that if enough Americans are killed, they will quit. From this logic flows the conclusion that America will be targeted again with the expectation that sufficient pain at home can politically force the United States to withdraw from the greater Middle East. How much pain the United States can tolerate is something on which the radicals cannot be certain.

Fifth, the organization of al Qaeda is probably widely distributed and closer to franchise operations than tightly controlled from the center. Planners operate in secret and are very compartmentalized to prevent their being turned and neutralized. Financing, despite the money laundering and preventive activities of law enforcement, exploit *hawala*, the principal means of transferring money in the Arab world. Money exchangers are highly trusted. Money entrusted to them is not sent directly to the recipient. Instead another money exchanger in that city or locale transfers funds from his account. Based on trust, accounts are balanced but not to double-entry bookkeeping standards of the West. Hence, the system is very difficult to interdict. The conclusion is that money is not a main worry for al Qaeda.

Sixth, jihadist extremists, regardless of internecine conflict and opposing agendas, have a common target—the United States and its allies. Therefore a bomb or an attack delivered against any of these targets redounds to the common advantage. Whether the terrorists who blew up the HSBC bank and British Counsel's office in Istanbul in November 2003 were with or against al Qaeda, the net effect surely helped more than one cause.

Seventh, the immediate aim of terror is to disrupt, divide, and isolate. In Iraq, for example, the destruction of part of the UN compound in Baghdad and the killing of the High Representative, the distinguished Brazilian diplomat Sergio

Vieira de Mello, forced the United Nations to reduce its presence. Subsequent attacks against the Italian *carabinieri,* Japanese diplomats, and South Korean civilian workers in Iraq had the same intent. Given the presence of al Qaeda cells throughout Europe, further attacks must be considered likely.

Taken together the intention of al Qaeda and other extremists is as cosmic as Lenin, Mao, and those who would change the world. Terror is a tool and an increasingly effective one in disrupting, dividing, isolating, and, of course, terrorizing. Iraq is a separate case and, ironically, an unexpected bonus for extremists. The United States must prevail in Iraq. If it does, however, fundamentalism will not be fully defeated. After that setback extremists will most likely move on to the next battle.

If the United States stumbles or fails in Iraq, then the fundamentalists will have achieved a major victory with very little cost. The biggest question is whether al Qaeda will let events play out in Iraq without committing substantial resources. Or will it take a more active role in opposing and disrupting the occupation? The Bush administration believes the latter, asserting that it is far smarter to fight the war on terror in Iraq than in America. In that process the jihadists will be attracted to Iraq where they can be hunted down or neutralized. The evidence so far does not favor the Bush view.

As will be discussed later, the current situation in Iraq may end up favoring the Fundamentalists. In the south the Shias under Grand Ayatollah Ali al-Sistani have already begun putting in place the foundations for an Islamic Republic. Clerics are organizing at local levels to take political control. Women are now required to dress in compliance with the Sharia, covering their bodies from head to toe. Alcohol has been banned and a few Iraqis who violated that ban have been killed as examples.

Neither the CPA nor the IGC in Baghdad have any authority or power to change these trends. Local leaders have grimly promised success either through the ballot box or other means—what Mao meant when he said political power comes from the barrel of a gun. The goal of bringing democracy to Iraq will not be helped should an Islamic Republic spring up in the south, possibly with direct links to its neighbor to the east and charter member of the Axis of Evil—Iran.

WAGING THE GLOBAL WAR ON TERROR[3]

The United States and its allies have taken dramatic steps and expended vast political, human, and monetary resources in fighting the war on terror. The third paragraph of the National Security Strategy of September 2002 over the president's signature makes the significant point that defending the nation has

---

3. See the appendix, which contains a summary of the actions the Bush administration has taken to date in waging the Global War on Terror and that are found on the White House web page, http:/www.whitehouse.gov/homeland/progress, under Progress Report on the Global War on Terror.

"changed dramatically." It goes on to note that: "Now, shadowy networks of indi- viduals can bring great chaos and suffering to our shores for less than it costs to buy a single tank. Terrorists are organized to penetrate open societies and to turn the power of modern technologies against us." Chapter III, titled "Strengthen Alliances to Defeat Global Terrorism and Work to Prevent Attacks Against Us and Our Friends," expands on describing the strategy.

Among a sea of available materials about the war and its conduct, the White House web site on the global war on terrorism is impressive in detail and filled with facts and figures that document many of the government's efforts and achieve- ments in this war. A summary is listed in the appendix. However, none of the open source materials address Rumsfeld's profound concern about whether we are winning or losing the war on global terror. To answer this question we must dig much deeper to know and understand:

- What America's strategy for fighting and winning this war is
- How that strategy has affected the conduct of this war and how we are organized to fight it
- What has changed in terms of what the various government agencies and departments are doing differently or have chosen to continue to do
- And, most important, whether or not all of this is working.

The strategy is not lengthy, particularly complicated or secret. According to the National Security Strategy, "the enemy is terrorism—premeditated, politi- cally motivated violence perpetrated against innocents." The strategy makes "no distinction between terrorists and those who knowingly harbor or provide aid." Also, the strategy is in three parts: "Attacking Terrorist Networks at Home and Abroad," "Reorganizing the Federal Government," and "Strengthening and Sus- taining the International Fight Against Terrorism."

"Our priority will be first to disrupt and destroy terrorist organizations of global reach and attack their leadership; command, control and communications; material support and finances." The fight will be waged on a regional and local level with allies and partners, and the strategy will include strengthening home- land security, as well as coordinating but not reorganizing much of government in this fight.

A simple listing of resources and the amount of paper committed to this strategy is revealing. On the nineteen pages of web site, only two are devoted to the international efforts to fight terrorism. Two-thirds of a page relates to Dimin- ishing the Underlying Conditions Terrorists Exploit.

In dollar terms, the administration requested and Congress approved $41 bil- lion for homeland security, $18.7 billion for rebuilding Iraq and Afghanistan and, beyond the aid to Israel, a $3 billion five-year assistance package to Pakistan. The Millennium Challenge Account (MCA), the Middle East Partnership Initiative

(MEPI), the Trade for African Development and Enterprise Initiative (TRADE), and the Middle East Initiative with a number of actions including a proposed Middle East Free Trade Agreement "to reduce economic disparities that fuel discontent, anti-American violence and terrorism" at most will have only several hundreds of millions of dollars allocated.

A billion is a thousand millions. The United States is deploying billions for direct defense of the homeland and offensive actions overseas and beyond American borders to disrupt and destroy terrorists and their cells. It is spending only millions or hundreds of millions for prevention and elimination of the root causes of terror. This ratio seems out of balance.

The assumption is that offensive actions will neutralize more extremists than are recruited to the cause, a seemingly unfavorable cost exchange ratio at best. Hence, based on dollar expenditures alone the logical evaluation suggests winning this war cannot be assured on the basis of how money is being spent.

Beyond criticism over dealing with symptoms rather than causes and declaring war on an inanimate enemy, evaluation of the GWOT can be conducted by examining five key and interrelated areas. While the administration's rhetoric and "spin" are fiercely supportive of and optimistic in reporting how the war is going, particularly as the November 2004 elections approach, analysis and fact can be better measures of progress. From these metrics, understanding of the state of the global war on terror and what more needs to be done can follow.

The first area is political-diplomatic and applies to the level of international support the administration has accumulated and has put to effective use in waging this war.

Second is how American law enforcement and intelligence agencies have been used in this war and how effective they have been.

Third is how safe and secure the United States is being kept inside its borders through the creation of the Department of Homeland Security and through bringing local and state capabilities to bear in this effort.

Fourth is the intellectual battle of ideas often seen as the propaganda and information wars.

Fifth is the military component of the war on global terror and taking the fight against terror to Afghanistan, Iraq, and many other places around the world such as the Philippines and Indonesia. Assessment of these areas yields answers to Rumsfeld's question about whether we are winning or losing the global war on terror.

BUILDING OR LOSING SUPPORT?

On September 12, 2001, the attacks on Washington and New York had produced unprecedented international sympathy and support for the United States. Messages of good will flowed in from allies and adversaries alike. NATO quickly and for the first time in its history invoked Article V of the Washington Treaty regarding collective defense. An attack against one was an attack against all. NATO was now in the war on terror.

Yet for all of this good will, in waging its war against terror the Bush administration managed to dissipate much of it. In moving against the Taliban in Afghanistan, the home base for al Qaeda, Bush pointedly warned that "you are with us or against us" in the global war on terror. However, few situations are ever that stark.

To some a terrorist is a freedom fighter. To others a freedom fighter is a euphemism for a terrorist. Some who supported America's offensives against al Qaeda and the Taliban as part of the global war on terror had radically different views about the Palestinian-Israeli conflict and whether Hamas and Hezbollah or the Israeli Defense Force were the real terrorist organizations.

The U.S. military's technological superiority, essential to the decisive military campaigns, ironically, was not without a political downside. If the United States were to rely on NATO allies in fighting any military campaign against terrorists, interoperability and the ability to fight alongside together raised severe operational problems. Aside from Britain and France, the latter having withdrawn from NATO's military structure during DeGaulle's presidency, other militaries were simply not capable of operating with the Americans in all or many circumstances.

The 1999 NATO campaign in Kosovo, Operation Allied Force, was relatively easy to conduct because it involved almost exclusively air forces. These forces had worked together before and, with the advanced AWACS and other command and control systems, could be integrated relatively quickly and effectively. There was also relatively light Serbian military opposition.

In more complicated campaigns requiring substantial ground forces, for valid military reasons, from the U.S. perspective, coalitions of the willing could hamper America's ability to use its overwhelming military power because allies would not be able to operate with the far more capable American formations. That operational gap would reinforce U.S. preferences to work with fewer rather than more allies. In Afghanistan, because relatively few ground forces were used, a larger coalition could have been made to work. But in Iraq, aside from the British, no allies could have kept up with the rapid advance and the very complex and heavily technologically based state of operations.

George Bush's personality also played a key role in affecting international support. Bush tends to personalize relationships. He "loathes," for example, North Korean leader Kim Jong Il for starving and maltreating his people. He "looked into Putin's eyes" and saw he could relate to the Russian president. And, reportedly, he has a very high regard for Israeli Prime Minister Ariel Sharon. When debate in the UN Security Council grew heated over passing the resolutions to authorize force, Bush seemed to personalize his differences with Schroeder and Chirac. In time broad international support wore thin.

Secretary of Defense Donald Rumsfeld contributed to this erosion in support. In one of his famous press conferences he made reference to a "new and old Europe." The inference was that the "new" Europe—namely the newer members from Eastern Europe—better reflected the future path for NATO than did the "old" Europe—principally Germany, France, Belgium, and Luxembourg—who opposed war in Iraq. The remark came at a time when a majority of Europeans were also opposed to the war. Interestingly, Rumsfeld's aides later said Rumsfeld's intent was to describe the differences between the "old" and the "new" NATO.

In September 2003 NATO took an unprecedented step. It assumed duties in Afghanistan for the International Security and Assistance Force (ISAF) deploying some four thousand troops. This was the first time NATO had deployed a force out of area, and Afghanistan was about as far away as one could get from NATO.

Iraq, however, was a different matter. In deciding that Iraq was an urgent danger, Bush chose to ignore the need to rally international support and instead put together a "coalition of the willing." The administration would claim that ninety states supported the United States and forty-nine were members of the coalition, demonstrating that international flavor of the war in Iraq. The fact is that outside of the United States, Britain, and Australia, few other states participated in the fighting and much of the support was rhetorical.

The donors' conference in Madrid that November was a disappointment. Of the permanent members of the Security Council, France, China, and Russia were not in favor of the war. While a number of NATO states sent forces for the occupation, and Japan pledged and then sent the first contingent of a forthcoming one thousand peacekeepers, the war was regarded by most observers as exclusively American with the British as a distant second participant. At the end of 2003 NATO began discussions on undertaking an alliance role in Iraq.

Although Bush's global war on terror continues in many other places, from a political perspective few states share the American view of the sole importance of that fight to the exclusion of other important policy issues. Indeed, some states see the United States as having overreacted to September 11 and now demanding the rest of the world to follow suit. As a result the United States is the only country that sees the global war on terror as its most crucial priority.[4]

The Bush administration was criticized in its haste to make war on Saddam for diffusing the broader effort on the war against terror. That criticism, popular among Democrats, missed the point. The United States had the physical capacity

---

4. Obviously, states such as Israel, Saudi Arabia, and Russia have very real problems of terrorism and regard those threats as critical; but they tend to be localized and therefore different from the broader global war, although there are some obvious links.

to pursue both wars concurrently. It did not have the political or moral authority, however. Furthermore, by prosecuting the war in Iraq as it did and not being adequately prepared for the occupation, the administration raised the stakes more than it appreciated. Iraq was never the "center of gravity" in the war on terror, but it has now become the central battleground. With very little effort on its part, al Qaeda and other extremist groups have been strengthened by American action in Iraq.

The war and the peace have proven expensive. At one stage, Andrew Natsios, director of the State Department's Agency for International Development told Congress the costs of rebuilding Iraq would not exceed a few billion dollars. That prediction was wildly off the mark, and both the war and the peace drained physical and intellectual resources.

If the United States stumbles or is not fully successful in democratizing Iraq, the biggest winners will be the fundamentalists, who will use those setbacks as powerful propaganda to advance their cause. If the insurgency in the so-called Sunni Triangle around Baghdad spreads to the Shia or, more likely, some form of an Islamist Republic is formed in the south, either will be a potential disaster for the United States. The tragedy is that despite good reason for removing Saddam, the United States chose not to mobilize greater international support. The urgency that the Bush administration believed justified removing Saddam sooner rather than later prevailed over the need for greater international support.

At this point this decision (or failure) has imperiled the U.S. purpose in Iraq of bringing democracy and freedom to the region. The Bush administration has no choice but to prevail in Iraq if only to move forward in the war on terror. Inadvertently, perhaps, by downplaying the need for international support in winning the peace in Iraq, the United States paid an enormous price and imposed on itself a huge burden. That burden of bearing the sole responsibility for the future of Iraq also impeded prosecuting the war on terror, but not for the reasons asserted by the critics. It will be American legitimacy and credibility at stake, not its power. It had the power and capacity to pursue the war on terror, as well as the war in Iraq.

Law Enforcement and Intelligence

Law enforcement and intelligence are critically important to the war on terror. Here the administration has had to move forward on two fronts. Internationally, coordination between and among a large number of states on intelligence and law enforcement has been undertaken. Interpol and other international law enforcement agencies have been made important partners. On balance, and given the sensitivity and secrecy of these relationships, it is fair to say that progress has been good. Terrorist attacks that have been prevented and the number of suspects and potential terrorists arrested represent some of the positive achievements.

But difficulties remain over intelligence and information sharing. Those divergences are especially true at home. The federal government has dealt with the "stovepipe and rut" problems largely through increasing interagency working groups and assigning intelligence specialists to law enforcement staffs, and vice versa. Nearly ninety joint counterterrorism task forces have been established.

There are inherent structural contradictions. First, the FBI has always been a law enforcement agency with a law enforcement culture. Successful prosecutions rather than criminals arrested are the preferred metric. Rules of evidence and proper prosecutorial procedures must be followed in order to win convictions. Otherwise cases will be dismissed. However, taking on the war against terrorism and the mission of counterterrorism has precisely the reverse metrics and rationale for conducting business.

Law enforcement cannot wait until after a terrorist attack to make an arrest, as is the normal course of action with criminal justice. Nor can law enforcement worry about following rules of evidence since prevention, not prosecution, is the aim. Making that cultural change is extremely difficult. Consider how long it took, for example, in the Department of Defense for "jointness" to take hold.

Second, the CIA and the FBI have a fundamental conflict of interest over counterespionage. It is the FBI's responsibility to conduct counterespionage. That means investigating the CIA. It is inherently difficult to assure full trust and confidence, crucial in winning the war on terror, across two agencies when one has the responsibility for investigating the other. The only real solution is to split terrorism and counterterrorism away from the FBI and invest it in a new or separate department. *Unfinished Business* outlined a number of specific recommendations for law enforcement and intelligence.

HOMELAND SECURITY AND DEFENSE

The third measure of how the war on terror is proceeding concerns self-defense and homeland protection. Creation of the Homeland Security Department brought together 170,000 personnel from twenty-two separate agencies and arms of the federal government. Turning that into a functioning entity is an extraordinarily difficult task.

One fact is telling. Newt Gingrich, former Speaker of the House of Representatives, critically observes that the department reports to some eighty-eight committees and subcommittees in Congress. Membership on those committees involves every member of the Senate and some three hundred members of the House of Representatives. Oversight is not only unwieldy, it is also impossible. Hence, the department has much political and bureaucratic inertia to overcome.

It may be years before the department will be able to make its full contribution to homeland security. The department has two additional problems. Despite noble efforts, liaison with state and local levels of government is still a work in progress. Also, despite strong statements from the Justice Department, coordination and exchange of information and intelligence across government is inadequate. When the department was formed in 2002 the biggest criticism from state and local governments was the absence of this exchange, particularly with the FBI. Two years later the complaint has not changed.

THE CLASH OF IDEAS

In many ways the battle of ideas and ideology in Bush's war on terror is the one that is being least well fought by the United States. There are good and bad reasons to explain why. Americans tend to believe they are usually on the side of justice and represent what Lincoln called "our better angels." Having fought and won two world wars, saving Europe along the way, and having persevered in the Cold War, Americans did not expect treasure or great reward. Selflessness was an accurate description of American policy. Many Americans saw ending Saddam's rule and liberating Iraq as sufficient reason for Iraqis and regional states to support and admire our actions.

Hence, it is often difficult to take seriously the intellectual and ideological challenges of opposing theologies and points of view, particularly those foreign to Americans' culture and values. Because the United States is protected by two oceans and insulated from the rest of the world, there has been a tendency to view others as we see ourselves. When the adversary was a large, clumsy opponent who hardly could get out of its own way, the ideological battle was less important.

President Ronald Reagan thought otherwise. Although ridiculed at the time for proclaiming an "evil empire" and making Soviet attention to human rights a major sticking point, Reagan joined the ideological battle. His demand, referring to the Berlin wall, to "Take down that wall, Mr. Gorbachev" will be one of the great statements of the Cold War.

So what is being done to challenge bin Laden's letter to America?

THE MILITARY

The military has been given a central role in this war. The reasons are obvious. The military has the physical capability in terms of force that can be used overwhelmingly or with laser-like precision. It has the flexibility and sustainability and is capable of being deployed virtually anywhere around the globe, anytime. It reports to the commander in chief and can go into action in the time it takes to send the order. Also, as the postwar occupation in Iraq showed, it has the ability to respond to new and fundamentally different tasks, such as battling insurgencies or hunting down Saddam's former regime members. Yet while the military possesses these and other capabilities, it is only one tool in the war on terror and a tool with certain disadvantages.

First, it is expensive. At least an additional sixty billion dollars was needed to cover the costs of the occupation during the first year. Much more money will be needed, more than has been anticipated or programmed.

Second, maintaining a sizable military presence requires extensive use of reserves. Nearly two hundred thousand guard and reserves have been called up. In some cases these call-ups can be for fifteen months. Since reservists have full-time jobs, the call-ups have imposed substantial hardships and strains on families, employers, and local communities. In one small town in South Carolina the mayor, chief of police, and fire marshal were ordered to active service. The upshot is that the all-volunteer force with premeditated dependence on a strong reserve component was not designed for this type of service. Fundamental changes will have to be made. Given the politics of making significant alterations to any aspect of the Department of Defense, from canceling weapons systems to closing unneeded bases, rebalancing active and reserve and national guard responsibilities and assignments will not be easy.

Meanwhile the military was not prepared for the peace in Iraq. For all the admirable aspects of transformation, fighting insurgencies and dealing with the pitfalls and hardships of rebuilding a defeated or failed state had been purposely assigned very low priorities and resources for those tasks. That the U.S. military had traditionally been assigned these tasks—from helping to settle the West to serving as occupying forces in many countries—and, as recently as Vietnam, that they took counterinsurgency operations very seriously did not count for much. Preparing for the "big war" and big battles has shaped the Pentagon's thinking for most of the Cold War, absent Vietnam, and for the entire post–Cold War world.

WHY NOT MOBILIZE?

The United States mobilized for World Wars I and II and rearmed for the Korean War. In a sense the Kennedy administration began a partial rearming and mobilization for the Cold War. However, Vietnam intervened. LBJ, confronted not with the choice of "guns or butter" but with the war or his "great society," unsurprisingly declined setting a priority. Both paths were followed. The nation paid a price at home and saw its economy sputter. Abroad the consequences were clear.

George Bush could mobilize for this war too. If not a draft, some form of national service could be required. More forces could be called up. National Guard and reserve forces could be assigned even more responsibility for homeland security. Americans could be called on to make greater sacrifices, and taxes could be raised to pay for the costs of the various wars, the reconstruction efforts in Afghanistan and Iraq, and even to pay for a new Marshall Plan to cope with addressing the causes of extremism.

Barring a catastrophic attack that would make September 11 seem trivial, it is clear that no president would be willing even to consider any of the possible steps noted above. Politically each would be seen as near fatal. There would be virtually no support in Congress or the public without a cause célèbre or intense effort by the White House to make this case to America. Indeed, Bush would find himself in a position not significantly different from LBJ forty years ago.

Why then raise the question of mobilizing for the war on terror? The answer is a further reason in understanding the inherent difficulty of waging and winning an undeclared war on terror. Ultimately no matter how much more additional money Congress is likely to appropriate, without the political authority and legitimacy to mobilize, there are limits on the resources and political capital that are available in waging this war. While the tendency of the United States has been to spend its way clear of danger, unless the threat of extremism turns out to be far less than is expected, money will not relieve this danger.

The crucial point is that the West is fighting an intellectual battle. Understanding the nature and motivation of the danger is essential. Prioritizing resources in line with this understanding is a second lesson. Finally, having the courage to change course based on a comprehensive appreciation of the strategic choices and consequences, something that has not occurred yet, is vital. The message is clear. We need to mobilize our intellects and intellectual capabilities, not our wallets. If we can do that, we can make the nation safer and securer. If we cannot, then the United States is in store for an unpleasant future.

What Else Is Wrong With the War?

Simply put, for all of the power, commitment, and promises of the United States, it cannot "win" the global war on terror. In the first instance, its strategic emphasis on remedying the symptoms can be likened to destroying the Nazi army a soldier or a squad or a platoon at a time. That cost exchange ratio favors the terrorists. Unless and until the causes are taken head on, there will be no way of limiting the influx of extremist recruits under the fundamentalist banner, regardless of whether they consider themselves "freedom fighters" or in the service of the almighty.

Second, war on an inanimate thing is not winnable. The success that has been achieved in winning wars against drugs, crime, poverty, inhumanity, and other societal ills is at best making gains and improvements. Total or unconditional victory is not achievable. The same applies to the war on terror.

Finally, there is no grand or comprehensive strategy that links the many and often disparate tools of government—from military and law enforcement/intelligence assets to information and public relations campaigns to training and educating the government and nongovernmental personnel whose professional portfolios touch on pieces of this larger problem. That strategy has certain limits. Disengagement is not one of them.

During the Vietnam War Vermont's Sen. George Aiken advised declaring victory and withdrawing American troops and presence from that beleaguered region. The United States cannot withdraw from its international responsibilities and commitments. However, it can declare that this part of the struggle is over and move to the next phase. On January 20, 2005, the next president of the United States has this opportunity.

A State of the Union for the Twenty-First Century and Against Jihadist Extremism (and why this is unlikely to happen)

How then should the next president deal with jihadist extremism? The following chapters delineate specific solutions and policy alternatives that are part of a larger, single, and integrated national strategy. But regarding the first steps that should be taken to make this war on terror winnable, the State of the Union Address would be the starting point. The first declaration that speech should make is that it is time to move to the next phase of the war on terror.

By edict the phrase global war on terror will be replaced with jihadist extremism and consigned to the history books. Given the military successes in Afghanistan and Iraq and the continuing efforts to rebuild and democratize both of those states, a new stage in defeating the evils of fundamentalist extremism has been reached. The analogy is the Cold War and the struggle against Communism.

The strategic objective of this new stage in the struggle against jihadist extremism and its dependence on violence and promoting instability through terror is to target the causes of this radicalism and redress or eliminate them. Force and violence can play only a limited role in this effort. Obviously, appropriate and aggressive use of military, law enforcement, and intelligence forces is important. More important is creating the international mechanisms and consensus to eradicate radicalism, and relieving the contradictory tensions is a critical aspect.

For example, unless or until the Palestinian-Israeli conflict is brought under control or finally resolved, al Qaeda and other jihadists will use it as a powerful means to recruit. Unless or until the more autocratic aspects of rule in states such as Saudi Arabia, Iran, Syria, and Egypt are contained, these will remain breeding grounds for radicals. Unless or until the Indo-Pakistani conflict over Kashmir reaches some form of settlement and Pakistan takes further steps to rein in the fundamentalist elements, radicals will flourish.

Choices also must be made about dealing with important states such as Russia—fledgling democracies with insurgencies as in Chechnya that threaten the stability of the regime and country and have been dealt with using harsh and often brutal tactics that violate American standards of human rights. There is no one-stop strategic shopping or one-size-fits-all solution here. All of these choices raise the most profound challenges for any strategy, grand or not.

The State of the Union is a first occasion to begin this process.

A First Recommendation

The United States must abandon the "global war on terror" as its major strategic priority. In its stead the United States needs a newer version of the old Cold War construct and the notion of long-term ideological, political, and strategic conflict. But "war" suggests the wrong context and means for waging and winning this struggle.

The United States is engaged in a struggle against jihadist extremism, the perversion and kidnapping of a religion for political reasons. The goal is not only to prevent a theocratic radical regime from seizing power and becoming a state, as opposed to a nonstate, threat but also to persuade billions of citizens of the world about the dangers that are posed to them by this ideology and bring them to oppose and resist theocratic radicalism.

This will require a fundamental transformation in how the United States goes about advancing its security. Specific recommendations follow. However, the government, meaning both the executive and legislative branches, must first develop and agree on the broader approach and then ensure that Americans in overwhelming numbers understand and support it. The executive branch must lay out a comprehensive and detailed plan that reshapes and transforms the national security organization in keeping with these dangers, challenges, and threats. Congress must approve that plan, including reorganizing itself for the tasks at hand. The public must also appreciate that more spending will be needed.

If, for example, in 2004 the nation spends roughly half a trillion dollars on national and homeland defense that is primarily aimed at direct protection of the United States, as opposed to eliminating or mitigating the causes of these dangers where they exist, it must also spend a greater percentage on the latter. Even 10 percent or fifty billion dollars would go a long way in making the world and, by extension, the United States safer.

Recommendations on ways to accomplish these tasks are central to the remaining chapters.

A Not So Joyous Christmas

On December 19, 2003, the Department of Homeland Security announced threat condition Orange was in effect. Orange meant that the danger of terrorist attack was high, the second highest level of warning. Tens of thousands of federal and local law enforcement and security personnel were placed at bridges, airports, and other critical locations where terrorists might strike across the nation. The warning was nationwide, even though many parts of the nation were not at risk. The costs were measured in billions of dollars a day. Although the federal government could meet these demands through borrowing or through deficit financing of the budget, states and cities did not have that luxury. Most states require balanced budgets. Hence, the costs were disproportionately directed to state and local pockets.

Airline security was heightened and nearly a dozen flights, first from France and Mexico and then Britain, were canceled or delayed. British Airways Flight 223 from Heathrow to Washington came in for special scrutiny. At least six flights were canceled or repeatedly searched before take-off. The administration cited credible but unspecific warnings about times, dates, and targets and that particular flight as reasons. No terrorist attacks took place. Obviously these precautions and preparations could have been responsible. The security authorities could have had good information and intelligence and acted appropriately. There were two other possibilities. The information could have been wrong, misinterpreted, or too ambiguous to call. Under those circumstances, who would take the chance? Prudence and caution under these conditions were understandable. After all, no president would find failure to prevent an attack helpful in an election year.

Last, the warnings could have been misinformation. Al Qaeda or groups without political agenda could have been playing with the system by planting false information to mislead, deceive, and force a dramatic response. Further, strategic or tactical disinformation on the part of the administration cannot be discounted as a means for confusing and misleading al Qaeda.

The problem with crying wolf is that eventually a wolf must be produced. Along with other security checks, such as Project VISIT, photographing and fingerprinting foreign visitors arriving at airports and seaports, the United States created the image of an armed camp, overly preoccupied with stopping terrorists. Foreign perceptions of American overreaction are not inherently helpful or harmful. But when the impression of incompetence or inflexibility is created, attempts to rely on international cooperation are likely to find less than willing foreign partners.

The general criticism leveled against the United States was that these security measures were incomplete. There was no way to continue delaying or canceling air flights indefinitely without paying a huge price in tourism and business or through retaliation in other countries. Indeed, VISIT did not check foreign visitors from more than twenty-four friendly states and would not have caught shoe bomber Richard Reid.

The impact of these security actions will become clearer over time. However, if the object of America's adversaries was to terrorize, they did so merely by virtue of threat. In cost-exchange terms, for the equivalent of a few intercepted e-mails and phone conversations, perhaps no more that a few dollars' worth, the United States incurred millions if not hundreds of millions of dollars' worth of expenses. Those expenses will most likely grow.

The point is that Bush's global war on terror offers a huge advantage to the terrorists in imposing costs if they are clever enough to exploit that advantage. To some degree, especially if it cannot be proven that attacks were prevented and at least a few terrorists apprehended, the psychological and political backlash can also be expensive. Indeed, America's credibility is at stake. Prudence and caution are understandable and justifiable. If caution is used to excess or appears wrongly exercised for political expediency, sentiments will change. Instead of advancing the war on terror, improperly applied precautions can have the opposite effect, making the American leadership look feeble, worried, and uncertain of how to deal with the danger in effective ways.

4

Allies or Adversaries?
Transforming and Reinventing Alliances

The end of the Cold War ultimately would challenge the system of alliances the United States and its allies had created to contain Soviet expansion and aggression. With the threat gone, no "clear and present dangers" carried even remotely the same weight of danger as did the Soviet Union. The first Gulf War in 1991 and its aftermath partially reoriented strategic priorities to the greater Middle East. However, no obvious, clear-cut basis existed for redrawing the role of the North Atlantic Treaty Organization (NATO), which was formed in 1949, and other coalitions—at least until late 2001.

This security dilemma for the United States and its allies was encapsulated in debate over NATO and how to sustain a military alliance created to deter a major military threat in the absence of that military threat. The Clinton administration began attacking that dilemma by enlarging NATO from sixteen to nineteen members. NATO ultimately grew to twenty-six members in 2004 with the admission of former East European members of the Warsaw Pact. However, the strategic rationale and missions were very much in flux, not only for NATO but also for other global strategic arrangements and networks the United States needed to continue, create, or terminate.

The war in Kosovo in 1999 came as close to fracturing NATO as any crisis in its history. The seventy-eight days it took to force Serbian leader Slobodan Milosevic to capitulate and withdraw from Kosovo was a "close-run thing." Having won under those circumstances, the alliance welcomed the prospect of a fierce debate on its future without being forced. Tragically, it took an event as dramatic as September 11 to make obvious the new dangers around which alliances and coalitions would need to be structured. For the first and only time in its history, NATO invoked Article V the day after the attacks and joined the United States in the war on global terror.

Restructuring the alliance remains a work in progress. NATO has taken some profoundly important steps in changing the character, capability, size, and role of the alliance. A critical step for success in this transition is to design a security structure not only to win the global war on terror but also to form alliances to deal with the underlying causes of extremism and radicalism, which are the collective danger to the international system and the individual states that comprise it. Reality, however, does not always produce change. Despite the promises of incoming administrations to cope with what they believe are the most important issues, fundamental change rarely happens. Continuity is far more common.[1]

Suppose, however, that the twenty-first century and victory in the Cold War a decade ago could resemble the first years after winning World War II. If the current security strategy and framework could be rewritten or recreated, what should be different and what should be maintained? Are the underlying concepts of containment, deterrence, and alliances still as effective against new threats in the global war on terror as they were against the Soviet Union? And if change were needed, could it be translated into action?

Using the transformation of the Defense Department as a guide, how might the United States transform its current security strategy, along with the structure of alliances and multilateral activities, to meet the demands of the new century coalesced by the collective dangers of Islamic extremism exploiting societal vulnerabilities for political purpose? Put another way, how can the United States overcome the paradoxical relationships between power and security through invigorating old or creating new partnerships to reduce or eliminate the shared vulnerability to disruption? Innovation and creativity are crucial ingredients. But bureaucratic inertia, long-standing institutions, practices and policies, and political resistance to change are formidable restraints.

Alternatives to Containment, Deterrence, and Alliances

To be blunt, it is difficult to see how a radical theology or ideology in which suicide is an acceptable practice and in which states and individuals are not held accountable for their actions can be contained or deterred by conventional means. The solution would be to attack not only symptoms, namely the terrorists and the responsible organizations, but also to remedy the causes.

The most practical way to proceed would be to form a new or expanded system of alliances and relationships, certainly in the abstract. Since the greater Middle East is the general geographic region from which these dangers emerge, it is treated in a separate chapter. This chapter examines how willing and sometimes not-so-willing partners and coalitions from outside that region might be incorporated in a broader system and strategy of relationships to prevent and eliminate these dangers.

---

1. As noted, the Kennedy administration did make major changes. The Nixon administration reached out to China, eventually making the Soviet Union the sole adversary in the Cold War. It remains to be seen whether George W. Bush's administration and its neoconservative instincts will prove to be another major inflection point that marks a significant change in U.S. policy.

A vast number of organizations in place today, around one hundred and fifty, play a role in the broader global security framework. Dealing with these nongovernment entities can test the limits of any government in even the most casual attempt to coordinate and interact with them. A review of these organizations is not possible in less than a very long book. However, several of the organizations are useful guides and starting points for creating a new framework.

The United Nations, the International Monetary Fund, and the World Bank sprung in part from the memories of World War I. NATO arose as an Iron Curtain descended across Eastern Europe and a Cold War ensued with the grave risk of becoming hot. NATO now consists of twenty-six members and a dozen more states in the related Partnership for Peace (PfP). The European Union (EU) more recently has been the major force for integrating now twenty-five states in Europe economically and politically. The EU is also developing a security force, still ill defined, that ideally should be integrated with NATO. Neither political integration of Europe nor EU military capability with NATO may happen soon or at all, especially after discord over the proposed constitution that was not ratified at the December 2003 meeting on precisely that agreement.

There are hosts of other institutions, such as the forty-member Organization for Security and Cooperation in Europe (OSCE); the twelve-nation Asian-Pacific Economic Cooperation (APEC); the eight-member ASEAN (Association of South East Asian States); and regimes such as the Non-Proliferation Treaty group, the Proliferation Security Initiative, and Missile Technology Control Regime.

As General of the Army George Marshall was fond of saying, "If you get the objectives right, a lieutenant can write the strategy." The objective of reconstructing and changing the current security framework must be to contain, deter, prevent, and ultimately eliminate the causes of extremism that rely on terror and violence to achieve cross-border political ends. Al Qaeda is a convenient expression of the fundamentalist radicalism that has hijacked Islam. But al Qaeda has been a catalyst. Many new cells, unconnected to al Qaeda, have sprung up very much the way cancer expands in the human body. Unlike traditional military alliances and security treaties for mutual and bilateral defense, these new structures have to have a broader range of cooperative elements that combine all policy tools from military to law enforcement and intelligence to economic aid and resources if the battle of ideas and ideology is to be won.

To define future security constructs, NATO, the largest and most successful alliance in history, is the first and best place to begin. NATO must be put in the context of Europe, the European Union, and in the broader context of the fight against extremism. Since the Cold War ended and the Soviet Union dissolved, the alliance has been in a process of transformation. Today it is not an overstatement to predict that this transformation can be the most significant in NATO history, but it also runs the risk of foundering. A central problem is that NATO's politicians and publics are largely unaware of the commitments made, the consequences of those commitments, and the benefits of success and penalties of failure.

FROM PRAGUE TO PRAGUE

In 1939 Albert Einstein drafted a short letter to Franklin Roosevelt advising him that it was possible to generate huge amounts of explosive power from the atom. Six years later two Japanese cities were laid waste by two atomic bombs. The nuclear age had begun.

No letter to the president may ever carry more impact than Einstein's. However, that does not rule out any future events with strategic consequences approaching what $E = mc^2$ wrought. In fact, one may be underway today within NATO, which is in a profound state of transformation since its birth in 1949 to protect the West from the gathering danger of Soviet expansion.

NATO was and is a military alliance to defend against military threats. For the first forty years the threat from the USSR was well understood. Originally defense rested on "massive retaliation" and the protection afforded by American nuclear superiority.

By 1968 that superiority was eroding. NATO agreed to shift its strategy to "flexible response." This doctrine mandated a balance between nuclear and conventional deterrence so that a Soviet attack would not automatically trigger nuclear war. Despite clear evidence of a Soviet buildup in conventional and nuclear forces, European allies only reluctantly embraced this strategy. But the so-called Prague Spring of 1968 soon convinced them otherwise.

Democratic reform seemed to bloom, but it was short lived. The Soviets intervened to end reform in Hungary and elsewhere and threatened the other Eastern bloc states with what became the Brezhnev Doctrine, named for the then Soviet leader. Soviet military force would be used to preserve Socialist control. NATO's new strategy was essential to preventing the Brezhnev Doctrine from encroaching west.

After the Soviet Union imploded, NATO began the search for a new strategy. The dilemma was to find valid rationale for a military alliance when there was no military threat even on the distant horizon. September 11 helped clarify a new understanding of danger and, in November 2002, NATO's heads of state met in Prague to change the alliance yet again. This transformation, if successful, will not only change NATO but also could create the conditions for decades of stability in the West.

The Prague declaration was a commitment to expand membership, missions, and capability. This year NATO grew to twenty-six states. The broader construct of "security" has replaced "defense" in defining missions, and new threats now run from containing the frightening juncture of terrorists and weapons of mass destruction to humanitarian relief, reflecting the realities of the twenty-first century. New capability will rest on creating a highly trained, ready, agile, and capable expeditionary force able to deploy around the world and known as the NATO Response Force or NRF.

The spear for this transformation is the NATO Response Force. The tip is the high readiness portion, about six thousand personnel ready to deploy in five to six days with at least thirty days of staying power. These are discussed below. However, the NRF must vastly change the way NATO organizes, equips, uses, and provides for its forces. Therein lies the difficulty.

In October 2003 at NATO's meeting of ministers and chiefs of defense staffs in Colorado Springs, a highly successful seminar war game was played on the possible implications of using the NRF. In January 2004 one hundred NATO flag and general officers, including ten of four-star rank, with responsibilities for the NRF met in Norfolk, Virginia, in Exercise Allied Reach to advance fielding and deploying the full force of about thirty thousand in a two-year timeframe. In NATO terms these were very big deals.

Why is this important? No matter how powerful the United States may be, Afghanistan and Iraq validated the need for allies and for multinational forces that can go into action even at short notice. NATO unanimously joined America in the war on terror immediately after September 11. Today NATO is in Afghanistan as the International Security and Assistance Force (ISAF) and is likely to go into Iraq as an alliance.

Europeans recognize the new dangers but not as urgently as they should. Looking south, they understand that Africa's population on the northern tier, the bulk Muslim, is the fastest growing in the world. Many will emigrate north. To the east, the greater Middle East remains a snake pit of terror and violence, in the shadow of oil and nuclear weapons.

This new NATO can form a powerful force to contain instability, violence, and terror. But as in the Cold War, military force is critical. The post-Prague NATO, with the NRF as its cutting edge, fills this role. The crucial question is whether member states will ultimately honor the commitments made at Prague. If they do, and it is by no means certain that they will, the new NATO will have great and positive consequence.

PRAGUE 2002

This is what the member states of NATO committed to at the remarkable Prague Summit held in November 2002 in Czechoslovakia:

> We, . . . the member countries of the North Atlantic Alliance, met today to enlarge our Alliance and further strengthen NATO to meet the grave new threats and profound security challenges of the twenty-first century. Bound by our common vision embodied in the Washington Treaty, we commit ourselves to transforming NATO with new members, new capabilities and new relationships with our partners.[2]

---

2. Prague Summit Declaration issued by the Heads of State and Government in the meeting of the North Atlantic Council, November 21, 2002.

The engine for this transformation was the newly created NATO Response Force. The drivers of this engine initially were Lord George Robertson, until January 1, 2004, NATO secretary general; Gen. James L. Jones, USMC, Supreme Allied Commander Operations; Adm. Edmund Giambastiani, USN, Supreme Allied Commander Transformation; and Adm. Sir Ian Forbes, RN, Deputy Supreme Allied Commander Transformation. By virtue of the personalities and experience of each of these senior NATO officials, transformation and the NRF have been given a powerful start.[3] However, there are many obstacles that lie ahead.

The first element of the NRF, a very high readiness force of about six thousand three hundred soldiers, sailors, airmen, and marines, was put in commission on October 15, 2003. This force is to be rapidly deployable virtually to anywhere of interest to NATO, meaning virtually anywhere on the globe. NATO, as noted, is already deployed as an alliance to Afghanistan, halfway around the world from Europe. The larger high-readiness force of about twenty thousand is still a work in progress.

With Jones pushing the operational development and testing of the NRF in Europe, Giambastiani and Forbes are using the resources in Norfolk, Virginia, of the combined headquarters for Joint Forces Command and Allied Command Transformation to support the NRF. A visit to NATO headquarters on both continents shows how strong the commitment is to make the NRF viable. The issue, however, is not at the military level.

Despite the promises and commitments made by each member of the alliance to transform, the political and strategic consequences of the NRF are profound. The NRF will, in essence, stand the alliance on its head. The alliance must reshape and reform its military capabilities for expeditionary missions. It must agree in advance to use these forces in anger without lengthy debate and interminable discussion that have been part of the alliance's modus operandi since its inception. It must be responsive, not reactive, and capable of taking the offensive in spite of its previous history as a defensive alliance.

If the NRF can be made to work with a ready, viable, and usable force at NATO's disposal, this will be a major achievement. To put an even greater challenge in play, can this process of fielding the NRF be accelerated or expanded to deal with other new security challenges and become the principal example of how

---

3. The NRF is the collective brainchild of two senior civilians currently at the National Defense University in Washington, D.C.: Dr. Hans Binnendijk and Dr. Richard Kugler. Both served as directors of NDU's Institute for National Security Studies and Binnendijk on the White House NSC staff as well. Both have extensive experience in Europe and NATO, as well as in defense studies. The idea was brought to the attention of the Bush administration in late 2001 and quickly met with approval, leading to the Prague Summit in November 2002.

old structures can be reworked for the future, with application to other organizations and arrangements? Or is that task more than a bridge too far and one whose crossing could overextend and therefore compromise making the NRF a success? Despite an absence of answers to these questions, absence is not good grounds to delay consideration because the potential benefits could be great.

NUCLEAR FRAMEWORKS AND PARTNERSHIPS

A second example for creating new alliances and relationships engages the nuclear powers on the need to prevent the spread and use of the most destructive weapons of mass destruction—nuclear and biological. The six-power discussions among the United States, China, Russia, Japan, and both Koreas that are under way to explore means to denuclearize the Korean peninsula provide an opportunity to examine creating a broader, permanent group (such as the Conference on Security and Cooperation in Europe [CSCE] in Europe during the Cold War), to advance these purposes, perhaps including the other nuclear powers. A further inquiry is to determine how or if other initiatives from the Middle East Partnership Initiative (MEPI), Millennium Challenge Account, and the Proliferation Security Initiative (PSI) can be turned into opportunities for expanding security and cooperation through these or other means.

These are not new ideas in the sense that, since World War II, the United States has relied on multilateral efforts for enhancing and protecting security. The issue is whether those tested principles can be made to work in an era in which the threats and dangers are radical and radically different. Whether the Bush administration and its successors will see the value in creative attempts to work out new multilateral security solutions and approaches even with former members of the "axis of evil" remains to be seen. At first President Bush did not seem overly enthusiastic in pursuing negotiations with North Korea or moving past humanitarian aid with Iran.

Critics have attacked the Bush administration for pursuing unilateral actions unfettered by reactions and warnings of others, including friends and foes. The Bush administration has rejected charges of unilateralism. An article in *Foreign Affairs*, the journal of the Council on Foreign Relations, by Secretary of State Colin Powell in the Winter 2003 edition argued strongly for the need for multilateralism and cited chapter and verse of why and how the Bush administration was following that line.

Still allies and critics do not easily forget the memory of the administration's unilateral actions rejecting the Kyoto Treaty, ABM and the International Criminal Court, and its initial attempts to bypass Congress and the United Nations in making war on Iraq. Nor was the rejection of bilateral talks on the North Korean nuclear programs in favor of "multilateral" meetings strong grounds to believe the Bush White House was really multilateral in its outlook.

The intense focus on the greater Middle East, the Herculean task of postwar reconstruction of Iraq, and the increasing difficulties of maintaining political control of that process have reignited controversy over White House preference for unilateralism and the need for much more international help. The realists and the idealists in the administration have not resolved the full direction of U.S. policy under what appears to be the growing crisis in Iraq. Do these conflicting approaches reflect the deep, continuing contradiction and tension within the administration? Or, aware of how difficult the task of democratizing Iraq has turned out, have the neocons been chastened and the president faced with little alternative to considering the benefits of multilateralism?

While compiling answers to these questions, a better understanding of how and where alliances and multilateral efforts can be revamped to support global security is important. If Bush is reelected, he may be tempted to start with a clean slate. If there is a different president, these are answers that presumably he will wish to have.

Consider three examples for transforming alliances: how NATO, using the NRF, can become the case study for this effort either in concert with the European Union or not; how a new initiative in the Far East focused on denuclearizing the Korean peninsula can aid this process; and how a new initiative that shifts focus from the war on terror to prevent and combat radicalism can be fashioned. Whether or not one agrees with the specifics of each, using innovation and creativity to conceive new approaches is the lesson to be taken away. Directly put, can strategic frameworks and alliance make the United States safer and securer or is tempered unilateralism a better policy?

CASE I: NATO—TRUSTED OLD FRIEND, VIABLE NEW PARTNER—AND THE EUROPEAN UNION

World War II ended American isolation from the world at large. Alliances and partnerships have been crucial security foundations ever since. After NATO was created in 1949, as Lord Ismay observed, "to keep the Americans in, the Russians out and the Germans down," a series of other alliances were put in place to surround and contain the Soviet Union. CENTO, SEATO, and ANZUS, along with the bilateral U.S.–Japan defense treaty, demonstrated the importance of alliances in American strategic thinking. Of course, CENTO and SEATO proved relatively temporary.

With the end of the Soviet Union, the future of NATO was far from clear. Preserving a military alliance designed to deter a military threat that no longer existed was not a simple task. Europe lurched toward a pact of economic if not political unification, drawing it together under the European Union. France and Germany expressed preferences for fielding an independent EU military force. Each of these actions tested the relevance of NATO.

The central question is clear: What is the role of NATO in the twenty-first century and, indeed, does it have one? On the answers to these questions rest, the future viability of the alliance.

The Clinton administration's actions and admonishments about the importance of alliances were well known and well stated. A strategy of engagement and enlargement was put in place. Most notably NATO expanded from sixteen to nineteen and now to twenty-six states.

Indeed, the Bush administration was very critical of the policy of engagement beyond dissociating itself from the Clinton administration. Initially the Bush team believed engagement yielded the United Nations too much political authority at the expense of American control. However, after September 11, the Bush administration would come to appreciate the importance of NATO, in part by accident.

The Prague Summit could not have charted a better or timelier course for NATO's future. In committing to these bold and imaginative actions, NATO took huge steps in responding to the realities and dangers that both challenge and threaten the safety and security of the alliance. The first question is whether or not NATO can transform itself from a defensive military alliance against a single, awesome threat anchored in Eurasia to an expeditionary and responsive alliance with global reach against unspecific threats and dangers that put society at risk, not through destruction but disruption.

The second is whether or not member states will honor these commitments in action not only in theory by providing the necessary resources but also by making the requisite changes. These obstacles and challenges NATO now faces, ironically, are more perplexing and, in many ways, more difficult than those posed by the Soviet Union when the threat was clear and present and the ultimate nightmare was a nuclear holocaust that would have destroyed society as we knew it.

NATO's mission for fifty years was direct military defense of the alliance. Defense and security were virtually synonymous. The threat, made unambiguous through deed and action, neutralized many of the powerful centrifugal political forces that existed among even friendly states and coalesced the transatlantic nations into a single determined defensive military alliance. That alliance turned out to be history's most unconditionally successful, bloodlessly prevailing against a superpower replete with a matching alliance and a vast military arsenal.

Today, of course, the Soviet Union has been gone for more than a decade. The challenge for the alliance has shifted from direct territorial defense of national boundaries to the much broader and more difficult one of ensuring national security against more ambiguous and diffuse dangers. Defense and security are no longer identical in meaning or implication, reflecting a crucial distinction for NATO as it deals with the worlds of today and tomorrow.

Defense meant fielding substantial military forces to contain or deter Soviet aggression and military attack. Today defense alone is no longer sufficient to assure security, which cannot be guaranteed merely by relying on what worked during the Cold War.

NATO clearly understands this challenge and this difference. Its members agree that one of the main reasons for its continued existence is to counter the dangers of "asymmetric" threats, particularly those arising from the nexus of international terror and the proliferation of weapons of mass destruction. Those dangers, including narcoterrorism, cyber crime, and a host of other threats, are real and concern not only the actual damage such attacks would cause but also the wider disruption that would follow such an attack or threat of attack.

For NATO and the United States, if they are to benefit from a vibrant and refocused alliance, the overriding important challenge is to make good on the commitment to transform from a defensive military alliance created for the sole purpose of containing and deterring the daunting military threat of a superpower adversary to an alliance that remains as effective and relevant in a world with far more diffuse dangers and in which enhanced security must be the outcome.

Can the Past Be Prologue in Resolving the Toughest Questions?

Clearly the most crucial test of all is keeping NATO as relevant and effective in the twenty-first century against new dangers and threats as it was in the twentieth century in winning the Cold War. In the 1960s when confronted with an increasingly capable Soviet nuclear and conventional military arsenal, the original alliance strategy of "massive retaliation" was in jeopardy of being outflanked. After strenuous and often heated debate, the alliance unanimously adopted a strategy of "flexible response," which meant that NATO would return to a balance of nuclear and conventional deterrence and thereby counter growing Soviet military strength. The notion was to respond and deter the Soviet Union at all levels of nuclear or conventional capability. The word "flexible" conveyed significant strategic and political meaning.

The concept of flexible response proved to be brilliant. The American and European sides of the alliance could emphasize either the nuclear or conventional balance as best fit each member's interests. For the United States, enhancing conventional forces meant that nuclear escalation was not inevitable. For Europe, dependence on the nuclear guarantee of Washington remained in force. The net effect increased alliance cohesion and therefore deterrence. The example of flexible response can apply now—finding the right strategy that conforms to political necessity and reality. A range of tough questions must be addressed along the way. Some of the toughest include:

- Will new and old members agree that the future is best served by a vibrant alliance and take sufficient action to ensure NATO remains relevant and useful in that future? Will those actions require consensus and unanimity in decisions as in the past, or can new modus operandi be worked out, allowing the alliance to respond but without every member having to agree?

- Can common understanding of the new dangers and asymmetric threats be shared across the alliance, or will there be divisions over the imminence and danger to NATO's security and hence little reason to make further change in the alliance? And can America's view of a "preemptive" strategy be accommodated in the NATO context, especially when there is absolute or even strong proof of looming danger?

- Will new and old members take the necessary steps to acquire these promised capabilities, including aligning national budgets to provide the required monies and restructuring and even redeploying national forces as may be needed? Or will this statement of intent issued at Prague prove to be merely a nicely worded document and not a call to arms?

- Will member states make further changes in both national and NATO organization and command structures beyond establishing Allied Command Operations (ACO) and Allied Command Transformation (ACT) so that the new capabilities will be ready for use on a timely and integrated basis and so that operational commanders will have the authority for planning, preparing, and employing these forces? Or will cumbersome and time-consuming decision-making processes prevent these new capabilities from being used when they are most needed?

- Will necessary solutions be worked in terms of the critical information- and intelligence-sharing procedures, technology transfer restraints, and defense-industrial issues that make the so-called two-way street highly congested when it becomes the most efficient means for procurement of arms and military services?

- Having committed to "transforming" the alliance, will there be a shared understanding of what transformation means, how it applies to each state, and how that understanding can strengthen alliance cohesion and capability, or will the term turn into a slogan with uneven effect? And having made the NATO Response Force or NRF the first major undertaking in this process of transforming, how will these questions be answered in that context?

- How much more can and will NATO expand its membership and how will it ultimately choose to incorporate Russia in its planning in accordance with the NATO/Russia Agreement?

A NATO Transformed, But Not Yet

Former President George H.W. Bush and his national security advisor Brent Scowcroft were prescient in titling their joint memoir *A World Transformed.* That book showed how fundamentally the world had changed during a single term of one president. Change over the past decade persisted and probably has accelerated. In NATO's case profound change was necessitated by the fall of the Soviet Union if the alliance was to have relevance. A new strategic concept was adopted in the 1990s, and the alliance put in place programs to assist old members of the Warsaw Pact—now democracies and market economies—in joining NATO.

At the Prague Summit in November of 2002 the alliance approved further sweeping changes to the organization of the command structure, including recasting the responsibilities of the old SACLANT and SACEUR by creating ACT and ACO. Also, the NATO Response Force (NRF) was approved for implementation. Of course each of these commitments must now be translated into action. Action requires further implementation that will affect national forces and budgets.

How far and how quickly NATO has come in only a few years is evident and yet surprising. NATO went to war for the first time in its history in Yugoslavia, culminating in the spring 1999 campaign in Kosovo. The campaign took seventy-eight days during which time the strength of Serbian political resistance tested the alliance to its core. But NATO prevailed.

On September 12, 2001, the day after three airliners were turned into missiles that destroyed New York's Twin Towers and a portion of the Pentagon in Washington, for the first time in its history, NATO invoked Article V. The terrorist attacks against the United States were deemed as attacks against each NATO member, and the other eighteen states joined America in the war on terror. As the war shifted to Afghanistan, NATO provided both forces and support. On August 11, 2003, NATO formally assumed the duties as the International Security Assistance Force (ISAF).

Now with the NRF in very high readiness and ACT and ACO established as the major commands, NATO continues to take giant steps that only a few years ago would have been unimaginable. But broader questions remain. Having agreed to these changes, will each member honor its commitment fully? And can transformation, coined by the Americans in general and the Bush administration in particular, provide the intellectual and operational basis for embedding a process for keeping the alliance as effective and relevant as it was during the Cold War? Without doubt, the intent is present. However, these commitments mean that major decisions must be made and major new steps must be taken.

Skeptics will argue that NATO has served its purpose. In this view, while NATO might have a role as an insurance policy, kept around if needed at some future date, the alliance has become dispensable. The assumption is that other institutions, from the European Union to the United Nations, can pick up NATO's responsibilities. If terror is regarded as more of a law enforcement and intelligence problem, then Interpol and intelligence services should have those responsibilities.

Expansion of NATO membership was acceptable. Training, organizing, and preparing for a future emergency are also unexceptional steps. However, if this view achieves widespread acceptance, NATO will become little more than a forum for military communications and exercises and not a strong, vibrant, and effective alliance. Ultimately, it could become moribund. Divisions that already exist within the alliance regarding the nature and immediacy of the threat will reinforce this passive view of NATO.

Others argue that, having won the Cold War, larger, possibly more daunting, tests still lie ahead. There is little indication that al Qaeda and other theocratic-radical groups have abandoned their goals, given up, and returned to their homes and normal lives. Current events from the Middle East to the tip of Indonesia suggest that terror is far from subsiding. Unless there is a powerful means to contain its spread and, where necessary, respond in kind or indeed before extremists can act, in this view, the world and NATO will be less safe or secure. The presence of weapons of mass destruction and the states that appear willing to supply them amplify the danger.

The conclusion of this second view is for a NATO with a global reach, a capacity for responsive action, and a range of capabilities sufficient to carry out these new missions successfully. Such a force should provide some measure of deterrence through its inherent fighting power. Transformation, then, is a necessity if this capability is to be achieved. The Prague Declaration is the strongest example and proponent of this view. Hence, the test is ensuring that these commitments are put into place.

THE CRUCIAL BEGINNING: THE NATO RESPONSE FORCE

From these perspectives the political and strategic significance of the NATO Response Force (NRF) is crucial. Space precludes full discussion of the NRF. The Prague Declaration and subsequent NATO documents lay out specific details, including rotation, composition, training, certification, and deployment. However, in political terms, the NRF might be effectively viewed as the first twenty-first century version of the older flexible response doctrine model. The NRF provides the alliance the capability most likely needed in the new century "expeditionary" and is designed for fighting not only major wars but also so-called lower intensity operations. It is, therefore, the "driver" of transformation. For the NRF to work, the alliance must consider profoundly different ways of doing business. This contrasts the "old" with the "new" NATO and requires transformation at the outset.

General Jones, SACEUR, has summarized the nature of the differences in capability and thinking between the NRF and the forces structure that won the Cold War. During the Cold War NATO was static, defensive, reactive, and regional. Military operations were designed on the use of mass and attrition, and the logistics were based on fixed supply points.

The NRF must be agile, responsive, and global. Operations will center on exploiting maneuver and precision. The supply and logistics systems will be integrated and distributed. The NRF must be well prepared, well equipped, and deployable. The first and indeed crucial step to transform the forces nominated by the nations to twenty-first century forces is to make sure that they will have dominant battlefield awareness.

To be responsive before a direct attack, NATO and its governments must either have preapproval or quicker decision-making processes than exist today. Clearly, as during the Cold War, when tensions with the Soviet Union grew, there must be a set of rules of engagement that are approved to permit effective deployment and allow follow-on and replacement forces or other means to take over the missions. This is all work in progress.

The NRF is based on tiered-readiness, meaning that each element of the NRF has a certain timetable for deployment. The Very High Readiness element, consisting of about six thousand three hundred combat personnel organized around maritime, land, and air components, is to be deployable in five to thirty days, giving it an expeditionary character. The High Readiness Force, substantially larger and more capable, is designed for deployment within ninety days. The follow-on force element is in development.

Given the new capabilities that Prague set for transforming NATO (to improve chemical, biological, and radiological defense; intelligence, surveillance, and target acquisition; air to ground surveillance; command, control, and communications; combat effectiveness, including precision munitions and suppression of air defenses; strategic air and sea lift; air refueling; and deployable combat and combat service support), it is up to each member to follow through to the best of its ability. The implications of the NRF and what each meant for the member states as an extension to the Prague capabilities commitment were submitted to the allies at an extraordinary session of the defense ministerials held in Colorado Springs, Colorado, in October 2003.

A NATO First

In 2002 Secretary of Defense Donald Rumsfeld applied a measure of transformation for the NATO ministerial meetings. Encouraged by Vice Adm. Arthur Cebrowski, director of OSD's Office of Transformation, Rumsfeld suggested to NATO Secretary General George Robertson a departure for the meeting the United States would host the following fall in Colorado Springs. Why not begin that meeting with a war game that would stimulate and inform the ministers on transformation in order that the notion could be better understood and put in the NATO context? Robertson was highly enthusiastic.

As transformation evolved and the NRF became a reality, the war game evolved into a seminar. The NRF would be the vehicle to demonstrate how transformation could be applied to NATO and the new strategic environment it faced. A substantial effort was put in place that drew heavily on the Pentagon, Joint Forces Command, Allied Commands Transformation and Operations, and the NATO staff in Brussels. All in all, the effort took ten months and involved hundreds of senior staff.

The purpose of the seminar was to simulate how the NRF might be used in a straightforward, invented scenario to take place in 2007. The small island state of Corona, located near the Red Sea and a member of NATO's Mediterranean partnership, was beset by a growing insurgency. The security of foreign nationals, many from NATO states, could not be assured by Corona's forces. NATO was asked to consider deploying the NRF to undertake the evacuation of foreign nationals.

During the evacuation the state of the insurgency turned into a full-fledged revolution. Corona's leaders were driven out of the capital by the rebels. The NRF's peaceful evacuation now turned nasty. Corona's president requested NATO help to continue the evacuation and to help friendly forces defeat the rebels. That required deploying the bulk of the twenty thousand strong NRF in what could easily turn out to be a major conflict. The implications to the NATO ministers were obvious.

In the midst of these considerations on the military intervention in Corona, the scenario revealed that the insurgents had access to weapons of mass destruction—probably chemical and biological and a "dirty" but not a usable nuclear bomb. The insurgents had also pirated two merchant ships and had loaded aboard both cruise and short-range ballistic missiles, presumably armed with weapons of mass destruction, seized from an earlier hijacking. The two ships had sailed into the Mediterranean and were closing to within missile range of NATO's southern member states.

With video of Hollywood quality and NATO officers in cameo and leading roles, the NATO ministers were presented with a very credible and informative look at the future and the types of security dangers that they may have to confront. There was no school solution, and the seminar stopped before the more worrisome scenarios were played out. There was no doubt among the audience of twenty-six ministers of defense and chiefs of defense staff that this was a brave new world and, hopefully, a brave new NATO. This new world was brought home at a dinner for the minister and chiefs hosted by the secretary's wife and the chairman of the Joint Chiefs of Staff.

Held at a secluded resort not far from the conference site, an unusual security problem was thrust on the American hosts. Colorado Springs had an infestation of bears. Bears were routinely spotted in backyards and rooting through garbage cans. The danger of a visiting minister or defense chief crossing paths with a large, hungry bear on the lovely gardens and strolling paths of the restaurant was clear and present. What to do?

Posting armed guards did not seem like a practical or politically sensible option. The press would have had a field day. Fortunately, in researching solutions, one of the senior Americans learned that bears are deathly afraid of lions and tigers. How this fear became embedded in bears' psyches, no one knew. However, a very practical solution was at hand. The Denver Zoo was able to provide, for about fifty dollars, enough lion and tiger excrement to plant outside the restaurant to cordon off the outdoor area.

The good news was twofold. No bears were spotted. And none of the guests trod in the wrong place. This may not have been transformation as Rumsfeld saw it, but it certainly worked.

In January 2004 this process was continued. At Exercise Allied Reach in Norfolk one hundred flag and general officers with responsibilities for the NRF were assembled for the purpose of thinking through the political, operational, and logistical steps necessary to field a force that was ready, agile, capable, and deployable. The same seminar war game played at the ministerials was put to the participants at Allied Reach. The intent was to move from the political and strategic levels to the operational and tactical. The importance of the NRF was driven home by remarks made to the attendees by Gen. Harald Kujat, chairman of the NATO Military Committee and Gen. Richard Myers, chairman of the Joint Chiefs of Staff, both of whom flew in to deliver those comments, and by NATO's two strategic commanders, Messrs. Giambastiani and Jones.

While the military leadership surely has the message, the public and politicians do not. Shortly before the exercise, a delegation of parliamentarians from one of America's closest European allies traveled to Norfolk for briefings on ACT, ACO, and the NRF. Initially the delegation expressed disbelief that politicians would support what the military proposed for the NRF and for transformation. Clearly the Prague Declaration and commitments made by NATO's heads of state had gone unnoticed or unread. However, the conclusion is clear. Far more disclosure on the NRF is vital if there is to be sufficient public and political support to make it work.

BACK TO THE NRF

NATO has precedent to continue the process of fielding the NRF and to handle key issues and obstacles. Politically the most effective approach is to hold discussions within the North Atlantic Council, NATO's highest decision-making authority, and the Defense Planning Group (of which only France is not a member) where each state commits to fielding specific capabilities by a certain date. As with the old Defense Planning Questionnaire (DPQ), this will be an imperfect system. However, by having each state concentrate on its niche and special capabilities and then agree to take on others, sufficient overlap should be created to give NATO the force structure it requires.

All of this should be done in closer consultation with the European Union. As both headquarters for the two organizations are in Brussels and there is an overlap of twelve states across NATO and the European Union, consultations cannot be precluded by physical separation. Indeed, recognizing the friction between France and America, senior French military officers have suggested that the United States might develop a special relationship with the European Union. In Washington there have been suggestions to appoint a senior military liaison, possibly with SACEUR wearing two hats.

Full transparency is a good way to increase cooperation, especially as European militaries would have both NATO and EU requirements. One long-term goal might be to make NATO a military arm of or resource for the European Union to direct this use toward the battle against radicalism and prevention of mass disruption through whatever means are deemed appropriate.

Consider how this process might work. Europe as a single entity is mutually dependent economically on each state and on the shared infrastructure for power and electricity; finance, banking, and commerce; and communications and transportation. When disaster strikes one country, whether through an act of man or nature, the effects are felt throughout the continent. Mad Cow and foot and mouth disease are examples.

Forty percent of Europe's hydrocarbons—gas and oil—are pumped from east to west in two pipelines. Those pipelines pass through many states and are unguarded. Cutting one or both at several points to make repair more difficult is not beyond the capacity of even a relatively technologically inferior terrorist cell. The effects would be economically catastrophic.

If such a severing occurred in winter, the impact would be exacerbated by the cold conditions. Regardless, the economic damage would be extraordinary and extend beyond Europe, as the world economy would be adversely affected, possibly to the point of depression or collapse. Other vulnerabilities include shared electrical power. When power was lost in Italy in 2003, the outage began in France, where the electricity was produced.

Clearly a more significant role of infrastructure protection and consequence management, i.e., responding to disasters, would seem to be a good interface between NATO and the European Union. As noted in Chapter 2, one reason for picking March 20 as D-Day in the war in Iraq was to allow British forces time to complete their consequence management duties in the aftermath of the foot and mouth crisis and serve as replacements for the striking firefighters. Military forces can do double duty in this regard as well. Consequence management is one responsibility that will be a growth industry, especially as homeland security assumes higher priority.

NATO could form the training arm for the EU forces in protecting critical infrastructure. In essence the European Union would serve as reserve and National Guard forces with or without the support of NATO. As the United States provides the bulk of the strategic airlift and global intelligence and surveillance capabilities for NATO, NATO can be the provider of similar logistical and support functions in these critical areas.

An Axis of Stability, Not Evil: the Northeast Pacific

The second illustrative case for redefining alliances rests in preventing nuclear war and the proliferation of those weapons. Northeast Asia is the geographic region of interest, with North Korea the immediate focus. A cynic would observe that President Bush's loathing of North Korea's Kim Jong Il notwithstanding, an invitation from the White House for the two to meet and dine together would probably make Kim a lifelong friend of the United States. That prospect is unlikely to happen. Kim's conduct, along with the absolute authority of rule in North Korea and a penchant for dangerous and often seemingly strange behavior, are not good assurances for a safer peninsula.

Through mid-2004 diplomacy seemed to be working in Korea. A war would be devastating on both sides of the thirty-eighth parallel, which divided Korea for logistical convenience after World War II to establish Soviet occupation in the north and American occupation in the south. The north would lose any war, Kim would be driven out of power, and, as with Saddam, would be captured or killed. Hence, despite the bluster, there was no rational reason why Kim would choose a war he would surely lose unless or until he had a viable nuclear option capable of striking the United States. That option will be a very long time coming.

This strategy is one of leveraging the regional powers, particularly China and Russia, to pressure Pyongyang. South Korea has no interest in complete reunification. Seoul recognized what it cost West Germany to absorb East Germany a dozen years ago. And there is no strategic reason to urge unification at this point. That prospect, along with nuclear weapons potential irrespective of what the north chooses to do, could prove destabilizing for Japan and probably Russia and China as well. Responses by any of those states could lead to arms races and the possibility of Japan deciding to develop a nuclear deterrent.

North Korea and its leader no doubt seek legitimacy. The only real face card the north possesses is nuclear capability. Pressure from Russia and China and the carrot of trade and investment from the south and Japan, along with assistance from the United States, can be useful measures to persuade Kim and his ruling circle that negotiations are far more attractive than hostility and recalcitrance. But this means that President Bush must subordinate his visceral dislike for Kim to the larger goal of denuclearizing the peninsula permanently.

This will require further meetings of the six, along with compromise on both sides. If stronger influence and pressure are required on the north, China can play an important role. China has seen the value of closer relations with the United States. When Taiwan was threatening to move toward independence, thereby provoking a crisis with China, the Bush administration pointedly reminded Taipei of the commitment to "one China" and the dangers in changing that policy, even rhetorically. Taiwan dampened its rhetoric.

China has reportedly moved thousands of troops closer to the Yalu River and the border with North Korea to deal with the problem of illegal refugees crossing into China. Should China decide to move, say, a full field army closer to the border as a signal to Pyongyang to consider negotiations as a sounder option, the message would be clear. Informing North Korea of possible restrictions on trade and other commerce by China and Russia can be helpful in negotiations. These pressure tactics will fail, however, if positive incentives are not offered and are not credible.

This process will probably take months, if not years. However, from the concept of using the six regional power framework to achieve some measure of stability and reduce the chance of war, nuclear or otherwise, there are other applications. Proliferation and the threat of a nuclear, rather than a dirty bomb, attack and the use of biological weapons can be countered with a parallel forum.

Pakistan is perhaps potentially the most dangerous state in the world, a heartbeat away, as it were, from an Islamic republic should President Pervez Musharraf be removed or assassinated. While Pakistan and India are dealt with more thoroughly in Chapter 5, bringing all the known nuclear powers together for the purpose of discussions and consultations on reducing the number and possible use of nuclear weapons is an idea whose time has come.

The United States, China, Russia, Great Britain, France, India, and Pakistan, perhaps joined by Israel and the small group of states that voluntarily gave up their nuclear programs (South Africa, Ukraine, and Georgia) as ad hoc members, should convene in a forum dedicated to reducing the number and the possible use of these weapons. This forum would exist outside the Non-Proliferation Treaty. However, by adhering to the treaty commitment to reduce nuclear weapons ultimately to zero, which nonnuclear states continually criticize the United States for ignoring, this group could ensure that the most likely sources of nuclear weapons would not be used in anger.

There are antecedents for this formula. During the Cold War, the so-called Pugwash group, consisting of U.S. and Soviet delegates, frequently met to discuss limiting the nuclear arms race. The group was named after the first place they convened in the state of Maine. Similarly the CSCE was a useful forum for dialogue. The shift from the threat of mass destruction to one of massive disruption provides the foundation for bringing together new groups of states with a common interest in limiting the effects of disrupting and harming society.

AN AXIS OF STABILITY IN THE BATTLE AGAINST EXTREMISM

The surfeit of regional and global security organizations offers an opportunity and resource in the fight to contain extremism. Clearly the MEPI, PSI, and MTCR are examples of new and existing organizations put to this use. There are two principal focal points—bilateral and multilateral means to achieve this end point. For simplicity, regional rather than global arrangements are preferred. In this regard the U.S. strategic global rebasing plan in which, over time, U.S. military forces will be redeployed and repositioned around the world to deal with the newer threats provides a further means to create and strengthen new relationships. As that plan is not finalized, it is not discussed further.

On a regional basis, the notion of using the European Union in concert with NATO as critical infrastructure protection and response forces should be considered carefully. A second idea also emanates from Europe and the European Command (EUCOM), the U.S. side of Allied Command Europe. Commanded by General Jones, an arrangement as old as NATO, EUCOM is taking major initiatives in carrying out its missions. Africa is a good case study.

Africa combines all of the current security problems and challenges. In the south, the continent has been devastated by disease, civil war, and genocide. On the west coast, huge reserves of oil have been discovered. The northern littoral has such a high rate of population growth that, despite the HIV/AIDS epidemic, Africa is the fastest growing continent in the world. The north also is largely Islamic. Its people have migrated to Europe in large numbers. With Ghadafi's about-face on abandoning weapons of mass destruction, perhaps new opportunities for strategic relationships are possible.

Recognizing this, EUCOM is in the process of not only changing how it deploys forces in the region but also examining new and different means of staffing in the region and the types of skills needed to deal with this multitude of problems and challenges. Traditional military staffs are coded with the "1" dealing with personnel; "2" with intelligence; "3" with operations; "4" with logistics; "5" with policy and strategy; "6" with interoperability; "7" with communications and information; and "8" with budgets, analysis, and resources. In JFC, a "9" was created to conduct experimentation and develop joint doctrine.

EUCOM is examining alternatives. One possibility is to field a staff organization that looks more like a mini–National Security Council. To be sure, officers from other agencies such as State, Commerce, CIA, and the FBI are routinely assigned to major staffs. The intent is to create a functional allocation of responsibilities beyond the traditional military ones. Civilian senior fellows with extensive private-sector experience in relevant areas will most likely be brought aboard.

Africa will be a test case for determining how innovation and creativity can be applied in using staffs not only more effectively but also more strategically. This is not solely a EUCOM venture. Admiral Giambastiani at JFC has an experimental staff with dedicated personnel and financial resources that are being loaned to EUCOM, an interesting example of transformation in action, about which more will be said.

The function of these staffs will extend far beyond past military duties of liaison and training. No doubt much will be learned. Done properly, innovative uses of specifically designed staffs can have a larger impact on preventing instability and violence, ultimately providing cures to the causes and symptoms of radicalism and extremism.

WHAT ELSE SHOULD BE DONE?

The United Nations is certainly a critical institution that theoretically should be able to play a larger role in making the world a safer and more secure place. The Bush administration, or certain senior members, has been openly hostile to it. In early 2003, for example, the administration spoke mockingly of the UN when Libya was chairing the human rights and Iraq disarmament panel . Libya's about- face could be instructive. However, to the degree that the UN can be a useful instrument, it is one that should not be discarded for ideological or other reasons.

Similarly Latin America, once derided by Henry Kissinger when he described it as a "dagger pointed at the heart of Antarctica," is a region that must play a larger role in America's security. Perhaps the EUCOM effort in Africa might be replicated in Latin America. But the reality is that each of these initiatives is a big issue by itself. Collectively the labor seems more than Sisyphean, especially in the highly politicized system that characterizes American politics today.

Short of a war or a more traumatic version of September 11, it will be virtually impossible for even the most popular administration to accumulate the necessary political capital to meet these demands. Hence, prioritizing or, more realistically, triaging achievable actions is essential. That requires estimating how much time the United States and its allies have before radical Islam can indeed achieve its goals of establishing a fundamentalist regime with access to Saudi money and Pakistani nuclear weapons.

There is simply no way to know this. The probabilities must be in favor of the long term. However, a single bullet or bomb or other extraordinary and unpredictable event could precipitate a faster timetable. Pakistan has been mentioned. A revolution or radical regime change in Riyadh or Cairo could have that effect. The opposite is also true.

There is an old aphorism that lacking extra ammunition, it is wiser to shoot the wolf closest to the sled. The greatest arcs of direct danger emanate from the greater Middle East, including Pakistan, and Korea. The greatest capacity for disruption however rests in Europe and the United States. Thus, the United States must construct a strategy that connects these regions and provides the tools and means to constrain and eliminate the dangers.

In both *Unfinished Business* and *Finishing Business* a new, much broader version of the old Marshall Plan was recommended. Much of that plan was intended for the greater Middle East and will be discussed in Chapter 5. Beyond that the United States must focus on Europe, using NATO as the key strategic lever for imposing necessary change and applying that to the European Union; to Korea in defusing the nuclear dangers; and in concentrating on expanding the six-power Korean talks to the broader context of preventing the likelihood of the use of weapons of mass destruction.

Meanwhile the Bush administration is committed to higher priorities of fighting the war on terror and winning the battle to democratize and stabilize Iraq. There is little appetite for expanding those hugely ambitious aims. But the administration has options. Simply put, it can declare victory and recalibrate its priorities.

That appears to be the case in Iraq. In 2004 as this book goes to press, the administration's final decisions on what to do have not yet been decided although, as the war in Iraq was easily predictable, so too are the general outlines of U.S. policy. The first assumption the administration will make, implicitly or not, is that time is on its side in Iraq. This means that eventually the insurgency will be brought under control. The new Iraqi police and security forces will be able to contain the residual of that insurgency possibly in a year or so.

Second, it will take time for the new constitution and elections to take hold and still longer for democracy and the rule of law to take hold. As a result large American presence will be needed for some time to come. That presence will be in the form of military force and an exceedingly large U.S. diplomatic mission, probably in excess of five thousand people.

Third, it will take time for the $18.7 billion appropriated for reconstruction to be awarded, put to use, and then to take hold. Bremer's senior staff told him a minimum of nine months would be needed before real effect could be seen. With the decision to slow down the awarding of contracts in order to put in place a more rigorous system of oversight, auditing, and accounting, the lag time could be a year or more, meaning late 2004 or even well into 2005.

Fourth, as political power shifts to Iraqi hands, the CPA function will transition to the State Department during the summer of 2004. With Colin Powell as probably the most popular person in America in charge of that effort, the president will have provided an important political buffer between him and scathing criticism that no doubt will be a central theme of the opposing campaign. That transition would also be an appropriate time to end the bifurcated division of power between CPA and CENTCOM, probably by making the new ambassador to Iraq, someone of impressive credential, entirely in charge.

Fifth, if these assumptions hold, the administration will turn its focus to winning the global war on terror. Iraq and Afghanistan will be less visible and therefore less taxing in time and other resources. Of course if the neocons get their way and Bush is re-elected by a large margin, Syria, Iran, and other irritants might get the same treatment as Saddam. That is very unlikely but still possible.

Under those circumstances NATO will drift along. Based on the extraordinary efforts of its military commanders and, one hopes, Robertson's replacement as Secretary-General, there is a fair chance that the NRF can be successful and NATO will make the complete transition to an alliance highly relevant to the dangers of the current and not the past century. However, any leverage with the EU and the opportunity to deal creatively with limiting the effects of massive disruption to critical infrastructure and other vulnerabilities will be lost. The administration will almost certainly turn many of those responsibilities over to the Department of Homeland Security, giving it an international mission as well. While that might make bureaucratic sense, it almost certainly will be a long time in coming as the new department learns its way in areas that have been formerly left to others.

Meanwhile the inevitability of some agreement in Korea grows despite the president's personal (and understandable) animus toward Kim. However, the opportunity to expand the six-power talks in a larger context will be lost, and, by continuing the focus of the war on terror on striking terrorists, the causes will remain in play and could well be growing.

None of this is a happy prospect even at a great distance. The opportunities in NATO and with six power talks on Korea hold promise. But whether these can be turned into means for making America securer and safer is one of the toughest questions the next administration will have to answer, presuming that question is even asked.

5
The Crescent of Crisis
Transforming and Reinventing Alliances

No matter who takes the oath of office on January 20, 2005, the United States has three basic strategic choices regarding both the fight against jihadist extremism and its approaches to the greater Middle East. First is continuation of the current Bush policies: intense effort on and even enlargement of his global war on terror and democratization and rebuilding of Iraq as the center-pieces of changing the strategic landscape of the region; reliance on the "roadmap" to navigate a peace between Israel and the Arabs; support of current regimes in Saudi Arabia and Egypt, rather than forcing change and risking revolution; and embracing both India and Pakistan in order to reconcile that conflict.

The center of gravity of this strategy is the greater Middle East, and the focal point is Iraq. If democracy can take root, the effect will be a springboard for gaining positive strategic consequences elsewhere. The presence of substantial American and coalition military forces in Iraq can be subtle or blunt instruments in this process of shifting the character of the regional landscape. However, the Bush administration is unlikely to neglect the two surviving members of the "axis of evil" and their Syrian junior partner. Iran will be dealt with in the context of the broader Middle East. North Korea will remain a separate flash point, along with the Taiwan Straits.

The second strategy is to declare a victory and reshape policy accordingly. Using Libya's about-face as one sign of victory, this strategy would still place first priority on preventing terrorist attacks. However, there would be a less bellicose attitude. Emphasis would continue on the roadmap in the Middle East and advancing the process of democratizing Iraq. In essence, this would be a "Bush lite" version of the current strategy, and the greater Middle East would remain the strategic center of gravity.

The third strategy is to embark on a fundamentally different strategy that remains highly engaged but shifts the center of gravity from Iraq and the greater Middle East and focuses explicitly on making the United States and its friends safer and securer. Simply put, this strategy takes the same Bush objectives of winning peace and stability and uses what Clausewitz called "other (far different) means" than democratizing the region to achieve them. The means for achieving these objectives would be first to build on current alliances and expand them, possibly creating others, to contain the most dangerous crises points—India-Pakistan, Israel, the Korean peninsula, and the Taiwan Straits.

Bush's global war on terror would be subordinated to these ends on the grounds that making the world safer and securer would mean placing greater emphasis on remedying the causes and not just the symptoms of terror. The term "axis of evil" would be consigned to the history books, along with Ronald Reagan's label of the Soviet Union as the evil empire. This strategy has no chance of acceptance if Bush is reelected without an extraordinary event—another September 11 or a breakthrough in the Middle East.

Other possible strategies include retrenchment and a milder form of isolationism. A Eurocentric or Eurasia-centered strategy is another. These are only noted, as no president is advocating or even thinking about these strategic options.

RISKS AND REWARDS

The first and current Bush strategy has considerable risks and rewards. Indeed, that may be understatement. The strategy is based on the belief that democratizing Iraq will ultimately spread democracy and political pluralism throughout the region. Local regimes will be compelled to become more open and pluralistic. The assumption, largely disproved by history, is that democracies tend to be stable and peaceful. In plain language, in this argument democracies do not make war on other democracies. Should this happen over time, the results would be no less dramatic than Nixon's opening to China and the collapse of the Soviet Union. However, stability within democracies cannot be assumed or taken for granted, as that has not been the rule.

Unfortunately Iraq has no history of democracy and pluralism. The country was united under Baathist rule and then by Saddam's brutality and cruelty, relying on party loyalists who regularly spied on fellow citizens and a system of rewards and punishments designed to increase total political control. Hence, the centrifugal forces that divide Shias, Sunnis, and Kurds have no natural means of being contained. The prospect that Iraq could fracture, with local warlords and religious leaders in charge of various regions, is very real.

Meanwhile jihadists and other radical groups working in parallel with regime loyalists and a dangerous criminal element have persisted in mounting an insurgency. Although the insurgency will eventually be controlled, and represents a tactical rather than a strategic and mortal threat, the real issue is preventing extremists from exploiting the failure of the United States to achieve its aims in Iraq. Also, the jihadists could benefit by temporarily entering Iraq and then returning with "bragging rights" to recruit others by recounting colorful tales of how America and the coalition were attacked and its members killed and wounded.

The principal targets for the jihadists are the strategic bookends, Pakistan and Saudi Arabia. The longer the United States is bogged down in Iraq and the longer and harder the slog, the more likely al Qaeda and other radical groups will use that as evidence of winning the war against the Great Satan. Also, with an upcoming election in 2004, America and its allies will be tempting targets for another September 11 incident to destroy the authority and legitimacy of the Bush administration at home, as was Ho Chi Minh's strategy to win the war in American living rooms. The potential flaw is this strategy's emphasis on imposing democracy in Iraq as the means of transforming the region. Not only might the strategy fail but it also might fail catastrophically.

The rewards, however, would be extraordinary. If the region were to be transformed by the democratic process, the benefits would truly make the region, the United States, and its allies far safer and securer in the future. The effect would be to attack the causes of radicalism. A more open society in Saudi Arabia, the Gulf States, and Egypt would presumably remove many of the grounds for dissatisfaction, disillusionment, and desperation on the part of citizens who would otherwise see no chance for fairness and justness. Pressure on Pakistan's government would be relieved, allowing transition to civilian rule. Furthermore, elimination of many of the causes of terrorism would help finally to defuse the Israeli-Palestinian conflict.

Democracy and Islam

Compatibility between democracy and Islam, or the converse and more simplistic view that the two will never embrace, is central to how events play out in the greater Middle East. Islam is a highly diverse, complicated, and heterogeneous religion. Part of Islam is fundamentalist. The Guardian Shia, or ruling clergy, in Iran hold strong fundamentalist beliefs, although these views are not as radical or revolutionary as Wahabi Sunni sects or bin Laden and other extremists. Part of these beliefs rest in the primacy of religious over secular law, the place of women in society, and a certain distance from other faiths.

Islam also varies geographically. Asian Islam tends to be less harsh in its fundamentalist attitudes, generally but not always following cultural characteristics. With 1.3 billion practitioners spanning much of the globe, there can be no single definition or prediction of the future relationship between Islam and democracy. However, certain observations about democracy and its viability are relevant.

Democracy requires both will and a functioning societal structure. The rule of law, some form of market economy, and popular acceptance of political pluralism are other preconditions. Former East European states such as Poland, Czechoslovakia, and Hungary, among others, could make the transition. Russia has found democracy a more difficult pursuit, largely because of characteristics and legacies that long predated the Soviet Union. Hence, for democracy to succeed—let alone flourish—in the Islamic world, greater strides are essential in making society function in accordance with the rule of law outside the Sharia: the workings of a market economy protected from corruption, patronage, and the excesses of earlier regimes; a motivated and educated public; and some measure of political stability. The key question is, where could and do these features exist?

In the greater Middle East there are no obvious candidates. Egypt, Syria, Jordan, Saudi Arabia, the Emirates, and Iran lack many of these ingredients. Turkey is the state closest to being a full-fledged democracy. Yet while Islamic, it is not Arab. The same distinction between Islam and non-Arab applies to Iran. Clearly the test case is Iraq. Pakistan, both Muslim and Arab, reflects the inherent difficulties of ensuring a lasting democratic system largely because of a combination of Islamic extremism and the inherent instability of any democratically elected regime.

Hence, unless the causes of instability, extremism, injustice, and economic inequality are addressed first or in parallel, implementing democracy is not going to happen easily, if at all. A further political reality that will impede democracy is the notion of majority and elected rule.

If democracy means that political power comes from a ballot box, how then will minority rights be protected? Iraq is the most important test case. The majority Shia, taking their lead from key clerics such as Ayatollah Ali al-Sistani, will demand popular elections for choosing a government. That is democracy after all. The minority Sunni, long in control of Iraq, clearly will resist losing power to the majority without guarantees regarding their rights and status. The same is true of the Kurds. The intellectual and political problem is stunning. One foundation of democracy, one person, one vote, majority rule simply may not be feasible or workable in Iraq today. That constraint exacerbates the absence of any sense of social cohesion in an infrastructure still devastated by Saddam and war.

One conclusion should be certain. The road to democracy in the greater Middle East is neither defined nor, at this stage, practical. Unless or until the causes of extremism and instability are addressed, the foundations for democracy will rest on air. Although air is necessary for life, it is not the basis for building pluralistic and functioning democracies. That recognition must be driven into policies that will determine where the greater Middle East should be headed and in deriving the various roadmaps for the journey. Otherwise there will be little chance of success and every chance of empowering extremists and radicals to pursue their aims, relying on terror as a critical means of achieving them.

A Road Ahead?

In earlier chapters the Bush strategy for the greater Middle East and this crescent of crisis was analyzed. It is impossible to predict what a second Bush administration might do in continuing or changing the strategic course it has set. Given the historical record of second term presidencies, not very much is likely to change. Any change most likely will be a reaction to events, or perhaps preemption of them, if the administration sees a further strategic opportunity to use force to transform states such as Syria, Iran, and, less likely, North Korea. One prediction is that Iraq (and to a lesser degree Afghanistan) will continue to constitute such a strategic, economic, and political burden, as well as continue to require substantial amounts of U.S. military ground forces, that other large-scale elective military operations are unlikely. Internationalization will continue. The United Nations most likely will assume a larger role in reconstruction. NATO's chairman of the Military Committee German Air Force Gen. Harald Kujat has urged that NATO as an alliance pick up a substantial role in Iraq, as it has in Afghanistan. Presumably that would be with a relatively small contingent, probably in the thousands at most.

On the other hand, should Bush be reelected, possibly with a good majority, the administration would very likely consider finishing the mission in the war on terror. Deploying a substantial force to western Pakistan and Afghanistan to hunt down and eliminate surviving al Qaeda members and bin Laden would be a part of that mission. Further, to bring stability to the Israeli-Palestinian conflict, some form of military intervention in Syria, should negotiations lose relevance, is not out of the question. In other words, the neoconservative view of using force to change the landscape in the greater Middle East will not have changed.

Should this latter situation occur or the administration determine that preemption of another dangerous threat is urgent, or that the United States must respond to attack elsewhere, it would have various options for finding the necessary forces. It could request replacement forces from Iraq and perhaps NATO and other foreign troops. However, should the number of troops needed to stabilize Iraq remain relatively large, say two or three divisions, because of the strains and costs on the individual alliance members, NATO would not be able to provide that level of forces to conduct this mission. Recruiting other states to provide significant numbers of troops to support Iraq's rebuilding is even less probable. In early 2004 the French Minister of Defense Michele Alliot-Marie declared that under no circumstances would France send military forces without a UN resolution or some form of approval.

In considering possible strategic approaches, price tags must be associated with each. The United States will spend more than twenty billion dollars reconstructing Iraq and Afghanistan. The question is, if the Arab-Israeli and Indo-Pakistani conflicts were resolvable simply by spending money, how many billions would it be worth to achieve lasting settlements—twenty, thirty, forty, one hundred, or more billions of dollars? After all, in 2004 the United States government will spend about a half trillion dollars on security. A percent of that, which could enhance the nation's safety and security, would seem a wise investment. Yet because of the debt and deficit, even if a figure could be calculated, would the United States and other willing states have enough political capital to invest that amount to secure a just peace?

Unfinished Business called for a Marshall Plan for the region that would extend from the eastern Mediterranean and the Israeli-Palestinian conflict, through the greater Middle East, to the Bay of Bengal, and beyond. That plan was far broader than the original European Recovery Plan and was designed to meet the different country-specific challenges across the region. Having appropriated eighty-seven billion dollars to pay for the cost of the war and reconstruction in Iraq and Afghanistan, it is questionable what appetite the United States will have for more ambitious plans to bring stability and peace to that region. Until the causes of extremism are fully addressed, winning the war against terror can never be completed. Yet if there is any chance of bringing democracy and, more realistically, stability to the region, a plan of this type is essential.

This chapter presents an overarching approach based on the third strategy noted above and then draws on three specific solutions to deal with the crescent of crisis. The first focuses on the Arab-Israeli-Palestinian conflict. The second concerns India and Pakistan. And the third describes a program for mobilizing and reconstructing Iraqi society through an innovative mix of available technology and common sense that has applicability in other regions in building a more coherent society, eliminating corruption, and putting in place measures to facilitate an enduring government. However, concentration on these specifics does not dilute the need to deal with each of the major causes of, and contributors to, radical Islam.

A STRATEGIC TRIFECTA

Great debate rages in the United States over how much positive effect a resolution of the Arab-Israeli-Palestinian conflict will have on bringing peace and stability to the region. Critics argue that the Arab world in general, and the Saudis in particular, have no lasting interest in seeing a peace that produces the recognition of Israel and the permanent ceding of Palestine and Jerusalem and Islam's holy places to the Jews. Hence, these critics argue, imposing a peace will only harm Israel and ultimately damage the prospects for Israel's survival, since Arabs will never fully accept a Jewish state. There is some evidence and much bloody history to support this position.

At the same time the effect of autocratic regimes in Egypt, Saudi Arabia, and other dynastically ruled states in the region continues to breed opposition, dissension, and disenfranchisement of large parts of those publics and societies. It was not accidental that most of the September 11 terrorists were Saudi. Disenfranchisement leads to radicalism, and poverty and unemployment are grounds from which extremism springs.

The strategic question is whether these disparate points can be linked in the effort to resolve the Israeli-Palestinian conflict. Turning the Bush strategy upside down, are there other ways to achieve the same ends without the need for imposing democracy, first in Iraq and then in the region at large? Can the various diverging interests be joined in ways that would satisfy the key states and groups involved? From the Israeli perspective, the nonnegotiable aim is to have permanent security under the rule of law in a pluralistic and democratic state. From the Syrian perspective, return of the Golan Heights, along with discussions that would lead to peace, are preconditions for further negotiations with Israel.

The Palestinians want a homeland and enough resources to make that state viable. In that context the more radical Palestinian elements see no means for achieving independence other than by eliminating Israel. There are elements in Israel who, because of desperation or conviction that survival is the issue, refuse to negotiate with terrorists and indeed Arabs. Meanwhile Israel's policy of targeted assassination as one way to curb terrorism may eliminate a few members of Hamas and Hezbollah but infuriates (and probably terrorizes) many Palestinians. A host of pressing and so far intractable issues, such as right of return, status of Jerusalem, and self-determination, continue to make finding peace a distant hope rather than a possible reality.

Saudi Arabia is driven by regime survival, now threatened from many directions. Western influence, influence of Wahabi clerics and traditionalists within the kingdom, oil, al Qaeda and radical Shia out to topple the regime, and growing social issues inside Saudi Arabia are compounded by depressed oil revenues and a continually declining per capita GNP. Poverty, once a negligible problem, is on the rise. Average income, twenty thousand dollars per family a decade ago, is less than half that today. There are also reports of increasing drug and alcohol incidents among the Saudi elite. The House of Saud is trapped between its traditional roots and constituencies, when oil revenues were plentiful enough to buy solutions and ensure stability of the regime, and the need to modernize at a time when the money required for that purpose is in less supply.

The meeting between Indian Prime Minister Atal Bihari Vajpayee and Pakistani President Pervez Musharraf in Islamabad in early January 2004 offered the prospect, however distant, of a possible rapprochement between these two bitter enemies. Obviously Pakistan is one of the two key strategic dominoes being targeted by religious radicals. Making peace or winning real improvement in relations with India strips away a platform and rationale for terrorists—the dispute over Kashmir—assuming that some resolution would become feasible even for the long term. By reducing the prospect of conflict with India, Musharraf would have more time, resources, and reason to turn to domestic issues and the danger of extremism. In this case a possible greater U.S. military presence and a much more determined joint U.S.–Pakistani military campaign would help to end the threat of al Qaeda permanently.

After the earthquake in Bam, Iran, and the thaw in U.S.–Iran relations to deal with the tragic aftermath that killed about forty thousand Iranians as 2003 drew to a close, there was an opportunity to reshape Gulf politics by creating some sort of regional security structure to ensure that extremists not perpetrate an act of terror that could be as disruptive or destructive as this earthquake. If that opportunity could have been exploited, opportunity could have arisen from disaster. If not, after the effects of this disaster ran their course, was there any alternative means to mitigate the hostility that has permeated U.S.–Iran relations since 1979 and the fall of the Shah? So far the answer has been no.

The key to putting together a unified strategy is an imaginative concept that can bring these issues and divergences together in a form of strategic "ju jitsu." To a lesser and probably far easier degree, this is what President Richard Nixon did in his first term in regard to China and the Soviet Union. Called triangular politics, the leverage point was to use China as a force against the Soviet Union by moving the United States closer and vice versa. By going to China in 1972 Nixon confronted Moscow with a new strategic alignment. Relations between Russia and China had soured by the late 1950s and gone septic after that. Several bloody border clashes had broken out. With an historical paranoia toward China (one Russian word for boogeyman is "Chinese"), the Soviet Union found itself driven to improve its relations with the United States to keep the triangular realignment from shifting the balance in what Moscow feared was the wrong direction.

Although the Kennedy administration was dismissive of Khrushchev's strategic policies regarding downsizing his forces, the Nixon administration either knew or bet that the rift between China and the Soviet Union was real. The strategic trifecta for the crescent of crisis admittedly draws on a set of assumptions not dissimilar to Nixon's to exert leverage in order to resolve a series of very difficult and dangerous problems. The goal is to put in place a strategy that will complete these many contending unfinished pieces of business.

BITING THE BULLET—PEACE IN PALESTINE AND ISRAEL

The Bush administration has gone a long way in preparing for a long-term and lasting settlement of this heretofore intractable conflict. A two-state solution is only a part of the answer. While other presidents have called for a separate Palestinian state, Bush has been the most vocal. Getting there, through a roadmap or other vehicle, is the problem. After the breakdown of the Wye Plantation talks in January 2001 and the subsequent *intifada* that has only made life more desperate for Arab and Jew, the conflict continued to deteriorate. Terrorist attacks claimed the lives of nearly a thousand Israelis. For the first time women entered the ranks of suicide bombers. Thus, over those three years, the Sharon government took a very tough stand against terror and terrorists. Many Israelis, both inside and out of the country, question whether this use of force, no matter the provocation, has indeed made Israel any safer.

During this period the Sharon government continued to establish settlements in the territory, which it occupied in 1967 after the short Six Days' war. The use of the Israeli Defense Force (IDF) to crack down on terror and terrorists provoked a strong and predictable backlash. Indeed, senior Israelis, including current chief of staff Moshe Ya'alon, were publicly critical of the negative consequences of the government's employment of the IDF. Further, internal scandals plagued Sharon. Accused of accepting a bribe when he was foreign minister, Sharon could have been required to stand down as prime minister, but the charges were dismissed.

Had the roadmap followed the original track in 2003, in 2004 Phase II would be moving toward the two-state plan. Both Israeli and Palestinian leaders rhetorically are committed to the roadmap. General Ya'alon has also raised the "possibility that we will reach a ceasefire within weeks," although that has not happened yet. Palestinian Prime Minister Abu Ala has not made his stand on this clear, and, if he were to fail as Abu Mazen did in 2003, the roadmap could face fatal, not just serious, damage.

There are three levels of action that could be taken. First is to continue with the roadmap. Despite all of the obstacles and the desperation on both sides over the *intifada* and Israeli military responses, the roadmap may be the only viable alternative. The United States will continue to apply diplomatic and political pressure, perhaps as it did in 2003, through making token reductions in the amount of aid supplied to Israel. Along with the other three members of the quartet, the European Union, Russia, and the United Nations, gradualism may carry the day or at least not precipitate a crisis.

Second, can the wall, or Security Fence, as the Israelis call it, serve as the basis for engineering a strategic solution? As a last resort, in its view, and despite tepid concurrence by the United States, the Israeli government approved construction of a barrier that physically will divide Palestinians and Jews. At present the barrier has also caused enormous political and symbolic backlashes.

The metaphor of the Berlin wall is obvious. However, since the barrier's construction is inevitable, is there a way of using this reality to exert strategic leverage through it to bring about a solution? Are there trade-offs, such as opening or dismantling part of this barrier to encourage peaceful Palestinian behavior, or does the solidity of the wall mirror the inflexibility of the government to move toward a diplomatic negotiation to end the violence? This is the option that is reviewed.

Third is to impose a physical intervention with outside military forces and peacekeepers to separate the two sides in order to establish some modus vivendi. Such an intervention would most likely be done in small steps. Proposed elsewhere, the political and strategic obstacles will be far larger than Israel's security fence.[1] However, there may be no alternative if there is any chance of a just and lasting peace.

Each level of action has ascending amounts of risk and reward. Many already believe that the second and third options are either impossible or so dangerous as to be unworkable. Since the first, continuing the roadmap, is well understood, the other two are fully and explicitly described.

A Possible Strategic Virtue of the Wall

According to the web sites of both the Israeli Ministries of Foreign Affairs and Defense, the fence or security barrier will be about 480 miles long when it is finished and cost about $1.6 million per mile, for a total cost of just under one billion U.S. dollars. The Israeli government states that more than 97 percent of the barrier will consist of a chain-link fence system, running basically from north to south, with considerable meanderings in between. Less than 3 percent will be constructed of concrete. The explicit purpose of the barrier is to prevent terrorist attacks against Israelis by separating Palestinians and the sources of terror:

> The Government of Israel has an obligation to defend its citizens against terrorism. The security fence will not annex Palestinian lands, change the legal status of the Palestinians, or prevent them from going about their daily life. It will not establish a border, which is to be determined by direct negotiation between Israel and the Palestinians.[2]

Israel also promises that the barrier is temporary and that its purpose is security in response to the "horrific wave of terrorism emanating form the West Bank." The Israeli cabinet approved the fence in July 2001. Since then there has been a predictable and very negative reaction from the Palestinian and Arab communities and from both friends and critics in and beyond the region.

That the arguments are simple does not make them easier to reconcile. The Israelis, supported by their friends and allies principally in the United States, see the barrier as the only means to reduce Palestinian suicide and terror attacks. Physical separation, used in Gaza where barriers to entry have reduced attacks, is now the only effective option left. Barriers and walls do keep possible terrorists out.

Critics and Palestinians whose daily lives have been or will be profoundly affected by the wall, making cross-border access difficult or impossible, have a long list of grievances and arguments as to why the barrier is so dangerous and destructive. The vast majority of Palestinians regard the barrier as a Berlin wall: a blatantly illegal and immoral means of isolating an ethnic group and, by sealing it

---

1. See *Unfinished Business.* Another strong proponent for intervention is former national security advisor Zbigniew Brzezinski.
2. Israeli Ministry of Foreign Affairs web site, December 29, 2003.

off from Israel, denying those people access to relatives, jobs, trade, commerce, and religious places of worship and significance. The barrier is also described as a naked attempt by Israel to ensure Israeli's permanent control of the West Bank and other territories occupied since the 1967 war under a Trojan Horse–like argument of countering terror.

The strategic opportunity rests in exploiting certain realities. Once the barrier is in place a natural reduction in terrorist attacks could well result because of the physical separation of both sides. With a lessening of terror the chance for accommodation might increase. Coordinated with the roadmap, the absence of suicide bombings and strong Israeli retaliation could lead to a respite in violence. This respite might be conducive to a dialogue leading to a long-term settlement. Unfortunately the negative political, social, and economic consequences arising from the security fence almost surely will outweigh the advantages.

If desperation is indeed a driving force in motivating both Jew and Palestinian, the latter to suicide bombings and other acts of terror and the former to retaliation with the IDF and a policy of targeted killings to eliminate terrorists first or in retaliation, then the vicious circle of violence will intensify. The barrier will simply impose constraints that ultimately will be overcome and may well cause terrorists to become more innovative and cunning and therefore more deadly in striking back. The political signal sent by the wall, along with new Israeli settlements in the occupied territories, will inflame, not dampen, the hatreds and enmity that for too long have made peace an impossible goal to achieve.

The Bush administration has signaled to the Sharon government only reluctant acquiescence to the barrier. Indeed, the administration privately objects. Because of the strong support for Israel, taking firm steps such as reducing aid substantially, not by just token cuts, is something most administrations have been reluctant to do. A second-term president might feel differently. Unless an administration is prepared to spend a great deal of political capital, possibly more than it possesses, it will have to work within the realities of the situation. If the barrier is in place, then seeking to find a means of exploiting it strategically to reach an agreement is a worthy effort.

DIRECT INTERVENTION

The highest risk strategy is clearly to intervene directly with forces on the ground. The general notion is to impose a force to separate both sides, first in a small area and, as confidence builds, to radiate outward. The Gaza Strip is a good starting point. Outside forces coming from many states and best handled either under the UN mandate or the quartet would provide peacekeeping, peace enforcement, and stability operations.

Before any forces were deployed, a series of actions negotiated in advance would take place. The Arab world would collectively and publicly recognize Israel and its right to exist. Agreements to exchange ambassadors would have occurred. The Golan Heights would revert to Syria. It would be demilitarized. To ensure demilitarization a detachment of American forces would be stationed on the heights. This force would be capable of defeating any Syrian attack—a deterrent and a guarantee for Israel.

As both sides reached gradual accommodation the zone for intervention would grow. If the security barrier were fully in place, then it would be dismantled as the intervention force undertook those duties. The United Nations, the International Monetary Fund and World Bank, the Arab League, and others would commit to providing the new Palestinian state with substantial resources for rebuilding and for economic development. Since any number of opposition and terrorist groups would oppose these developments and terror attacks would not end or necessarily decline with the arrival of outside forces—as in Iraq, they might increase—there must be on the part of the outside forces and the UN a full and complete long-term commitment. As noted in Chapter 4, the issue of Israeli nuclear weapons would be incorporated into the nuclear states disarmament discussions.

The shortcomings and difficulties with this bold approach are not difficult to appreciate. The Israelis could be the most obstinate of the parties and simply refuse to accept the idea of foreign soldiers on their sacred territory. The Arab governing circles may find it impossible for domestic and religious reasons to be so public in recognizing Israel. Money is tight. Iraq did not receive the funding that many thought was needed to rebuild. Why should these funds go to a new Palestinian state or to Israel? Reluctance and recalcitrance may well mark the two poles of acceptance of this strategy by any number of participants needed to make this work.

Within the United States reaction will run the gamut from intense opposition to support. But the monetary costs and prospect of casualties to the intervening forces will pose strong limits even on those favoring such a bold strategy. However, the issue is simple to cast in definitive terms.

If the global war on terror and the battle to defang jihadist extremism can only be won through solution or mediation of the Israeli-Palestinian conflict, is there an alternative? The Bush administration believes that the path to winning the war on terror goes directly through Baghdad. In this strategy the route is to Jerusalem with stops in Riyadh, Cairo, Damascus, Amman, and the United Arab Emirates. The Bush administration is prepared to spend more than one hundred billion dollars in its strategy to democratize Iraq. How much then is this strategy worth spending?

Critics will also observe that, should the Bush concept of democratizing the Middle East fail, trying to pacify perhaps an unsolvable conflict will also fail. There, as Israel has nuclear weapons, the risks could be greater.

This criticism cannot be dismissed or ignored. However, the absolutely critical question remains: Can the United States, the region, and much of the world be made safer and securer by resolving this Israeli-Palestinian conflict? If the answer is yes, then the course is clear. And if the answer is yes, then the White House will have no option other than to get its political checkbook out and begin writing checks.

A Breakthrough With India and Pakistan?

Terror, Islam, nuclear weapons, and six decades of strife with India make Pakistan one of the most potentially dangerous flash points in the world, a bookend to the crescent of crisis and a strategic domino that al Qaeda and other radicals wish to topple. Fundamental Islam has powerful roots and support throughout the land. President Pervez Musharraf is a pragmatic and secular leader who came to power in 1999 in a military coup. Military rule must be replaced with an elected and legitimate civilian government, and the bulk of the population is anxious to see to a democratic and open society.

Despite the assurances of the government to return to civilian political control, it is unclear when that will happen. With more than ten thousand *madrasses*, many of which teach the most radical forms of Islam to very young and easily influenced males, and an underlying base of fundamentalist military officers, the opportunity for rapprochement with India will face fierce opposition. Indeed, Pakistan is literally a heartbeat away from chaos should one of the many assassination attempts against the president finally succeed. Further, no matter how secure Pakistan's current leadership believes their nuclear weapons to be, in the hands of a new and radical government, no future guarantees can be assumed.

Pakistan, with a critical geostrategic location at the eastern corner of the crescent of crisis, bordering on Afghanistan (itself falling back toward control by warlords and the Taliban), will be, in the wrong hands, a nightmare for peace and stability in the region. Enmity and passion over Kashmir provide further grounds for fueling Pakistani nationalists and radicals who refuse to submit to Indian predominance in that highly contested and divided state.

The United States has been promoting and catalyzing these promising first steps between India and Pakistan. Deputy Secretary of State Richard Armitage, highly respected in many places, has made this an imperative and, over time, through personal diplomacy in Islamabad and Delhi and with support by Secretary Powell, helped achieve this important meeting. The issue is how to exploit this warming and what steps must follow to achieve a lasting, stable relationship in the subcontinent. Money would help. Dealing with nuclear weapons is another way to help.

As the United States and others are putting tens of billions of dollars into Iraq and smaller amounts into Afghanistan, Pakistan needs similar help. The notion of a Marshall Plan applies. As for nuclear negotiations, these are addressed in Chapter 4.

As Pakistan and India continue to improve relations, the United States, possibly unilaterally or through a new arrangement such as a regional security and cooperation conference, should be prepared to support this movement with a substantial aid-and-development package. At a time when the nation is in debt and the debt is growing, finding billions will be next to impossible. What this package would provide will be hotly debated. However, the general direction for such an approach should focus on several key aims.

Despite signs of some growth, Pakistan's economy is not strong. The Gross Domestic Product (GDP) is about seventy billion dollars. With a population approaching one hundred fifty million, of which 75 percent are Sunni, about 20 percent Shia, and less than 3% Hindu, the per capita GDP is $470. The standard of living and the bulk of public education remain meager. About half the young males entering school do not complete their education because of poverty.

The key to defusing the India-Pakistan conflict is development in Pakistan. Without dramatic improvement and change in Pakistan and the neutering of radical Islam, the United States will NEVER win the global war on terror. That assertion will be hotly debated. However, without removing one of the key regional breeding grounds and causes that propel terrorism, it is impossible to see how this war can be brought to a successful end.

This means that tens of billions of dollars will be needed. Determining where and how those funds are invested so that progress can be made and corruption and waste minimized is extraordinarily difficult. A UN-and region-led advisory board working alongside the United States is essential both to oversee operations and to ensure that the programs are put to appropriate use.

There is urgency. At least a dozen attempts on Musharraf's life have been made. More no doubt will follow, especially if some trade-off over Kashmir seems inevitable, as fundamentalist Islamists will find that situation intolerable. Revelations illustrate the dangers. Pakistan's two most famous nuclear scientists—Abdul Qadeer Khan, the father of Pakistan's bomb, and Mohammed Farooq—secretly and without any official sanction provided assistance to Iran and Libya, including blueprints for uranium enrichment. Fundamentalists in the army will also see time running against them. The way to prevent losing any authority over Kashmir is by eliminating the moderating force toward India—General Musharraf. The death of President Zia in 1987, along with U.S. Ambassador Arnold Rafael and defense attaché Brig. Gen. Herbert Wassom, aboard a Pakistani C-130 in what was at best highly suspect and most likely an assassination is a reminder that the game is played for keeps in that part of the world.

A Case Study: Community Communications Centers [3]

There are no easy or simple solutions in rebuilding Iraq or other devastated states and putting in place a plural, stable, and enduring government under the rule of law, let alone a functioning democracy. Germany and Japan may be cited as cases to the contrary. In Japan, the total surrender of the nation made the occupations simpler. Germany had past experiences with democracy. But even in France it took more than two years after the Germans were driven out in 1944 to draft a constitution and another decade before the Fifth Republic finally corrected the errors in that constitution.

History will determine whether the Bush administration exaggerated the case for war in Iraq and whether the attempt to impose democracy will work or fail. Regardless, the United States has legal, moral, political, and social responsibility for rebuilding Iraq. There was no choice for the United States, no matter whether its actions were in the larger strategic sense or in carrying out its legal responsibilities, except to rebuild that defeated and occupied state. If successful, it is also possible that this system of communications centers could find application in other states, such as Afghanistan and in Africa, where there is an absence of societal cohesion and the desperate need to repair that condition.

The most profound problem in Iraq was not the deplorable state of the infrastructure or Saddam's callousness in using basic resources such as food, water, and electricity as tools to control and run the country. The problem was not the insurgency that threatened to simmer for months or longer. The fundamental problem endemic to Iraq and to many other failing and underdeveloped states is the absence of any sense of social cohesion or functional society. Indeed, quite the opposite was the case. Kurds, Sunnis, and Shias, after Saddam's brutal rule, had no common reason for community. This was not the United States in 1776 with a band of brothers, turned founding fathers, determined to bring forth a nation dedicated to life, liberty, and the pursuit of happiness.

For Westerners in general and Americans in particular, understanding the significance of the absence of a basic sense of society is difficult because the experience is so fundamentally different in the West and in modern states. The most practical way in the past to overcome this dysfunction was by brute force and terror, although former Yugoslav President Marshal Tito demonstrated that force of personality could work. He, through personality and clever manipulation of regional differences, managed to keep Yugoslavia together without recourse to extreme forms of brutality. The Soviet Union was most helpful in containing the centrifugal domestic forces in Yugoslavia. Tito's death, followed by the disintegration of the

---

3. The community centers were devised by Alexander Globus, a business executive and investment banker. In the summer of 2003 Globus was referred to me by Thomas McAvoy, a distinguished corporate executive who served as past president and vice chairman of Corning Glass and on the boards of a number of Fortune 50 companies. Intrigued by the project, I agreed to serve as a senior advisor. Because of a series of bad reasons and misjudgments, the project was canceled by the CPA in Baghdad although it was approved by the highest levels of the Pentagon. To a much lesser degree, South Africa utilized a similar approach in providing information and outreach to distant tribes and with some success but with far less ambition.

Soviet Union, unleashed the destructive forces and passions of societal discord with tragic results for the Balkans.

Are there political, technological, and economic means to deal with and check societal dysfunction? Or is this Hobbesian state of conflict and violence inherent in failing nations? Community communications centers were designed with this in mind. In a sense, the concept is experimental. The basis for the strategy is to build some, put them in place, and evaluate the results.

Also missing in Iraq was the means for the Iraqi Governing Council (IGC) and the subsequent government to have direct interaction with the people. The IGC, largely for security reasons, was protected and isolated from the population it was supposed to represent. Contact was limited at best. During Saddam's regime (and this is absolutely true), the government used carbon paper as the principal way of communicating written orders and reports—an Iraqi version of "carbonpaper.com." An official would write on a thick stack of carbon papers and then distribute single copies to aides, who would often jump into taxicabs to deliver the message to other ministries and offices. The absence of a sense of modernity in administration and isolation in practice are not the best bases for establishing a functioning society.

In a broader sense, the ability to mobilize a population in support of rebuilding their country has application in many other states from Afghanistan to Zaire. Technology is not the barrier, but it can form the solution. It is critical to bring together the many components that will mobilize the public and help create a sense of society where none existed. From that sense of society, trust and confidence between government and governed can build. The more trust and confidence, the greater the likelihood that a coherent society can follow, essential for any pluralistic system under a legitimate rule of law.

A DAUNTING TASK

The United States is responsible for rebuilding and reorganizing Iraqi society. As the occupying power, it has that legal obligation. Beyond centuries of outside rule and decades of Baathist despotism, the extraordinary difficulty of creating virtually a whole, free, pluralistic, and functioning society is further complicated by corruption, resistance to change, political uncertainty, disease, anarchy, criminality, Baathist loyalists, and the lingering insurgency. More significant is that life under Saddam destroyed public spirit, mutual responsibility, and trust—indispensable in sustaining any sense of societal community. For rebuilding to work and to create a sense of society where none had existed these actions must be carried out and set the basis for the requirements that the community centers must meet. The priorities are:

- Create a national and legitimate political authority to which power, authority, and sovereignty can be transferred as quickly as feasible.

- Establish order, rule of law, and a judicial system to support a civil society and an enduring government of and by Iraqis.
- Restore and provide; water and electricity and provide transportation, health care, education, social services, and law enforcement.
- Ensure the equitable distribution of billions of dollars in aid and the fair allocation of national resources.
- Promote economic activity by jump-starting production and wholesale and retail distribution; facilitate employment and job creation; and establish a national currency and banking system for efficient conduct of commercial and private transactions.
- Neutralize Baathist influence and reduce the chance for corrupted government administrations.
- Put assets and lines of business out of reach of corrupt organizations and individuals.
- Prepare Iraqis for self-rule and the ultimate departure of U.S. personnel.
- Establish a sense of community that has been absent from Iraqi society for decades.
- Convince Iraqis, as well as the international community, of the enduring commitment of the United States.

What is lacking in the current reconstruction effort is the means to bring a new Iraqi government closer to its people and convince them of its commitment to a free and open society that is basically fair and just. To help in this process, community communications centers provide some of the physical means to achieve these goals. The aim of these centers is to establish a substantial number of wireless communication facilities that provide Iraqis with fixed, telephone-based automated access to government and to the outputs of good government such as voting, health care, food aid, job placement, education, banking, and other services without which a modern society cannot function. Such activities would also allow Iraqis to communicate with one another and with virtually anyone in the world. Automation will significantly reduce civil servant personnel requirements at these centers.

Facilities and centers are rough equivalents to phone booths and telephone-driven cyber cafes, usable regardless of reading skills. Larger community centers resemble post offices and social service centers where staff can provide assistance that automated systems cannot. Community centers house administrator stations where civil servants can meet with citizens to discuss specific issues. Community centers also house video presentation rooms and other facilities where important information can be easily and uniformly conveyed by the government.

These centers would bring to the public the basic services essential to creating a sense of society, using existing, off-the-shelf technology in the form of facilities to resolve the central problem of how government communicates with its citizens when there is no infrastructure for that purpose. The converse is true: how do citizens learn about and use basic government services—from food stamps and stipends for survival to drivers' licenses, voter registration, job application—and functions inherent in a viable society when no such system exists?

In the main, from these requirements for interaction and services between government and citizen, the centers would be built on four basic components. Specific communications facilities provide basic access to Touch-Tone telephones, messaging services and e-mail and other informational technology, both hard- and software that enable broad interaction and communication. These facilities would be roughly approximate to local Western Union offices. Numbering between eight thousand and nine thousand, these would be dispersed throughout the country in urban and rural locales.

Second are the larger community centers. These would support the smaller facilities. All are low-cost, prefabricated packages that can either be located in existing buildings in Iraq or in new structures and even in large trailers. Manned by relatively low-skilled civil servants, the centers would provide assistance beyond automation. Around one thousand would be needed. Clearly these centers, small as they are, if effective, would become prime targets for insurgents determined to disrupt the rebuilding of Iraq. Clever location to discourage or make attack more difficult could minimize security problems, and, by low-cost replacements would not be prohibitive, even in large numbers.

Third are wireless base stations. Community centers and facilities are fixed sites and therefore complement mobile and cellular communications. Wireless base stations connect these centers to each other and to data centers that serve the various communications systems by providing the computer links that store the necessary information to run the system. Base stations can be housed on top of buildings and towers to maximize transmission range and, like the centers, are inexpensive.

Fourth are the data centers housing the computers, voicemail systems, databases, and information technology. Data centers would be well protected, probably underground or in readily defensible locations to reduce vulnerability and could be relatively few in number.

Fewer than ten thousand communications facilities and centers scattered throughout the more populated areas of Iraq can reach more than two-thirds of the population. The total cost of installing a complete system is less than a billion dollars. As Iraqis pay for these services, the system is self-financing and, over time, this system can create a large revenue stream for the government.

Community Communications System Described

Each facility requires modest preparation, minimum amount of interior space, and independence from external power sources or existing wiring. Thousands of

Iraqi civil servants will be needed to man these facilities, thus reducing unemployment. Few of these positions will require specialized skills, and middle management requirements will be modest, given the automation of these facilities. The necessary software exists.

The basic design features that empower this system both to mobilize Iraqis in rebuilding their society and to increase social cohesion rest on four pillars. First, the systems are turn-key and use off-the-shelf technology available in the commercial world and widely used. Technical research, development, and evaluation of this system are not needed. These systems can carry out routine societal functions, including conducting elections and censuses, banking, health care, aid distribution, routine business operations from contracting to providing services, and virtually all other administrative activities. These interactions are first steps in developing a sense of community and societal cohesion.

Second, the system provides a permanent interface between government and the public. In modern societies, much of this is done at home through basic services such as mail, telecommunications, and computer networks. That infrastructure does not exist in Iraq. Nor does Iraq have a systematic and credible means for communications between the government and its citizens.

Third, the system is widely and easily accessible. Parallels with the old Western Union offices apply. These facilities could become social centers as well.

Finally, the computing resources in the data centers that form the nerve and brain tissue that make this system work are national assets. These data centers will provide the information necessary to assist Iraqis in exploiting this capability and in providing the basic framework for rebuilding the nation by connecting Iraqis with other Iraqis and with their government in obvious ways and with real benefits.

Communications facilities house fully functioning telephones that are used primarily through standard Touch-Tone response and voicemail systems. Such systems have proven their effectiveness and are increasingly used in modern societies. Furthermore, these systems require a small fraction of the transmission capacity of a full telecom infrastructure and, therefore, can be completely supported by a much smaller and cheaper wireless network. Finally, when using the system participants can automatically receive important messages and instructions from the Iraqi civil authority.

Despite the lack of complexity of individual components, the infrastructure offers powerful capabilities. For example, a subsystem that allows the government to send citizens interactive telephone messages does not, on its own, give the impression of great utility. But consider that local and national elections can be easily implemented through this interaction.

A simple phone-driven banking system can manage accounts for Iraqis using credits denominated in food, communications, housing, and other resources the government or aid agencies propose to grant, track, and distribute. Furthermore, cashless transactions enabled by these types of accounts are effective both in undermining black markets and in establishing the worth of a new currency. An interactive report for automatically identifying personnel problems could be added to this system, thereby greatly reducing the need for skilled management throughout the government.

Administrations will require a multipurpose card to guarantee the identity of the individual using these services. All of these components combined with small amounts of custom programming and the occasional participation of low-level personnel will be beneficial to the nation. Census information, registration for drivers' licenses, social services, and even employment can be carried out through this system. Any task that is facilitated by the ability to inform; be informed about; communicate with; and pay, tax, organize, and mobilize the citizenry to give Iraqis a better life can work here.

These centers cost fewer than one billion dollars and include the creation of public facilities, along with integrated wireless receivers and data centers.[4] In addition, as some form of identification and metric are essential, the net effect of these centers will be the registration of about two-thirds of Iraq's adult citizens. This would cost less than distributing cell phones, along with all of the equipment necessary to operate, connect, service, and bill mobile systems. Such a fixed system would complement mobile communications rather than replace or substitute for them.

The crucial questions and challenges are sociopolitical and cultural. Will Iraqis participate in this collective effort that aims to build social cohesion and what will their reactions be? Will the end results lead to better integration and interaction between the governed and their governors? And will these facilities either prove to be so acceptable that terrorists have no reason to target them or will their value invite attack and disruption?

Rewards and Incentives

Critical to making this system work is to know who uses it, to validate those identities, and to ensure they are protected. This would require some form of registration, and registration has powerful political overtones. National identity cards offend certain civil libertarians and are reminders of the tyrannical ways of Saddam's regime. The cost of proper identification metrics beyond simple fingerprinting, such as retina scans and other characteristics, can be prohibitive.

But the practical benefits of citizen registration are numerous and easily communicated. Fair and convenient access to food, civil services, available jobs, vot-

---

4. The estimated project costs comprise $150 million for domestic Iraqi goods, $125 million for full registration of virtually all adult Iraqis, $50 million for domestic labor, $400 million for foreign goods, $60 million for foreign design services, $50 million for software, $100–$200 million for systems integration and service, and at least $100 million for security.

ing, and bank accounts and the use of communication facilities are immediate examples of some of the benefits. Other significant gains, such as increased access to retail goods and the money to buy them, and improved community security, will develop over time. Simply listing the benefits of new government integration, however, does not fully convey the effect it would have on a citizen's life.

Iraqis are an accomplished people with a remarkable history spanning thousands of years. The impact of decades of despotic rule, exacerbated by two catastrophic military defeats and a needless and bloody war against Iran, weigh heavily on the national psyche. Arguably one of the key challenges in helping Iraqis rebuild their country is overcoming the sense of humiliation that many Iraqis have endured from years of privation and indignity at the hands of a totalitarian regime.

Consider how this will work. Suppose an Iraqi has registered with the civil authority and received his multipurpose card to use the system. If that individual were due payment, instead of cash, a direct deposit of Iraqi dinars would be made to the registrant's own account or sent to a locally approved retail outlet through a cashless transaction. Beyond ensuring an efficient and effective means for payment, corruption and graft would be made physically more difficult by an absence of cash to be stolen, bribed, or extorted.

Transfer of foodstuffs, humanitarian aid, and other government-delivered goods could be carried out near local communication facilities. Local attendants could quickly and efficiently scan citizens' multipurpose cards to confirm identity and to validate the transfer. In other cases, cards could be used as cash alternatives to make purchases in stores and thus help build a functioning market economy. The government could offer employment, education, and other opportunities at these facilities where citizens could register and apply for them, creating and fostering a viable and useful interaction between the governed and their government.

Telephones at communications facilities may not be as convenient as home or cellular phones. However, every citizen within a particular district would have simultaneous, fair, and equal access to this basic service, and the basic aspects of a normally functioning society can be derived from this access. Physicians, for example, could leave messages for patients, schedule appointments through automated systems, or prescribe drugs through registrants' accounts. Iraqis could request and schedule services from the government without necessarily having to wait in line. The communication facilities also could be the location to register and vote, whether for candidates to high office or on whatever issue the government chooses to place on a national referendum.

CONCLUSIONS

The United States won the war in Iraq. But peace is at risk unless people, programs, and resources are directed to ensure the development and maintenance of a capable and service-oriented government that would promote community action and protection from Baathist resurgence, divisive factionalism, and organized crime. Failure would be catastrophic for Iraq, for the region, and for the United States.

The need to mobilize Iraqis to rebuild their country, combined with the current chaos and violence, presents a fleeting opportunity to turn the tide. The community communications centers present one means of seizing this opportunity. Clearly Iraqis may reject this approach. Centers designed to bring Iraqis together may be resisted because of a natural reluctance to go in harm's way without reason, regardless of the state of the insurgency. Iraq is the pivotal point in determining America's ability to shape events.

If the Bush administration fails in Iraq to improve the lot of Iraqi's and to make this nation safer, as predicted in this book, the results will have almost certain strategic consequences. Those consequences are likely to be profoundly negative. Extremism will be fanned. America will be bogged down. Iraqis will become more resentful and therefore more likely to resist the occupation. A fractured state among Sunni, Shia, and Kurdish factions is a Yugoslavia in the making but with twenty-five million people. The bookends in Pakistan and Saudi Arabia could be toppled. The centers proposed here might have little impact. pt to explore.

The tragedy is that this concept, despite support from the highest levels of the Pentagon, was disapproved by the CPA. Indeed, "fast track" legislation approved by Congress and signed into law by the president as part of the Iraqi reconstruction package in November 2003 for the purpose of accelerating the contracting process in Baghdad (and providing a way for small companies to compete with the giants such as Bechtel, Halliburton, and SAIC) was ignored by the CPA. Investigations by several inspectors general are under way. Whether or not any of those investigations leads to criminal charges is yet to be determined. The tragedy is that the constipation and sclerosis of the bureaucratic process in Washington was exported to Baghdad. If the coalition fails to bring stability to Iraq, in large measure that failure will have arisen from the manner in which reconstruction was handled and the obstacles, inherent in Iraq and part of the process, that prevented those funds from being spent efficiently, quickly, and effectively.

6
The Common Defense
Transformation, Democratization, and Other Challenges

The Bush administration came into office vowing to transform the U.S. military for the twenty-first century. Nearly four years later, objective assessment of the state and progress of transformation remains in the eyes of the assessor. However, much has been accomplished in transforming how the military is, and will be, used in war. Less has been achieved by the Department of Defense outside its priority mission mandated by Title X and legally directed "to be prepared for the conduct of sustained operations incident to combat."

The most significant progress has been in agreement by the senior military on the importance of transformation. Reading the various documents emanating from the Pentagon, starting with the Defense Secretary's Transformation Planning Guidance issued in April 2003 and reflected in each of the services' transformation road maps and plans (and "Military Transformation A Strategic Approach" issued by OSD's Office of Force Transformation in the fall of 2003), reveals a robust and probably enduring basis for insinuating transformation into the bosom of the military planning process for sustained operations incident to combat.

There are, however, several other important but unanticipated factors at work that affect evaluating the progress of transformation. The president's directive to transform the most capable military force in the world into a force that placed priority on different capabilities was, in a few words, an awesome and daunting challenge. As Japan's sinking of battleship row demonstrated on December 7, 1941, the same military system can be transformed from strategic centerpiece to a supporting role in a single morning.

Transformation has many facets. The most important and most illusive is the intellectual component. Both leap-ahead and evolutionary technologies, from repeating rifles and breech-loading artillery to aircraft, nuclear weapons, GPS, and precision munitions, have transformed war and military forces. The need to foment permanent change in order to accommodate to or anticipate dramatically changing environments is self-evident. As events in Iraq so vividly revealed, transformation cannot succeed if it is applied only to military combat and war-fighting capabilities.

In 2003 the Iraqi Army was routed in four weeks. The insurgency lingers. The danger of Iraq fracturing along religious and ethnic divisions cannot be prevented by military superiority in firepower, accuracy, and lethality, no matter how overwhelming. That lesson is unmistakable: to win both the war and peace, transformation must apply across the entire national security spectrum and every relevant department of government, a challenge more daunting and complicated than events taking place in the Pentagon.

Moving from an intellectual appreciation and acceptance of the need for institutionalizing a process of transformation taking concrete actions is not easy. The initial jargon of transformation that military forces had to be more "agile, flexible and lethal" was not a blueprint for creating those forces or answering the questions, more agile and lethal than what and why should future forces need more of those capabilities than it currently plans to develop? Because traditional lines of demarcation between military, law enforcement, intelligence, and diplomatic elements of security have blurred, transformation of only one arm of government cannot ensure a safer and more secure nation.

Indeed, the most trenchant of question for the Pentagon was, transforming the force to what? In simple terms, what should the military force be capable of achieving that it was not and what was it doing that should be foregone? After nearly four years of promoting transformation, the current and projected force is not significantly different, qualitatively and quantitatively, in capability from what the Clinton administration planned. Granted, transformation was not a process that occurred overnight, absent an exceptional event such as Pearl Harbor or even September 11. However, as Rumsfeld asked regarding whether we were winning or losing the war on terror, how will we know that we are transforming at a sufficient rate to stay ahead of the competition?

There is no doubt that considerations of military risk have dramatically changed under the Bush administration and its dynamic secretary of defense. The use of fewer rather than overwhelming forces in the first two wars of the twenty-first century is the most dramatic example of accepting much higher risk. Yet aside from the "Blue Tracker" system that enabled higher headquarters to keep instant track on virtually all friendly units, no other transformational systems were employed in Operation Iraqi Freedom.

Only two major weapons systems, the army's Crusader, a self-propelled artillery weapon, and its new helicopter, Commander, have been canceled by the Bush administration so far. Although each of the four services produced convincing briefings to document how seriously transformation had been adopted in shaping the future force, signs of clear operational differences between the Five- and Six-Year Defense Plans developed under this administration and the last Clinton administration plan are not as telling as the Bush administration would have liked.

This will be a critical year. In 2004 "transformational capabilities," such as air- and sea-lift, unconstrained by traditional dependence on sea and airports for access and removing the stovepipes and ruts that impede ready and instant access to information and intelligence, will be defined and funded. Identifying and then buying these capabilities will begin to make transformation a more permanent phenomenon. Further, getting these capabilities through the process and approved by Congress, especially as federal deficits and national debt grow, may prove as difficult as democratizing Iraq.

Transformation has been principally a military, war-fighting phenomenon. But the management, procurement, support, maintenance, logistics, personnel, and myriad essential non-war-fighting elements have not received the complete attention or the full force of transformation yet. That has been a result of the bureaucratic and political inertia of a system of government that has rightly been described as dysfunctional and not the result of any failure on the part of Rumsfeld or the Pentagon. As the painful process of base closings demonstrated, rational efficiency-making actions are at the mercy of the more powerful political forces. Unless or until Congress is a full member of transformation, necessary changes to how and where efficiencies, such as base closings, and discretion in making the best use of financial resources cannot be implemented, imposing further constraints in achieving genuine and lasting transformation.

Noted here and elsewhere, transformation did not extend to postwar conditions known as stability operations, where military force plays a crucial role in providing security and stability. The insurgency in Iraq seemed to come as a surprise to the administration; the lessons of previous wars and insurgencies, particularly in Vietnam, should have been part of the military toolkit. Other government agencies, particularly Congress, have been spared the burden of transformation (although the administration would argue that creation of the Department of Homeland Security and major organizational changes in the Executive Branch regarding counterterrorism constitute a form, if not direct application, of transformation).

There have been serious gains. Intellectually the battle has largely been fought in recognizing that transformation is a continuing process. The military at virtually all levels recognizes the need for transformation, and for the time being, that war has been won. However, as with the failure to remain current on counterinsurgency operations, there are no guarantees that future administrations, particularly when the other party assumes power, will remain committed to transformation, which could well reject it on purely partisan grounds unless the process is institutionalized. "Whether transformation" could easily become a great debate, and if this process is seen as partisan, its longevity will be in doubt.

New administrations have their own ideas, agenda, and vocabulary. Kennedy's flexible response replaced Eisenhower's massive retaliation. Clinton's bottom-up review, initiated by his first defense secretary, former chairman of the House Armed Services Committee Les Aspin, superseded Bush 41's Base Force defense review and made enlargement of alliances, engagement, and counterproliferation higher priorities. For the current administration, transformation is the order of the day.

The combatant (four-star) commanders in the field have been empowered to push the boundaries on transformation in conducting their planning and operational responsibilities. Joint Forces Command under Adm. Edmund Giambastiani has been assigned the duty and responsibility for making transformation operational. Chapter 4 covered transformation in NATO. The best practical examples of the dynamism of transformation are most obvious in the field, where commanders can act without many of the constraints of Washington and the Pentagon. On the basis of close coordination, with Joint Forces Command as catalyst and facilitator between and among the combatant commanders, transformation thus far must be judged very successful.

TRANSFORMATION IN BRIEF PERSPECTIVE

The Bush administration took office promising to transform the American military for the twenty-first century. Reaction among the senior American military was mixed at best. Although there was confidence in the knowledge that America's military was both the most powerful and most capable in the world and that it was the best professional force in its history, the appeal of transformation was not instantaneous or obvious.

America's senior military leaders have been among the most knowledgeable and shrewd observers of the political process in Washington. Achieving three- and four-star rank requires, as it should, an understanding of the political realities, the limits on what can and cannot be accomplished, as well as the precious nature of political capital. The senior leadership is still old enough to have entered service on the back end of Vietnam. It witnessed the extraordinary efforts in the 1970s and 1980s to rebuild the military with an all-volunteer force. By 1991 it rightly was proud of those accomplishments. Desert Storm and the victory in the first Gulf War were crowning achievements of how far the military had come since the disastrous Vietnam War ended. Then chairman of the Joint Chiefs of Staff, Gen. Colin Powell was the personification of that exceptional progress.

When Donald Rumsfeld came back to the Pentagon for a second tour as secretary nearly twenty-five years after leaving it the first time, it had changed far more than he probably realized. Out of office Rumsfeld had been too valuable to be kept out of harness. During that interim he served in a number of advisory positions and chaired two commissions on defense. However, for all of that experience, only service inside the Pentagon could have revealed how much the Department of Defense had changed.

When Rumsfeld sent his first budget to Congress in 1975 it was tens of pages long. Today's defense budget is hundreds of pages long. The regulatory environment not only for buying weapons but also for ethics, conduct, and personal behavior is a world unto itself. The Goldwater-Nichols Defense Reform Law of 1986 mandated fundamental changes to the department, including the imposition of jointness. The political definition of jointness was based on a simple argument. Because the services were inseparably linked on the battlefield, operating as independent fiefdoms in the Pentagon was a prescription for disaster. Maintaining separate services for bureaucratic reasons was understandable; fighting wars as separate services was unconscionable.

As Rumsfeld was to learn, Congress had changed dramatically, too. No longer was obtaining support from a single or even a handful of senators or representatives who chaired the Armed Services or Appropriations Committees sufficient to make changes or implement specific programs. The seniority system that Rumsfeld knew when he was in the House, which was on the way out when he was first secretary, had been replaced. Congress was a far different animal, even when controlled by the same party as the president's.

Initially Rumsfeld's abrasive and aggressive manner and habit of raising tough questions that challenged conventional wisdom alienated many of the senior military. In private, senior generals and admirals complained loudly. Despite the work of many Pentagon panels examining transformation and interminable meetings called, a great deal of heat and little light was being created. The secretary's instructions were often so broad as to be unworkable. What did greater lethality, agility, and flexibility mean? What force structure had to change and why? And what was the basis for knowing that transformation would indeed prove to a more capable force?

By the summer of 2001 rumors began circulating that Rumsfeld's days in office were numbered. Names of possible replacements appeared in newspaper and television stories and in Washington's political gossip columns. September 11 changed all that. Like the phoenix, Rumsfeld not only rose from the ashes pundits had consigned him to but also found himself catapulted into a national figure and the administration's most prominent spokesman, after the president, on the war on terror. With the famous press conferences that captivated viewers and intimidated the press with crisp, often humorous, and occasionally biting answers and the victory in Afghanistan, President Bush assigned his secretary the nickname Rumstud. That fame was accentuated in the run-up to and conduct of Operation Iraqi Freedom.

Regarding transformation, the most significant achievement of Rumsfeld's performance as what the press described as America's "minister of war" was the change in attitude of the senior military leadership on active service toward him and toward transformation. Rumsfeld gained the grduging respect and then admiration of his military subordinates. The army was, in Rumsfeld's view, the slowest to transform. The retired military community took great offense, especially over what many believed was the mistreatment of former Army Chief of Staff Gen. Eric Shinseki by the secretary.[1] Service transformation documents, as well as the private comments of senior military officers, reinforce the opinion that acceptance of transformation and Rumsfeld's leadership have become widespread. The issue turned from "why transform?" to making transformation work for the long term. However, because the United States is committed, probably for a very long while, to democratizing and rebuilding Iraq and keeping substantial numbers of military forces stationed there for security reasons, the priorities for transformation and for democratization inevitably will, or have already, collided. This is discussed later.

The latest and current definition of transformation is sensible, straightforward, and simple. As Rumsfeld observed, "There will be no moment at which the department is 'transformed.' Rather, we are building a culture of continual transformation so that our armed forces are always several steps ahead of any potential adversaries." The single definition of transformation is "a process that shapes the changing nature of military competition and cooperation through new combinations of concepts, capabilities, people, and organizations that exploit our nation's advantages and protect against our asymmetric vulnerabilities to sustain our strategic process, which helps underpin peace and stability in the world."

Transformation was designed to address three major areas: how we fight, how we do business, and how we operate with others. By far, the most progress has been in the first. To the credit of the department, in April 2003 OSD sent a proposed bill to Congress entitled the "Defense Transformational Act for the Twenty-First Century." The purpose of that bill was to deal with the issue of how we do business.

Fixing these problems of doing business date back to Washington's presidency. For better or worse, only part of the legislation was approved and signed into law, commissioning the National Security Personnel System, which at least gave the department more authority over its civilian workforce. The regulatory morass remains a jungle and is expanding. For example, the political necessity of preventing the trinity of waste, fraud, and abuse from contaminating the contracting process in rebuilding Iraq greatly delayed the issuing of bids and spending the $18.7 billion appropriated to that end.

1. In mid-2002 Rumsfeld announced his intention of appointing Army Vice Chief of Staff Gen. Jack Keane as Shinseki's relief, eighteen months in advance. This was unprecedented and was taken as a direct attack on the chief. Later, Army Secretary Thomas White was asked to resign, a further sign of Rumsfeld's displeasure with the army. The retired community, loyal to the chief and the secretary, both West Point graduates and decorated Vietnam War veterans, held Rumsfeld to blame for trying to ruin the army. That hostility persists. Rumsfeld then chose retired Gen. Peter Schoomaker as the next chief.

Transformation under Rumsfeld has yielded at least four major achievements. First and foremost, it has made the conduct of war more analytical, scientific, and intellectually based. Net-centric warfare is the current phrase often used to describe the operational construct. Net centric in its simplest formulation means the intelligent use of data and information to leverage military effectiveness. However, effects-based targeting and a more studied approach to military operations is the first legacy.

Described in Chapter 2, effects-based targeting means defining desired outcomes and effects and then applying military force to achieve them. To some degree militaries have always approached war from this perspective. However, excessive focus on Clausewitz' dictum that denying the enemy the will to resist rested in destroying the means led to attrition and force-on-force types of operations. Effects-based and net-centric warfare modify this traditional operational principle and thus reflect major transformation.

Second, the senior leadership, to use a favorite Rumsfeld term, "gets it!" This means that although there is no permanent definition of transformation that can always be translated into forces and capabilities and no endpoint in this process, the senior military understands that continuous change requires a continuing process for making change. The bureaucratic and organizational form this process will take is still unclear. Joint Forces Command has the lead in refining the specifics. However, there is consensus on the need for this process, which is a major transformation in thinking.

Third, transformation has permeated the field. Combatant commanders are directing staffs to reexamine all aspects of operations, management, administration, and organization—unlike the Cold War, when there was a fixed and relatively consistent series of policies for countering the Soviet Union and change was not as important. Nor was a continuing process of change necessary, as it took years for the threat to evolve, new systems to enter service, and political capital to build to introduce different strategies.

Asymmetric threats, the global war on terror, new challenges from AIDS to instability, humanitarian disasters, and a range of events that the military might be assigned are now legitimate grounds for planning. All of these require transformation. Operational commanders from the Pacific to the Atlantic are reacting. The formation of Northern Command, as part of homeland defense, also suggests new areas in which defense will be involved. The enduring scenarios of conflict in Korea or the Taiwan Straits will also be the focus of transformation.

Fourth, transformation had been applied to overseas basing and strategic redeploying of American military forces. The unarguable logic was that strategic deployment devised for the Cold War had to be transformed for the twenty-first century. The general principles were to shift U.S. forces, bases, and access to new regions of importance—the greater Middle East, East Asia and the Trans-Caucuses, and Central Asia.

For fifty years, American deployments were concentrated in Western Europe, Japan, and South Korea to contain and deter the Eurasian challenge posed by the Soviet Union. Now that strategic interests have clearly changed and America's military forces are becoming more agile, flexible, and lethal, bases and potential access overseas must keep pace. The current plan will take upward of a decade to implement.

The general thrust is to reduce American military presence in Europe, bringing much of the U.S. Army's V Corps home. That could lead to a reduction of about fifty thousand troops, an annual loss to Germany of about five billion dollars in revenue. Germany has already hired lobbyists in Washington to minimize or prevent that redeployment.

Iraq almost certainly will be a heavy user of American forces for a long time to come. Chairman of the Joint Chiefs Gen. Richard Myers predicted American forces would remain in Iraq through 2005. Some envisage a far longer stay. In Korea, U.S. forces will be redeployed farther south, no longer on the thirty-eighth parallel and the border with the north. Elsewhere in the Pacific, forces will be redeployed in keeping with the new strategy, and the Trans-Caucuses will have increased U.S. presence and so-called lily pad bases, so named because these will be jumping-off sites in and outside the region.

MAKING TRANSFORMATION WORK

There are shortcomings in transformation that must be addressed. Of the four pillars, the first two—enhancing jointness and exploiting intelligence—may be the wrong criteria or focus. Jointness is now the mantra of the Department of Defense. Virtually no briefing goes forward from a single service without the cover of advancing jointness. No officer, according to the law, with very few exceptions, will be promoted to senior rank without having served in an accredited joint billet. But jointness per se is not the right or only answer.

Clearly, each service and the capabilities it provides must be integrated into a common doctrine and operating concept so that fighting power meets the needs of the end users—the combatant commanders. That is unarguable. However, there are limits on jointness.

In 1973 the Israeli Defense Force (IDF) was the most joint military in the world. The army and air force were seamlessly integrated to repel attack as instantly as possible. After all, given the tiny size of Israel, trading space for time was not a satisfactory option for success. In October when the Yom Kippur, or War of Atonement, began with Egypt's surprise crossing of the Suez Canal and Syria's assault south of the Golan Heights north of Israel that threatened to divide the nation, the IDF reacted piecemeal. The air force courageously attacked the advancing Egyptian forces in the Sinai, and the army raced to blunt Syria's ground attack.

Rather than operate jointly as they had trained, the Israeli forces had no option but to operate independently. As a result the tactical expediency caused Israel to suffer far greater losses and come close to being defeated. Then Chairman of the Joint Chiefs of Staff Adm. Thomas H. Moorer dryly observed that the "Israelis planned for a short war and damn near got one." The meaning was obvious. Joint operations were precluded by the surprise attack.

In Iraq today joint operations are not being conducted. True, Special Forces are drawn from each of the services. Navy and air force aircraft support the ground commanders. Intelligence and special investigation units are multiservice. However, the postwar is a ground campaign waged by ground forces. Jointness is simply not relevant here, unless the intent is to require each of the forces to supply people to conduct the counterinsurgency campaign alongside the army and the marines.

Regarding intelligence, the bulk of transformation here might be better aimed at the intellectual aspect of conducting operations and less at the technological and systems capabilities for conducting surveillance; reconnaissance; and the general gathering of data, information, and intelligence. The U.S. lack of sufficient Arab linguists for building peace is an indicator of where and how transformation can work to close this gap. Another area of deficiency among the forces and the occupation that followed the war, where transformation is critical, is the lack of cultural and social understanding of Iraq and its people. Education and training are fundamental. The current as well as past emphases are on technical solutions. If the war on terror is ever to be won, the emphasis must be on intellect and understanding the nature of the danger and how it can be contained and eliminated.

The strategic redeployment plan will have to overcome substantial political, economic, and cultural obstacles. Relocation from Germany is perhaps at the top of the list. Tensions in NATO over the Iraq war and its aftermath are still fresh, and uncertainty over the future relationship between NATO and the EU is still an issue: any American redeployment must be accomplished in this context. A large, possibly permanent deployment to the greater Middle East has already shifted the strategic center of balance from Europe southeast to the crescent of crisis, intensified by the global war on terror.

This redeployment can have highly positive strategic value if properly executed and implemented, which must be the aim. The question must be how this proposed redeployment can be made part of a transformation effort that will enhance American and global security and stability.

Finally, transformation within the department has not yet made a dent in reducing the growing costs of providing these forces and capabilities. In 2004 about four hundred billion dollars will be spent on and by the Pentagon. A good chunk, nearly a quarter, is the cost of operations in Iraq, Afghanistan, and the war on terror. However, as in the private sector where economies of scale, technology, and productivity have trimmed costs—the computer and electronics industries being the most obvious—transformation must have an impact on the amount of money and how it is spent on defense.

If major war can be fought with far fewer forces, then, because people are the single-largest expense in the budget, surely fewer are needed and, if the logic works, so, too, should less money be spent. The other side of the argument is the postwar situation that may require more people, though not necessarily all from the Department of Defense. How can transformation help here? This question leads to several of the fundamental paradoxes that make keeping the nation safe and secure more daunting tasks now than during the Cold War.

TRANSFORMATION AND THE FIRST PARADOX—TRANSLATING STRENGTH INTO SECURITY

The greatest test for transformation is coping with this first contradiction: despite being the most powerful state in the world, the United States has also become exceedingly vulnerable. What can transformation do to lessen this tension and resolve this contradiction? In other words, how does transformation affect the shift from an era of mass destruction to one of mass disruption and how can military forces be better configured and prepared for this different environment? Or is transformation only a process that can work in enhancing war-fighting because of the political, economic, and cultural complexities that are part of the non-war-fighting roles?

History provides practical insights. Rather than serve as a predictive mirror for the future, history provides useful metaphors and lessons that must be transformed into current contexts. For much of the nation's history, America's military had two principal roles. Defending the United States against attack from within and without and helping to settle and develop the vast uncharted territories that stretched to the Pacific were the bases for raising an army and maintaining a navy. While American forces, particularly naval, saw action abroad, the military focus was on the United States, certainly through the Civil War.[2]

In responding to the needs of homeland defense, the Pentagon created Northern Command. Its chief purpose was to provide military support to homeland security and coordinate department resources with those agencies charged to defend the United States against terrorist and other forms of attack. But with more than a million people in the National Guard and Reserve components and a civilian

2. The United States fought various declared and undeclared wars in its first decades, with the War of 1812 and the brief War with Mexico in 1846 being the most well known. The role of the army and navy was principally domestic. For decades, coastal defense was the navy's raison d'etre, while the army fought Indians and helped chart and settle the West.

workforce of at least another million, the Department of Defense has an enormous capability to take on these new tasks. The problem is shifting from the Cold War structure, in which the reserve component was responsible for much of the combat support and combat services support functions needed in war, to more useful and relevant tasks required by the dangers of the new and different threats facing this country.

The toll on guard and reserve forces in Operation Iraqi Freedom and the postwar occupation were obvious. The all-volunteer force had not been designed for that purpose. The assumption was that to win future wars the United States had to mobilize, meaning there would be full public support, a direct lesson from Vietnam. Wars of the future would not be half-fought.

Now with more than thirty-five thousand guard and reservists on active duty in Iraq and nearly two hundred thousand called up, in some cases for more than a year, the commitment in Iraq has negated the reasons and obligations for which these personnel had originally agreed to serve. Short of a world war, reservists never expected or were intended to serve lengthy spells of active duty. The administration has recognized this and is taking steps to balance the active-reserve mix. This is an area where transformation is critical and where major transformation can and must be achieved. However, changing the reserve mix will abut congressional and local prerogatives and politics in the fiercest way. Hence, the proposed changes must not only be sensible and acceptable but must also be forced through a political process that will resist many of these changes on the basis of inertia alone.

Here is one transformational solution. The U.S. military should have functions beyond its Title X requirement to train, man, and equip for sustained combat operations. Unlike Britain in its defense review of 2003, which assumed that Britain would never fight a major war such as the Falklands in 1982, alone and without allies, the United States cannot make that assumption. It clearly has the capability to fight and win one or more wars in different locales that occur more or less simultaneously. Major debate over whether the right number is one, two, three, or more wars is meaningless. There is no right number.

At present even the remote prospect of major conventional war exists in only four regions: India-Pakistan, the Korean Peninsula, the Taiwan Straits, and the Middle East. The first two are the more likely cases. In the event of a crisis between Taiwan and China, presumably naval and air forces would be engaged without the need for large numbers of American ground forces.

In fighting a war on the Korean peninsula, the south should bear the brunt of providing ground forces, supported by American air and, as needed, other forces. America's overwhelming strike and firepower capabilities are the ones that make the biggest strategic and tactical differences. While U.S. forces would be hard-pressed for service to separate the combatants and defuse the conflict if India and Pakistan were to fight a major war, surely the capability for possible intervention could not be ignored if there were a revolution in Pakistan and a fundamentalist regime were to take power.

It is this category of revolution or regime change in a state opposed to American and Western interests that should be a key focus of transformational thinking, as this is the goal of the extremists who are at the root of the terror against which the war is being waged. What can or should the Pentagon be doing to prevent or contain the possibility of revolutionary and extremist regimes from seizing power in states such as Pakistan, Saudi Arabia, and Egypt. Or is this not a DoD worry but a national policy and strategy choice?

For the time being, there is no answer to this last question. So, absent presidential directive, what might the Pentagon do in applying transformation in each of these possible mission areas: war-fighting in particular scenarios, war prevention and limitation, prevention and mitigation of hostile regime change, postwar stability and security operations, homeland security, and other tasks that may be assigned in the global war on terror? While there can be debate as to whether this list of tasks is too broad or too narrow, for purposes of analyzing how transformation might be expanded, assume away these valid caveats.

FIGHTING WARS

This mission clearly is the first among equals in setting requirements and tasks for the Department of Defense. The first mission is to fight and win wars. In this case, based on both Desert Storm and Iraqi Freedom, against a likely adversary with an armed force of about half a million, a "corps-sized force plus" of 150,000–170,000 including all land, sea, air, special, and space forces seems a reasonable planning number. Given the conservatively cautious and traditional concern that only having the capacity to fight one war at a time may embolden adversaries to strike elsewhere, it is reasonable to assume the need for at least two of these war-fighting sets of forces as a minimum.

Obviously logistics, lift, and the ability to support two simultaneous contingencies are crucial and have been weaknesses in the past when there simply was not sufficient capability to go around. However, as the basis for war-fighting planning, having two separate and independent force sets ready for action is a fair starting point.

In creating these forces, CS and CSS elements in the reserve would be migrated into these active force components. That would not entail the complete transformation of the guard and reserve. It would, however, call for a substantial change.

A rule of thumb in force planning is the so-called 3:1 ratio—for every forward-deployed force, two are required in the rear as replacement and in training. In this case an arbitrary decision is made to reduce this to 1:1. For the two corps-sized plus forces, a total of 325,000–350,000 personnel would be needed. Using a

1:1 standard, a total war-fighting force of about 700,000 is needed. These forces would be self-contained and not require reserve augmentation.

The specific shaping, structure, and organization of these military forces are not part of this discussion because, while the devil is in the details, the purpose of this analytical approach is to generate discussion on general principles and underlying assumptions. If agreement can be reached or alternatives sharply defined, it will not be difficult to develop force structures for each. Clearly any force would be geared to high-intensity combat. It would possess ample numbers of tanks and armored vehicles, artillery, reconnaissance and surveillance, combat aircraft and helicopters, and amphibious and airlift support. It would be deployable within thirty to sixty days, with at least sixty days of sustainability as general sizing goals.

Debate over future force design will be intense. While based on Iraqi Freedom, the organization of Marine Expeditionary Brigades (MEB) appears the most practical to emulate with integrated sea, air, and ground forces. The new army formations based on Stryker Brigades and other innovative proposals such as Army Col. Douglas McGregor's five thousand–person strike forces (patterned after the U.S. Army's World War II Regimental Combat Teams) should all be evaluated.

Because the navy and now the air force are organized to be expeditionary, the critical consideration is ensuring their integration into the force packages, which have been improving over the years as both Enduring Freedom and Iraqi Freedom demonstrated. However, in this mix, emphasis should be put on assets such as the Joint Strike Fighter rather than the F-22, on the basis that air superiority can most certainly be ensured with fewer numbers of higher performance aircraft, while support of the ground mission assumes greater importance—a recommendation that will be strongly opposed by air power advocates.

More special forces and special forces–like forces would also be fielded. These would have greater application in the other mission areas that follow. There also needs to be an intense examination in the principal strategic outcomes and effects to be obtained by using military force.

Throughout history, military forces were designed and used to fight like forces, insurgencies, and revolutions withstanding. In that conflict, the Clausewitzian objective of disarming the enemy of the capacity to fight by destroying or neutralizing military power was paramount. However, as noted earlier, the prospect of seeking to affect, influence, and even control the adversary's will and perception should bear closer scrutiny. Forcing the enemy to act as we wish or to restrain from taking actions that we do not want to happen should be aims for experimentation and analysis.

Termed as shock and awe and Rapid Dominance, transformation should be directed to discover the limits of how far both concepts can be taken in fighting wars and in waging peace. On one hand, it may turn out that attrition and force-on-force operations are the only certain way to win wars. On the other hand, given the overwhelming fighting power the United States possesses, transformation can lead to new or different means to apply that power more effectively, efficiently, and at least cost to ourselves, to innocents, and to the adversaries.

WAR PREVENTION AND LIMITATION

By far the most difficult of tasks is prevention and limitation of war. During the Cold War, nuclear deterrence was surely an effective and frightening way to prevent war between East and West. That period and conflict may prove unique in history. There may be, for example, no way to prevent war short of nuclear retaliation. In most cases, from the five Arab-Israeli wars to the three Indo-Pakistani conflicts to the most recent Gulf War, limitation could be a more urgent requirement that prevention, itself perhaps unobtainable.

Transformation is relevant here. This is not a case of force size and shape. It is a matter of bringing other capabilities to bear. The NATO Response Force, for example, if successful, may prove to be a force that can prevent and limit conflict by its existence and the willingness of NATO to use it before the fact or crisis erupts. In other words, this mission is largely a matter of intellect and intelligence—knowing when and where force can be used or threatened to prevent or limit conflict. Part of these considerations are inherently linked to preventing hostile regime takeover of states of interest and value.

HOSTILE REGIME CHANGE

Ironically perhaps, the fundamental purpose of Iraqi Freedom was to reverse the legacy of a hostile regime by changing it. But larger challenges lie ahead. If the bin Laden/theological credo is indeed aimed at regime change and substitution with a fundamentalist or extremist leadership, what is the role, if any, of military force in preventing that outcome? There is a rich history of Cold War experiences in which the aim of American policy was to keep the status quo and the friendly regime in power. The Shah of Iran is the most vivid example of failing to prevent a hostile regime change.

Today the most obvious candidates are Saudi Arabia, Pakistan, and Egypt. More subtly, the future Iraqi government is far from determined. It is not impossible to foresee an Islamic-like regime or one that surely favors a strong fundamentalist leaning. Bayonets, of course, can prop up a regime. As we are relearning in Iraq, however, that is not a lasting solution.

In dealing with the issue of future regime stability, because of its forward presence, the military has always had access to virtually every state in the world through either military assistance groups that were part of country teams under the U.S. ambassador or through whatever military-to-military relationships had been crafted.

Using Africa as a test bed, the European Command has begun exploring different and creative ways of using its presence to deal with the security challenges. Africa, in many ways, is a laboratory for innovation, as that continent contains the emerging security challenges. In the south, HIV/AIDS, extreme poverty, and autocratic regimes have created humanitarian crises. On the west coast, discovery of what appear to be huge oil reserves offshore will have enormous geopolitical and economic consequences. The northern littoral is not only experiencing the most rapid population growth in the world but is also linked through religion, history, and proximity to both Europe and the crescent of crisis. Hence, understanding how and where discreet use of military presence and influence can deal with these challenges and advance American security interests is important.

Whether military-to-military contacts, as with the PfP, can prove useful in helping to democratize and modernize these societies is the crucial question. Expanding the breadth of military contacts and nonmilitary assets from other departments including State, Treasury, Commerce, Health and Human Services, other government agencies, the private sector, and nongovernmental organizations is an important step to explore. The experience of NATO expansion is a good model. The historical utility of military assistance and training suggests that creativity in using these instruments can have high payoff. So far these are still works in progress.

What is envisaged in military transformation is expanding the traditional foreign area specialties by embedding these skills more broadly throughout the forces. Officers were once required to seek advanced degrees to broaden their perspectives as prerequisites for promotion; foreign area training and language skills should become mandatory for a larger portion of the force. In addition to warfare and combat specializations, there is no reason why foreign area skills should not be required of more serving personnel. In that regard, service personnel must be allowed time to receive that training, rather than receive it when off duty.

POSTWAR SECURITY AND STABILITY

One of the more glaring gaps in U.S. strategic policy was preparation for the postwar period in Iraq. It is unfair to criticize the administration on grounds that postwar stability and reconstruction were ignored or received insufficient attention. It is fair to observe that the planning was not up to the task. Some of the reasons were noted earlier.

Transformation must now be stretched to remedy this ill. More than the Department of Defense (DoD) must be embraced in this effort. Unless there is a fundamental transformation of the government's ability to deal with nation building, stability, peacekeeping and peacemaking, and reconstruction operations, the United States will be able to win decisively in war and then risk losing all in peace. For DoD, there are important things to be done.

Royal Navy Adm. Sir Ian Forbes, former deputy commander, Allied Command Transformation, put it this way: "Balancing soft and hard power" is the challenge. Soft power, coined by Harvard Dean Joseph Nye, refers to the nonforceful elements. Hard power is the converse.

It is extremely difficult for any force to switch immediately from war to peace or from projecting hard power to projecting soft power. These conditions require often profoundly different operational outlooks, skill sets, and training. This distinction does not mean that many individuals are incapable of carrying out both assignments, but rather that entirely separate units are probably required. There must be duality of training to support both sets of capabilities, which will require having a dual-track system in which service personnel can rotate between war fighting and other units without foregoing promotion opportunities.

The Department of Defense should enhance experimentation on specific requirements for forces and capabilities for missions other than war-fighting. A great deal of effort has gone into this over the years: missions have been variously called low-intensity conflict, operations other than war (OOTW), and military operations other than war (MOOTW). It is time to determine if specific units should be manned for these purposes.

The toolkit must go beyond military skills. Civil action, police, law enforcement, engineering and construction, health care, infrastructure repair and regeneration, education, and myriad other necessary tools should be incorporated. Other departments would have to provide skills, or skills could be bought and borrowed from the private sector.

A brigade-size force of five thousand to ten thousand would be a good test bed. The services have all done this type of experimentation. In the 1980s the army assigned the Ninth Division stationed at Fort Lewis, Washington, as a test bed for experimentation. One of the benefits arose from experimental tactics of looking deep in the enemy's rear to one hundred to two hundred kilometers in planning operations. A number of the Desert Storm Corps and division commanders had been veterans of the Ninth Division, using that experience to rout the Iraqi Army in deep battle in 1991. More of this experimentation is needed. The costs in dollars and personnel, as trained and experienced professionals are essential to effective experimentation, will not come cheaply and will exact a price on other units—a trade-off that cannot be avoided.

The purpose of transformation is to determine and evaluate whether separate forces for this type of work are necessary and, if the answer is yes, to provide recommendations on the shape, structure, and composition of those units. If it turns out that such capabilities are needed, it is not an ironclad requirement for them to serve under the Defense Department, even though defense might contribute the bulk of personnel. Regardless of where they served, defense must have the resources to ensure this force is properly trained, equipped, and manned for the assigned tasks.

Personnel could be encouraged to rotate from war fighting to these other units on a regular basis. This interoperability would enhance both sets of forces by expanding the experience base. This model should be shared with allies. For example, the NRF could be a leader or follower and work with these forces in these nonmilitary tasks dealing with preventing and restraining war and supporting friendly regimes.

Transformation has done well thus far in making U.S. forces more adept at their primary combat tasks. The next challenges are to transform the decision-making and resource and supporting functions so that more can be done with less or with about the same level of resources. The further challenges are to extend transformation in related areas: preventing and limiting war; stability, security, and rebuilding operations; and providing some means for promoting stability of friendly regimes within acceptable standards of human rights and democratic principles.

THE CLASH OF CULTURES: TRANSFORMATION AND DEMOCRATIZATION

Ironically, transformation now faces an unexpected obstacle in that the two most important defense goals of the administration have collided. Transformation of the military was the first goal and on the top of Secretary of Defense Rumsfeld's personal agenda. The second was the war in Iraq and democratizing that country in the aftermath. In the process of transformation and with the war, this second goal rose to the top of deputy secretary Paul Wolfowitz' agenda. Now the two are in conflict. While the intent of transformation is to induce change "even at eighty miles an hour," as the president noted, there are limits to transforming and at the same time maintaining a large part of the force either deployed or preparing to deploy to Iraq. Hence, winning the transformation battle and peace in Iraq, unless handled with great skill, can prove incompatible.

Transformation is very much at risk and politically subordinate to imposing the peace in Iraq. Massive personnel and monetary resources are going into the latter. With so many forces and so much focus of the senior leadership rightly committed to the peace, transformation must be affected. It will prove impossible to move as quickly with transformation as Rumsfeld wished until Iraq is stabilized and a firmer projection of the long-term resources required there can be calculated.

Rumsfeld's question of whether or not we are winning the war on terror must apply to Iraq. Are we winning or losing the battle to make Iraq whole, free, and productive? If both transformation and postwar aims for Iraq are to succeed, then perhaps transformation should be applied to how the United States is indeed operating in Iraq.

Before the planned turnover of political power and sovereignty to Iraqis in July 2004 occurred, there were two distinctly different answers to the question of whether we were winning or losing. The administration forcefully argued it was succeeding and dismissed or downplayed negative press reports to the contrary. Citing all manner of statistics from schools and hospitals reopened to oil and electrical production back on line, the administration made a strong case that Iraq was on the road to recovery. In fairness, the White House had consistently informed the nation that this was not a short-term campaign or an easy job to complete.

By mid-summer 2003 the insurgency had taken hold. More Americans were killed or wounded in battling this insurgency than in the three weeks it took to occupy Baghdad and rout the Iraqi Army. Violence has not ended, and by most measures is getting fiercer. The insurgency could turn into civil war. Despite Saddam's capture on December 13, 2003 senior officers expressed caution and predicted that the insurgency would continue for some time. The greatest risk was the spread of the insurgency to Kurds and Shia, which would have set the coalition against a national uprising. Thus far that has not happened. As long as there is an insurgency and that security is a major issue and detriment to reconstruction, bringing stability to Iraq remains extremely difficult.

At this writing there are three principal hurdles that must be overcome if the United States and its coalition partners are to win in any sense of the word in restoring law and order and some form of pluralism to Iraq while putting in place the infrastructure to support this larger effort of rebuilding the shattered country. These hurdles grow larger each day as intense counterinsurgency operations turn from friend to foe. Simply put, unless there are visible signs of progress soon, the United States will run out of time and Iraqis will run out of patience.

The first hurdle is the lack of legitimacy of the Iraqi Governing Council (IGC) and its inability to reach unanimous agreement on basic political solutions for future governance. Unlike Afghanistan where Hamid Karzai emerged as a unifying leader, no single figure in Iraq has yet been identified for a similar role. Afghanistan still is far from peaceful. The IGC is seen as aloof, consumed in its own political machinations and incapable thus far of providing the necessary political judgment and leadership required in establishing a pluralistic form of government under the rule of law.

Part of the problem is security. One member, a woman called Hashid Sistami, was assassinated and another wounded. Hence, these are politicians who cannot routinely interact with the public outside very protected meetings.

The second obstacle has been the failure so far to put in place the underpinnings for creating a cohesive sense of society to rally and unify the diverse ethnic, religious, and national factions. The community communications centers or local town halls were offered as one immediate means of dealing with the absence of cohesion. However, integrating American and coalition efforts in the rebuilding process is another way of introducing foundations for creating the sense of a cohesive society.

Third has been the delay in spending the $18.7 billion reconstruction package approved by Congress and signed into law by the president. CPA administrator Ambassador Bremer was advised by his senior staff to expect at least a nine-month period from the time money was actually being spent until some positive effects were felt. Unfortunately, in late December 2003, a hold on all requests for proposals was ordered.

The White House—nervous about ensuring proper oversight and accounting for these funds and stung by accusations that Halliburton (the firm Vice President Cheney had chaired) and Bechtel (with deep ties to the Republican Party), had been unfairly awarded huge contracts for work in Iraq and then had proceeded to overcharge the government hundreds of millions of dollars—directed the Department of Defense to transfer contract oversight to the Army Corps of Engineers. Many of these allegations turned out to be unfounded. But an unfortunate result was further delay in releasing the money to carry out the reconstruction work it was appropriated for.

To deal with these obstacles, the administration should have considered these solutions. Regarding the IGC, the president would have been wise to dispatch a personal envoy or envoys to negotiate directly with the IGC and work out suitable solutions regarding the structure and composition of the interim government. Someone of the stature of the vice president or secretary of state or equivalent former official was needed, and that person or persons would have to use force of personality, logic, common sense, and other persuasive measures to induce unanimous agreement by the IGC on the road ahead. Then these decisions must be given the widest public distribution so that average Iraqis would be able to understand and support the steps toward a pluralistic government. Public diplomacy remains a key. It is also one area that must receive more attention and resources if the United States is to succeed in Iraq. Most Iraqis watch al Jazeera and al Arabiya on satellite television and not the U.S.–funded local channel.

Second, unity of command, taught from the Harvard Business School to the National War College, should be imposed on the CPA and supporting military forces. Either Bremer or Abizaid or another individual must be placed in overall command of both the security and reconstruction efforts. Ordering a four-star officer to take over command of the forces in Iraq, allowing Lt. Gen. Sanchez to concentrate solely on winning the insurgency, was sensible. However, duality in command continued.[3] The opportunity to rectify this deficiency was in the early winter of 2004 as marine units took over security responsibilities from the U.S.

3. Here was an unfortunate contradiction. Ambassador Bremer reported to the Secretary of Defense. But he clearly was very sensitive to guidance from the Secretary of State and the White House. After receiving a great deal of input from many senior officials in Washington and establishing an excellent personal relationship with the president, Bremer quite understandably reacted to these competing pressures by increasingly taking charge. This collided with the Secretary of Defense, who, by

Army. Waiting until July, when the transition of power to an Iraqi government was to take place and a U.S. ambassador installed to centralize and control security and reconstruction may have been too late. Why the administration favored this division of command still remains an unanswered question.

Third, delays in awarding contracts and getting money to flow had to be stopped by fiat if necessary. Special legislative authority, such as in the Transportation and Aviation Security Act of 2001, should have been requested. Clearly the political and practical need to minimize corruption, theft, and inefficiency in spending the public's money was important. However, Iraq was not the United States in doing business. For example, the principle of low-cost contract award simply will not always work. Tribal or local chiefs will submit awards they expect to be approved with or without competition. In essence, the extra cost is for buying or renting loyalty and influence and is the cost of doing business in that part of the world.

Failure to gain results in relatively short periods of time had pernicious political effects on Iraqi perceptions of American intent. True, billions could have been wasted through corruption, theft, and inefficiency. However, the long-term costs of avoiding these risks doubtless will prove far more expensive.

Failure to cope with these deficiencies can only lead to greater total costs in blood and treasure in winning in Iraq. But failure could also have more serious and pernicious effects. If the United States were forced to withdraw or reduce its commitment and leave to Iraqis the responsibilities to cure their ills and they failed, the Bush administration could face a defeat greater than Vietnam. Worse, the degree to which radicalism would be aided by this defeat would have strategic consequence. Failure also would intensify the collision between transformation and democratization and dampen or damage the effects of both. If the United States does not succeed in Iraq, or if the costs of success become a major drain on American resources, transformation will be a victim.

The Transformational Road for the Rest of Government

One long-term step must be institutionalizing transformation across government. Education and training are among the most useful means to achieve that aim. A quarter of a century ago the Department of Defense created the National Defense University (NDU). That institution has amalgamated the three service war colleges, the staff college, and the National War College and Industrial College of

---

December 2003, could say that Defense no longer had the responsibility for rebuilding Iraq. It would support. And the spending priorities required by law and sent to Congress on January 5, 2004, were not fully shared by Rumsfeld, exasperating this tension. Hence, rather than place Central Command under Bremer, which was the most likely way to solve the unified command problem, Rumsfeld preferred to leave the matter open until State took over in July 2004.

the Armed Forces, along with other institutes and research centers under a single umbrella of NDU.

What is needed is a National Security University. Indeed, the theme of national security should be extended throughout each of the government agencies that have specific roles. The reasons for this are clear. National security no longer can be neatly compartmentalized or placed in General Jumper's stovepipes and ruts.

National security can no longer be considered strictly in terms of national defense. Intelligence and law enforcement are clearly critical components made more so by the demands of the war on terror. Establishment of the Department of Homeland Security has also breached past boundaries and responsibilities. But Commerce, Treasury, State, Health and Human Services, and, as BSE or Mad Cow disease showed, Agriculture all have crucial roles. Consider just one illustration of how distinctions have become blurred.

Stand a squad of U.S. Special Forces or the army's super-secret Delta Force alongside a SWAT team from any major metropolitan police force and try to find major differences in equipment, armament, and training. The visible similarities from flack jackets and helmets to automatic weapons and side arms are obvious. Both teams also have special training to deal with all forms of terrorism and other crises. In this age, characterized by the danger of mass disruption, national security is now a cross-government task. There must be means of ensuring that the relevant parts of government are given the education and training necessary to carry out these new assignments.

Several options can achieve these purposes. The NDU system could be expanded, possibly doubling the number of students at all levels to accommodate the other agency and departmental needs. Or the Department of State, using the Foreign Service Institute, could become the principal agent for this NDU construct. It would also be sensible to integrate this structure with NATO and other allied educational institutions, and the student body should be expanded to include more foreign nationals.

The curricula must be revamped and changed. Greater understanding of the broad needs of national security must be translated into specific courses and training. Area or regional awareness and even language training should be part and parcel of this system. America simply has to have a larger reservoir of individuals who are better educated on national security and the international component, including far greater understanding of foreign states and publics. This transformation should extend to the service academies and ROTC units in making national security the broader focus.

There is no reason that total enrollment of cadets and midshipmen at the service academies could not be significantly increased along the lines of national security and not a defense or service perspective. As it is, most of the real professional training is done after graduation, when young officers learn the skills involved in sailing ships, flying aircraft, and running ground operations in war and in peace. So, too, ROTC, units should be greatly expanded and possibly new types of Officer Candidate Schools opened for national security training.

Graduates could elect to have a reserve military commission. They would have a commitment to serve in government in a national security–type assignment in any of the relevant agencies or in Congress for a specific time period. This would not be the same as the draft. However, far more Americans would have military and security training and education, thus increasing people with these skills in the population over time. As these individuals returned to the private sector, as draftees did in earlier years, American society would benefit from their experiences and background. Transformation would be ingrained and institutionalized as the process by which Americans go about providing for the common defense and collective security.

Whether the Bush administration understood fully what transformation meant when it was still a campaign slogan, transformation has been successfully grafted onto the military. Military applies to both the United States and its NATO allies. Whether politicians and publics are fully aboard here and in Europe is still dubious. Two further recommendations are important.

First, the process of transformation is absolutely vital. It is to the military what competition and competitive advantage are to the private sector. When the Bush administration leaves office, in 2004 or in 2008, transformation is a legacy that must be maintained irrespective of party in power.

Second, transformation is the key to keeping NATO viable as an alliance. The less support transformation receives, the more vulnerable the alliance becomes to the natural centrifugal forces that exist within it. Whoever is president in 2005 and beyond cannot ignore or underestimate the power of this word and what it means. Whether the United States wins or declares victory in the GWOT, that statement will be meaningless under all circumstances if the energy behind transformation is dispersed in the victory celebrations. Unfortunately that war threatens to linger for a very long time, lending even greater urgency to the case for transformation.

7
Patriots, Cops, and Spies

O ne of the most inflammatory, highly controversial, and potentially intractable issues surrounding the global war on terror is the potential impact and lasting effect on individual freedom of increased law enforcement and intelligence activities aimed at keeping the nation safe and secure. The Patriot Act, known as HR 3126, "Uniting and Strengthening America by Providing Appropriate Tools to Interrupt and Obstruct Terrorism," passed on October 24, 2001, has been a lightning rod in this debate. Attorney General John Ashcroft has become its personification, accused by critics of overly zealous pursuit of security at the expense of freedom and defended by supporters for the same reason.

This conflict is between two equally valid objectives: increasing government capacity at a time of war or crisis to root out dangerous terrorists at home and abroad through expanded law enforcement, and policing powers and preventing excessive government intrusion on basic liberty in combating terror. Islamic extremists and others wishing this country ill have not yet recognized the potential destructive power of this conflict as it continues to force America and Americans to war with each other over how far defending the homeland against future acts should intrude on normal life. Put another way, of all the ramifications of September 11 and the subsequent wars in Afghanistan and Iraq, the most serious may rest in this conflict between national security and civil liberties. Extremists could do as much damage to America's way of life by forcing major restrictions on civil liberties as by using explosives, bombs, and the other tools of terror.

A state at war certainly has good reason for impinging on individual civil liberties in order to protect the nation's security. Lincoln's suspension of the writ of habeas corpus in the Civil War is one of many examples. The internment of 120,000 Japanese and Japanese-Americans immediately following the attack on Pearl Harbor is another. However, a nation whose leaders have pronounced rather than legally declared a state of war can be trapped by potentially precedent-setting decisions necessitated to balance security and freedom, decisions that may not get the balance right. This is where the United States finds itself.

On September 14, 2001, Congress passed the resolution authorizing President Bush to use all necessary and appropriate force against those responsible for the attacks three days earlier. That resolution fell well short of a formal declaration of war. Congress has not declared a war on terror since. The president has no constitutional authority to do so and sent forces into action as commander in chief.

But commitment and rhetoric over Iraq and defeating terror are so strong that war it may be, even de facto. The Korean War, the Vietnam conflict, and the War to Liberate Kuwait were all waged without formal declarations, relying on supporting congressional resolutions instead. However, the global war on terror is not war in the strictly legal sense. This difference has already been exposed in the case law surrounding military tribunals and enemy combatants. And this distinction will come up in the future as these and other cases move up the chain of the federal court system.

The war on terrorism will go on for years, probably without a legal or final conclusion. Historically, in the United States, civil liberty violations and impingement on individual freedom during wartime have been rectified after the end of hostilities. With an unending war, contemplating and rebalancing of freedom and security by the legal and political system are made inherently more difficult. Another September 11 scale of attack will almost certainly bring another round of reactive and preventive legislation.

To appreciate the intensely important issues at stake, first there needs to be an understanding of the available tools at hand, how they have generally been employed in the balance between freedom and security, and how history sets the context. Second, the specific changes and impact of the Patriot Act must be identified. Third, several of the politically explosive issues, including enemy combatants, detainees held at Guantanamo and Iraq, and military tribunals, must be explored. Finally, what can and should be done in the future to balance and protect the tension between freedom and security, while answering the question of how at risk civil liberties are under actions deemed necessary to win the war on terror.

THE PROFOUND CONTRADICTIONS

There is nothing new about terrorism. What is new was September 11 and the legitimate fear that terror and weapons of mass destruction had finally become a grave threat to the security of the United States. What also was not new was that both the Bush and Clinton administrations shared a common view of danger. The difference was that the Clinton administration chose to deal with terror principally as a law enforcement and intelligence matter augmented by military force and, when needed, military strikes with Tomahawk cruise missiles and other "standoff" weapons to minimize American casualties. The Bush administration took a diametrically opposite view to what was principally a law enforcement response.

Military force and a proactive, preemptive series of actions designed to defeat terror and terrorists (and those that support them) far from America's shores took precedent. Law enforcement in the form of the Department of Justice and the Federal Bureau of Investigation were ordered to make their number one priority countering terrorism at the expense of fighting crime. Terrorism, of course, always required some preventative law enforcement actions. However, here rested a first contradiction.

Law enforcement, based on due process, well-understood binding regulations, and restrictions on excessively intrusive conduct and strict rules of evidence, depended on a prosecutorial strategy to apprehend, try, convict, and ultimately punish criminal activity. The rules of law and evidence were crucial. Unless evidence was admissible in court, defendants could not be convicted. In general these prosecutorial requirements were scrupulously followed, and conviction was the metric of success. The threat of arrest and punishment, including the death penalty, also had some deterrent value on wrong-doers, although this has always been a debated issue.

The contradiction is glaring. Success in the war on terror will rest on prevention as much as and realistically more than on conviction. Convicting the perpetrators of September 11 would have been trivial compared to preventing the attacks in the first place. Rules of evidence and procedures required in criminal prosecutions have been and will be constraints in prosecuting terrorists. Waiting for an act to be committed, as horrific as September 11 or worse, before making an arrest will not be acceptable to publics or politicians. As terrorists are prone to suicide, the traditional deterrent value of law enforcement would seem negligible or meaningless.

The absolute requirement to prevent a terrorist act, possibly with nuclear or biological agents, motivates government and law enforcement to rely on "other means" for fulfilling their duties, including intrusive investigation and monitoring of sources of funding and organizations that are not obviously terrorist. Gaining information cannot always be done under strict rules of evidence if an attack is to be prevented. These understandable pressures to go beyond traditional law enforcement rules and techniques mirror what has happened in the past in criminalizing a broader set of crimes.

The Racketeer Influenced and Corrupt Organizations (RICO) statute to counter organized crime and the war on drugs, described below, illustrates how the law has been used to go beyond the original guidelines (although Congress did direct that RICO was to be broadly interpreted). With RICO there clearly have been impositions on and even severe deprivations of civil liberties.

As counterterrorism has become a higher national priority, greater congressional oversight on the tension between security and freedom will be essential. As we will see, the Patriot Act itself was not a blank check written by Congress for the attorney general or the administration. Congress did not state the need for broad interpretation as with RICO. Some provisions will expire automatically (sunsetted) and others require reports to Congress. However, because of the short period of time it took to draft and pass the Patriot Act, there was little debate and virtually no reflection on the consequences; some provisions lack appropriate oversight. The prospect of an activist judiciary to protect these rights cannot be assumed if history is relevant.

There is a second contradiction. A key ally is also a powerful enemy. This Janus-like relationship is over technology. The marvels of instant telephonic and electronic communications are both a grave danger and a crucial tool to prevail. The cell phone and e-mail give terrorists extraordinary ease of access and communication. But every electron-driven device leaves a trail. The contradiction is balancing the need to keep this technology from contributing to the ability of extremists to do real harm while not intruding so far as to impede technological progress and to trample genuine civil liberties and rights of privacy.

This contradiction is a subset of the inverse relationship between the absolute power of the United States and its vulnerability. American security and liberties must be protected. American technology must be allowed to advance. The Patriot Act is the symbolic and politically charged blender that brings all of these ingredients together, but it requires constant oversight and at least annual review.

Third is the contradiction between the government's ability to obtain information and intelligence from detainees and the rights of these detainees to some form of due process and habeas corpus. In January 2004 Defense Secretary Rumsfeld acknowledged these contradictions in an interview with the *Washington Post*. Keeping detainees, whether enemy combatants or material witnesses, for extended periods, Rumsfeld argued, was justified by the information that would be disclosed to the government and used to pursue the war on terror. The counterargument is that information is perishable and, after more than two years in confinement, what further valuable intelligence could be gleaned from detainees that warranted imprisonment?

WHO OR WHAT IS A TERRORIST?

Under the law who or what is and can be classified as a terrorist? A street gang member armed with an automatic weapon is a clear and present danger. To innocents in the vicinity, that person certainly seems terrifying, especially if the weapon is being fired or threatened. But that does not make the gang member a terrorist.

International and domestic terrorism are defined by Section 2331, Title 18 of U.S. Code. Both forms involve violent acts or acts dangerous to human life that are a violation of the criminal laws of the United States or of any state, or that would be a criminal violation if committed within the jurisdiction of the United States or of any state. The activities must appear to be intended to intimidate or coerce a civilian population; to influence the policy of a government by intimidation or coercion; or to affect the conduct of a government by mass destruction, assassination, or kidnapping. Still, these definitions are ambiguous and do not differentiate between, say, a member of the Irish Republican Army or other localized terror organization and al Qaeda.

International terrorism occurs primarily "outside the territorial jurisdiction of the United States, or transcends national boundaries in terms of the means by which these acts are perpetrated, the persons they appear intended to intimidate or coerce, or the locale in which their perpetrators operate or seek asylum." Domestic terrorism is similar in definition and deals with acts that occur within American territorial jurisdiction.

These definitions are imperfect. A local gang shooting up a 7-11 convenience store, for example, could not be classified as terrorists since the crime does not fit any of these three criteria. But if that gang were to use the proceeds of that robbery to finance al Qaeda or some other terrorist organization, they could be prosecuted under the Patriot Act. Clearly the broader the definition of international terrorism, the more authority investigators will have.

In political rather than legal terms, terrorists are those out to use crossborder violence against the United States and its allies. It is the transnational and crossborder activities that largely define terrorists. Also it is clear and therefore problematic that the bulk of these terrorists come from the crescent of crisis and are almost all of the Islamic faith. Hence, the war on terror and against terrorists has a political context that shapes the law and law enforcement tools and policies in waging and winning that war.

A LITTLE HISTORY

U.S. history is replete with examples of the constant tension between security and freedom. Abuse of civil liberty is most common during and after periods of great domestic stress and crisis and often during military conflict. In most instances civil liberty abuses were rectified after the crisis or hostilities ended and the nation returned to a peacetime normalcy, thereby negating the need for special laws to cope with the special circumstances. Theoretically, denial of due process and other rights is not always or automatically redressed and can remain in force for generations. If the crisis were for an extended period, measured in decades and not years, then the consequences of placing the priority for security over liberty would forever change the nation's social and legal fabric.

At its inception the United States struggled to maintain independence from powerful European nations, particularly Britain, France, and Spain, themselves at war. The Alien & Sedition Acts of 1798, which criminalized unpatriotic and unpopular speech—that is, speech critical of the government—were passed. Under these acts about a dozen people were prosecuted, found guilty, and forced serve prison terms. After Thomas Jefferson became President in 1801, he issued pardons for all of those found guilty by the acts whose provisions expired that year.

The Enemy Alien Act of 1798 authorized the president to detain, deport, or otherwise restrict the freedom of citizens from a country with which the United States was at war. The law is still in force on the books and has been invoked as authority in today's war on terror. However, the law has not been used since World War II because it requires a formal declaration of war.

Censorship in war has also been common. During World War I, Congress made it a criminal offense to speak disloyally or use defaming language about the U.S. government, the Constitution, and the flag. Some two thousand people were prosecuted for violating that law. The Supreme Court upheld the constitutionality of the law in several cases afterward. Flag burning has been permitted as an expression of free speech, suggesting how perceptions and the law have changed over the intervening decades.

Internment of foreign nationals of belligerent states during World War II is well known. In the three days following the December 7, 1941, Japanese attack on Pearl Harbor, over two thousand Japanese, German, and Italian aliens living in cities along the West Coast were arrested and brought into custody. None were suspected of breaking any law, nor were they permitted to challenge their detainment. During 1942, 120,000 Japanese and Japanese-Americans, two-thirds of whom were U.S. citizens, were relocated to ten detention camps. Interned in barracks with fences and armed guards, they were kept there until the war ended.

In 1944 a twenty-two-year-old Japanese-American held in these camps managed to move the case of forced relocation of Japanese to the Supreme Court. The plaintiff alleged gross violation of the Fourth Amendment citing race and national origin as reason for illegal confinement. In the subsequent Korematsu decision the Court ruled 6-3 in the government's favor arguing that military necessity, not race, was the determining factor for internment. This decision has never been reversed, although it is regarded as bad law.

Earlier laws regarding immigration are also important and reflect case law before September 11 and the passage of the Patriot Act. Immigration proceedings, including deportation, are not protected by due process. The Supreme Court has held that deportation is not a criminal punishment; therefore immigrants are not afforded constitutional protections such as the automatic right to a lawyer, presumption of innocence beyond a reasonable doubt, the right to a jury trial, or the standard rules of evidence. The Court has ruled that aliens have the right to a fundamentally fair hearing, but the details remain ambiguous.

Since September 11 the Department of Justice (DOJ) has detained aliens who violated civil immigration laws and were from countries such as Afghanistan, Saudi Arabia, and Egypt. Justice repeatedly stressed that in contrast to what many claim, these individuals had violated immigration laws and could be detained. DOJ presumptively classified these individuals as germane to the September 11 investigation, and the FBI and INS began probing possible links to terrorism and terror cells. Nearly 800 detainees were taken into custody and placed primarily in prisons in New York and New Jersey. Among these and other detainees there have been well-publicized examples of abuse and allegations of violations of due process and law by U.S. law enforcement officials.[1] Overwhelmed by the size and scope of the investigations and the need to determine whether to bring criminal charges against each of the detainees, the Justice Department has been buffeted with questions over due process and whether innocent detainees were being unfairly confined even though they had violated immigration law.

Finally, the Foreign Intelligence Surveillance Act (FISA) of 1978 applies. This law requires judicial approval before government engages in electronic surveillance or physical searches for foreign intelligence purposes. FISA court proceedings are classified, and the courts are presided over by U.S. District Court judges. There is a three-judge FISA Court of Review and final review by the Supreme Court. Since it became operational in 1979, FISA court has approved about 1,000 applications for surveillance and denied only one.

The Racketeer Influenced and Corrupt Organizations (RICO) Act is also germane as grounds for concern over where intrusion into civil liberties by the war on terror may lead. RICO was originally enacted to end the influence of organized crime on legitimate businesses by precluding ownership or control of these firms by criminals and criminally linked individuals. But RICO grew far beyond the original intent and has often been used to prosecute white-collar and other interstate crimes outside the original context. This expansion is cited as an indicator of the potential risk to civil liberties posed by legislation designed to fight terrorism and used more broadly.

RICO's Title IX criminalizes three types of conduct: legal acquisition of an enterprise with money derived from a "pattern of racketeering activity"; illegal acquisition of an enterprise through a pattern of racketeering; and operation of an enterprise through a pattern of racketeering. But why did RICO expand so wide? The bill's sponsor, Senator McClellan, admitted on the Senate floor that "it is impossible to draw an effective statute which reaches most of the commercial activities of organized crime yet does not include offenses commonly committed by persons outside organized crime as well."

1. Several glaring examples of abuse must be noted. A Canadian citizen of Arab descent was arrested upon his arrival at Kennedy International Airport, detained, and then deported to Syria where he claimed he was tortured. He was held for ten months, and Canada protested the illegal deportation of one of its citizens. In a separate case a Moroccan man accused of aiding the September 11 hijackers was acquitted in a German court for insufficient evidence. Abdelghani Mzoudi was found not guilty, in part because the U.S. government refused to provide detainees it held as witnesses for the prosecution on the grounds of national security.

As it turned out the law was written to cover many common offenses irrespective of offenders and irrespective of the presence of organized crime. The law specifically instructs courts to interpret RICO broadly. This interpretation is why courts permit RICO to cover nonorganized criminal activities and allows a defendant not part of organized crime to be prosecuted under this statute.

What the Patriot Act Has Done and What It Has Not

The Patriot Act has ten titles that aptly describe where the law has jurisdiction.

- Title I, enhancing domestic security against terrorism
- Title II, enhanced surveillance procedures
- Title III, international money laundering abatement and anti-terrorist financing act of 2001
- Title IV, protecting the border
- Title V, removing obstacles to investigating terrorism
- Title VI, providing for victims of terrorism, public safety officers, and their families
- Title VII, increased information sharing for critical infrastructure protection
- Title VIII, strengthening criminal laws against terrorism
- Title IX, improved intelligence
- Title X, miscellaneous

The largest changes legislated by the Act related to the gathering of information and intelligence essential to preventing future attacks, particularly in light of new technology that enables terrorists to exploit the advances in cellular phones and the power of the Internet. Most of the changes affected surveillance powers via search orders. Before the Act, law enforcement and intelligence investigations used different procedures for obtaining court-ordered search orders—a "Chinese wall" separated the two. Intelligence did not involve criminal prosecution, so different ground rules were sensible. But granting law enforcement those same rules raised the possibility of abuse.

After September 11 this wall between law enforcement and intelligence was seen as impeding counterterrorist efforts, as cell phones had made the old requirement for single-number wiretapping authority obsolete. The Act largely abolished many of the search order restrictions for law enforcement. Clearly civil rights groups and concerned citizens are worried about abuses that could arise over surveillance such as occurred in the 1960s, when the FBI conducted counterintelligence operations against U.S. civilians.

The goal of the reforms in the Act was to provide the Justice Department with the tools to prevent future terror attacks. The primary mechanism was a series of reforms to the Foreign Intelligence Surveillance Act (FISA) that gave Justice access to surveillance authority previously only available to intelligence investigations. FISA search order requests must state facts supporting probable cause that the "target" is a foreign power or the agent of a foreign power, that facilities being surveilled are used by the target, and that the significant purpose of surveillance is to obtain foreign intelligence information. Requests for FISA have far less specificity and require no argument of probable cause suggesting a crime. Under criminal search orders the suspect is notified. Under intelligence search orders this information is classified. Search warrants lasts ninety days instead of thirty, and the results are kept secret in court proceedings of a secret court.

Before the Act a FISA search request had to demonstrate that the target was either a foreign power or the agent of a foreign power. The Act permits the option of either meeting the "agent of a foreign power" standard or showing that the information being sought is in connection with an international terrorism investigation. The argument for this power stemmed from the reasoning that planning and execution of a terrorist attack do not always involve a spy or even a foreign citizen. Hence, relying on an international terrorism investigation gives law enforcement and intelligence agencies the scope to enlarge wiretapping and electronic surveillance.

Clearly this authority is not without controversy. Domestic surveillance by CIA often violated the law in the 1960s and 1970s. In fact the FISA court system was created to prevent intelligence investigations from wandering into domestic surveillance. Removing the foreign power requirement makes monitoring U.S. citizens far easier. The burden of proof to obtain a FISA search order is low. Granting DOJ access to FISA search orders on grounds of law enforcement–related issues will increase the number of search orders and the ease with which they are obtained. Abuse is a major issue: the FBI admitted misleading FISA court in 2000 and again in 2001 in requests for search orders, and its record of errors in cases from Waco to Ruby Ridge to the physicist Wen Ho Lee is not reassuring.

In 2002 the FISA Court ruled against Justice on the grounds that FISA applications could not be used for criminal investigations. However, the FISA Court of Review heard the appeal and reversed the decision 3-0 to allow application in certain criminal investigations as consistent with congressional intent in the Patriot Act. Most importantly, the ruling specified that the FISA process cannot be employed in ordinary crimes unrelated to terrorism but can be employed for ordinary crimes related to terrorism (such as theft and fraud) that recycle the stolen funds and assets to terrorists.

The Act's provision affecting business records has received much attention in the context of libraries and bookstores. The Act changed the scope of FISA search orders to include "business records" as broadly defined. Records included medical records, purchasing records from credit card companies, and membership lists from major organizations to library, and bookstore records. These investigations are authorized to obtain more than "records," meaning "any tangible things (including books, records, papers, documents, and other items)."

If broadly interpreted, the Act does not require identifying a specifically targeted person for obtaining a business record search. Hence, the government could, by legal request, possibly intrude into vast databases. No specific facts on the person of interest, probable cause, or description of the items sought through the search are required under the new FISA procedure. In normal criminal investigations, warrants are not attainable without satisfying these two steps. This provision is sunsetted.

Roving wiretap authority allows a wiretap to continue even when the target constantly changes communication devices (cell phones and e-mail addresses, for example), regardless of location, without obtaining a new warrant. Congress authorized roving wiretaps for criminal investigations in 1986 and 1998, and roving wiretaps have been authorized against drug dealers since 1986. The Act extends roving wiretap authority to FISA-ordered wiretaps. Obviously the intelligence community needed the ability for continuous wiretaps to prevent a suspect from evading detection. Possible abuses were potentially curtailed by reports to Congress twice a year on their use, and the provision is sunsetted.

While individual changes to the FISA are not of themselves a danger to civil liberties, the combination and accumulation are worrisome. For example, Justice is now able to obtain all of the book sale records from a seller without the purchasers' knowledge, without appeal, and without proving probable cause of a crime. Before the Act, Justice would have to use the criminal procedure that included due process rights, such as notification an individual of a search warrant.

The Act also made reforms to the "pen register/trap and trace" powers. A pen register allows investigators to determine outgoing identification information, i.e., the person or number being dialed. A trap-and-trace device allows investigators to identify incoming caller information—that is, who is making the phone call. The Act allows pen registers and trap-and-trace devices for nontelephone communication, including computer networks, e-mails, and cellular phones. This authority is granted only for identification information, not the content of the communication.

The Act permits criminal pen register/trap-and-trace orders to extend beyond geographic areas of the jurisdiction of the issuing court, a necessary response to cell phones and modern mobile communications. The reasoning is obvious. Authorization was needed to trace e-mails and cell phone calls. Before the Act courts had not consistently allowed this surveillance. Further, the requirement to obtain a new court order for each jurisdiction to conduct a wiretap was made unworkable by mobile communications and use of multiple cell phones and cell phone numbers.

Regarding nationwide wiretaps, opponents use the opposite geographical argument against it. Because of time, cost, and distance, Internet service providers and other communications companies who are to comply with the law cannot always challenge the wiretap order if the court originally issuing the order is on the other side of the country. Judicial oversight can also be limited since a single federal court issuing an order for surveillance in essence is granting a "blank check" anywhere in the country. The provision is not sunsetted.

The final major area of reform under the Act was for delayed notice search and seizure warrants, known as "sneak and peak." These types of search warrants were permitted for terrorism investigations through the Act. The rationale was clear: the nature of the terror threat necessitates flexibility in carrying out searches. Courts have long ruled that "knock and announce" notification is part of a "reasonable" search and seizure, as in the Fourth Amendment. There is no statutory limit to the length of delay before executing a warrant, provided a judge is persuaded that there is a particular risk in notifying the target. But a judge must approve the warrant, delay, and duration. Courts had been granting warrants for terror-related investigations and also in the drug war and against organized crime.

The average length of delay has been about a week and as long as ninety days. However these warrants apply only for terror-related investigations. Extensions must be approved by a court, and, through the end of 2003, DOJ requested 247 extensions. No extension was for more than one day. The Department of Justice reported that it has used delayed search forty-seven times to date, as of mid-2003. Courts have granted forty-seven of forty-seven requests. Of fifteen delayed seizure requests for the same period, Courts denied only one.

DEPARTMENT OF JUSTICE INTERNAL REFORMS

Attorney General John D. Ashcroft made several internal reforms to facilitate prosecuting the war on terror and preventing future attacks. Many of the reforms were issued as a new set of investigation guidelines for the Department of Justice, substantially altering those originally written in 1975 by former President Gerald Ford's attorney general, Edward Levi, and known as the Levi guidelines. The most important change relaxed the criteria for FBI agents who now can more freely attend public protests and religious functions and can scan the Internet as part of investigations and information gathering.

Criticism and concern are clear. Without careful control and oversight, abuse in the form of fishing expeditions is present in which FBI agents lack specific reason for an investigation but discover information that can be used to prosecute unrelated cases. The counterargument is equally clear: increased flexibility is essential to uncovering information for preventing terrorism.

The Levi guidelines restricted FBI agents from investigating these First Amendment protected activities without "specific and articulable facts" that indicated criminal activity. The changed guidelines allow agents to attend and monitor public activities on the same basis as the public. For example, despite the label of profiling, Muslim religious activities open to the public should not be closed to the FBI. In this argument the government's claim is that this access is no different from that of an ordinary citizen. However, there are strong grounds for concern, given past abuses during the Cold War and the Vietnam War when the government did impinge on and in some cases break the law in surveilling legal activities.

Earlier guidelines did not grant FBI agents authority to surf Internet sites for the purpose of collecting information unless pursuant to the investigation of a specific case. The new guidelines have relaxed restrictions on agents to monitor the Internet in conducting counterterror information and intelligence gathering and without specific or probable cause. Because there are so many web sites that can provide information, such as that of Hezbollah or Hamas, the government argued that greater freedom is warranted. The argument is repeated that this power is identical to that of a private citizen who freely surfs the Internet.

The new guidelines also extend the period of investigation to a year with proper approval within the Justice Department. While many of these changes can be justified, given the need to keep up with the exploding technology and the Internet, the guidelines were reset without full consultation with Congress. Attorney General Ashcroft later noted in testimony that congressional consultation on these changes "was not substantial or significant." The government's argument was that these changes were consistent with congressional sentiment reflected in the Patriot Act, making consultation unnecessary.

To a significant degree the attorney general is a large part of this debate over security and freedom. Ashcroft, a former senator, has been brutalized by critics who claim that he has purposely ignored the law in his pursuit of the war on terror. Critics claimed that Ashcroft was also unfit for this office (noting that he was defeated in a bid for reelection by a dead man or—more precisely—by his widow, Mrs. Jean Carnahan, who assumed her husband's candidacy after the popular governor was killed in a plane crash during the campaign). In addition critics believe Ashcroft's support of overly aggressive law enforcement and his stands on the death penalty and against women's right to choose disqualify him for his current responsibilities as the nation's top lawman.

His supporters, principally President Bush, vehemently disagree. Regardless, the reality is that partisanship and politicization have skewed the debate over law enforcement and civil liberties and have made finding the balance between defending the United States in the war on terror and safeguarding constitutional guarantees far more difficult. In this regard the political process has confounded and not relieved this tension. How this debate plays out will depend heavily on the pending election and the selection of the next president. On that basis future changes to the Patriot Act are likely to be determined.

Patriot II

The Bush administration in general, along with the president and his attorney general, appear very interested in a second Patriot Act and are lobbying to revoke many of the sunset provisions in Patriot I. The argument is that additional legislation is crucial to winning the global war on terror. A draft Patriot II Act produced by the Department of Justice but not introduced as legislation was leaked to the press. The Center for Public Integrity provided what it believed were some of the key draft provisions:

- Prohibition of Disclosure of Terrorism Investigation Detainee Information: Increases DOJ's ability to deny releasing material requested under the Freedom of Information Act (FOIA) on suspected terrorists in government custody.
- Distribution of "Worst-Case Scenario" Information: In the Clean Air Act the Environmental Protection Agency requires private companies using potentially dangerous chemicals to produce a worst-case scenario report detailing the effects that the release of these controlled substances would have on the surrounding community. This provision would restrict FOIA requests for these reports, which some argue serve as "a roadmap for terrorists" and reduce public access to "read-only" methods for citizens living or working near the plant.
- "Terrorist Identification Database:" Authorizes creation of a DNA database on "suspected terrorists" and groups suspected of supporting terrorism.
- Presumption for Pretrial Detention in Cases Involving Terrorism: Would authorize imprisoning suspects accused of terrorist acts without bail.
- Expatriation of Terrorists: Establishes grounds for expatriating American citizens if, with the intent to relinquish his nationality, he becomes a member of, or provides material support to, a group that the United States has designated as a "terrorist organization."

Whether or not there will be movement in an election year 2004 to draft a Patriot II Act, the powerful issues on all sides of the interaction among security, freedom, and technology mean that future debate and action are inevitable and essential. That ensuring national security and defending the nation are the highest priorities of government is unarguable. However, protecting the Constitution from assaults and guaranteed individual rights are also of the highest priority. The critical question is whether the current political process is capable of working out acceptable means to redress the profoundly important issues at stake. On that the future well-being of the country may well rest.

GITMO, UNLAWFUL COMBATANTS, AND MILITARY TRIBUNALS

The global war on terror raised legal issues that had not been seen in decades. With some seven hundred prisoners captured in Afghanistan during Operation Enduring Freedom, the Bush administration chose the naval base at Guantanamo Bay, Cuba, and designated Camp X-Ray as the place to detain and interrogate these former Taliban and al Qaeda fighters. Initially these detainees were not classified as prisoners of war, in part to circumvent the Geneva Convention regarding treatment and conduct. The designation also allowed the government to incarcerate these prisoners for long periods of interrogation. The intelligence and information obtained from these interrogations were deemed as highly important, highly classified; the public had no way of confirming whether the government claims were valid.

International reaction abroad was negative. After further consultation the administration decided that captured Taliban prisoners would be classified prisoners of war and al Qaeda fighters would remain unlawful combatants. As a result 660 people from 44 countries were held at Guantanamo Bay. None are U.S. citizens.

Legal rights are nonexistent for prisoners designated as unlawful combatants. Rights of habeas corpus, duration of detainment, sentencing, and treatment of these unlawful combatants are not covered by international agreements or the Constitution. For the first eighteen months of captivity, thirty-two attempted suicides were reported. Both Britain and Australia with citizens in detention in Camp Delta have strongly protested and asked for repatriation. During a state visit to Britain in late 2003 Prime Minister Blair specifically requested of President Bush that he agree to transfer the British citizen from Guantanamo Bay. Bush declined, to the dissatisfaction of Blair and the British public.

The legal issues surrounding the Guantanamo Bay prisoners are complicated and unsettled. In early 2003 the D.C. Circuit Court ruled that detainees in military custody at Guantanamo Bay had no right to challenge their status in U.S. courts, provided they were captured outside the United States, were not American citizens, and were incarcerated outside the United States. In December 2003 the Ninth Circuit Court of Appeals ruled against this argument in a separate case, noting that U.S. civilian courts had jurisdiction over Guantanamo detainees. However, that decision was appealed and the Supreme Court agreed to review the issue of the Executive Branch's authority to imprison foreign citizens seized in combat and held on territory under the sole control of the United States. The administration also allowed an Australian defense lawyer to meet with and defend an Australian held at Guantanamo Bay, and the administration is negotiating with other governments on the status of their citizens.

The Bush administration has committed to try these unlawful combatants in military tribunals. In November 2001 Bush issued a military order directing the Defense Department to create military tribunals to try non-U.S. citizens held at

Guantanamo Bay. The decision whether to try detainees in military tribunals or in civilian courts rests entirely with the executive branch unless Congress passes legislation otherwise. The Bush administration's decision to try detainees in military tribunals has aroused fierce opposition internationally and domestically. To some, tribunals are regarded as blatant violations of the rights of detainees who would normally face trials in either courts martial or civilian court.

These military tribunals have been criticized as legal black holes because there are no preexisting due process procedures and, while defendants have the right to representation, the government does not need to use the standard of reasonable doubt and other accepted legal practices. The government chose military tribunals in part because of concern that more open legal proceedings could be subject to reprisal by terrorists and could not fully deal with classified evidence. Further, the publicity generated would be harmful to prosecuting the global war on terror.

To insert fairness into these proceedings, in March 2002 the Department of Defense issued a statement of procedures for tribunals. These included a measure of due process in that there was to be presumption of innocence; conviction made only on the basis of guilt beyond a reasonable doubt; and the right to appointed counsel, the right against self-incrimination, and the right of appeal to a distinct appellate tribunal. There is, however, no right to confront accusers, and secret evidence is admissible.

Military tribunals have been used before, during, and after military conflicts. A crucial issue is the need for congressional and legal authorization. The Bush administration argues this was obtained in, and is implicit in, the congressional resolution authorizing use of force, although that resolution was not a declaration of war nor did it expressly authorize military tribunals. In Ex Parte Quirin the Supreme Court upheld the power of President Franklin Roosevelt to order the trial of eight German-born residents of the United States in military tribunals as unlawful combatants. However, Roosevelt had express authorization of Congress. The Bush administration has cited the power as commander in chief and Quirin as the constitutional authority to proceed with military tribunals.

ENEMY COMBATANTS AND MATERIAL WITNESSES

The Bush administration has used two legal designations—enemy combatant and material witness—to circumvent normal due process requirements. Using his authority as commander in chief the president has designated three individuals as enemy combatants. This status denies due process and many legal rights guaranteed for American defendants, including habeas corpus and assured right to counsel.

The enemy combatants are Jose Padilla and Yasser Esam Hamdi, both American citizens, and Ali Saleh Kahlah al-Marri, who is not. Hamdi was captured in Afghanistan by Northern Alliance forces in November 2001. Held at a navy brig in Norfolk, Virginia, Hamdi challenged the government. The case, *Hamdi v.*

Rumsfeld, is being appealed. A three-judge panel of the Fourth Circuit overruled the lower court's decision on the grounds that it lacked authority to review the designation. But the ruling was tailored specifically to the Hamdi case. The Supreme Court has not yet decided on whether or not to hear the case.

Padilla was taken into custody in May 2002 on landing in Chicago on a flight from Pakistan. Initially arrested as a material witness for the investigation of the September 11 attacks, the government later alleged Padilla was trained to explode a "dirty" radioactive bomb inside the United States. In June 2002 Padilla was designated as an enemy combatant, and moved him to military custody.

In November 2003 the deputy Solicitor General hinted that Padilla could see a lawyer after his interrogation was complete. On December 18, 2003, the Second Circuit Court ruled that the administration exceeded its authority in detaining Padilla, a U.S. citizen, and in designating him an enemy combatant. The court ordered the transfer of Padilla to civilian authorities within thirty days. The Justice Department petitioned the full panel of the Second Circuit to decide disposition on the grounds that allowing Padilla access to counsel too early hampered the ability to gather intelligence through interrogation. This legal proceeding turns on the need for obtaining information and for guaranteeing the defendant's rights under the Constitution as a U.S. citizen.

Regarding certain illegal immigrant detainees, the Material Witness Statute of 1984 applies under this statute, normally applied to reluctant and uncooperative witnesses whose testimony is material in criminal proceedings, detainees have the right to counsel and a bond hearing. As of December 2002, the *Washington Post* reported, forty-four people were being held as material witnesses. Twenty were never called to testify before a grand jury. Detentions lasted from a few days to more than four hundred. Some detainees had difficulty in contacting attorneys in the first few weeks of detention. Civil liberty groups argued that it is unconstitutional to hold detainees in maximum security settings and that this is a legal loophole exploited by the Justice Department to hold certain individuals of interest for longer periods than would otherwise be possible.

GETTING THE BALANCE RIGHT

The United States will lose the global war on terror if, in the process of waging that fight, the Constitution is trampled and the liberty assured the American public since 1789 is subsumed in the rush to defend the United States from terrorist attacks. Politics and partisanship are unavoidable. Attorney General John Ashcroft is regarded as a hero by some for taking strong stands to enhance the authority of law enforcement in countering terror. To critics he has willfully ignored the Constitution and the will of Congress. While the truth lies somewhere in between, the nation is at risk both to those attempting to do harm and to those allowing excessive and unnecessary intrusion on the right of life, liberty, and the pursuit of happiness.

Unfortunately none of this can be legislated. However, Congress must play a more intrusive role in providing oversight and checks and balances to the executive branch. Virtually any administration is anxious to find effective solutions in the war on terror that ease the inherent difficulty in preventing and responding to acts of terror carried out with suicidal intent. The tendency will be to err in favor of government agencies entrusted with these tasks and to impinge whenever and wherever necessary on individual rights on the grounds of protecting the larger common good. This tendency is colorblind when it comes to party affiliations. For example, the hunt for communist agents during the Cold War and in the fight against organized crime in this country was as vigorously pursued by Republican administrations as Democratic ones. J. Edgar Hoover, the long-time and much-feared director of the FBI, managed to conduct these investigations irrespective of whoever controlled the White House.

Congress must establish by law a permanent external oversight body such as the Securities and Exchange Commission (SEC), Federal Reserve, and other independent agencies, a group charged exclusively with monitoring this constant tension and conflict between these competing and often diverging aims of guaranteeing security and freedom. Congress obviously has committees and subcommittees charged with similar responsibilities. It can and does hold hearings and investigations, although not frequently enough. The GAO and CBO can also do studies and make reports. Unfortunately, these amount to too little, too late.

Perhaps called the Freedom and Security Commission, this independent body would closely monitor the interplay of government, including law enforcement, intelligence, and other agencies, as it relates to waging this war on terror and would report back on a regular basis to Congress, the White House, and the public. If this commission does not believe it is receiving the access and authority it requires, then it should have subpoena power as well as independent status to permit it to go to the media and the public as necessary.

Some will argue that creating yet another commission merely ignores the larger problem of government. Balancing security and freedom is inherently the responsibility of elected officials in the White House and Congress. However, the facts indicate otherwise. The Federal Reserve and the SEC were created because the political process was either not sufficiently capable or, in the case of the federal government, perhaps too capable of dealing with the broad area of fiscal and monetary policy. Left to its own devices, the normal political process would distort and manipulate laws, policies, and regulations, not always to the benefit or interest of the public.

There are other critical steps that must be taken. Regarding the prevention of terrorism, it is clear that improved tracking methods and procedures for visitors to the United States are needed, including correcting the deficiencies in programs for visas, aliens overstaying visits, and illegal means of entry. Efforts to improve coordination of terror watch lists among different agencies and departments and among countries are also essential.

A stricter definition of terrorism and a more focused use of that designation are essential if pretrial detention for individuals charged with these offenses is to be authorized and ultimately found to be legal. Information technologies for improving and sharing databases in the intelligence and law enforcement agencies are available. However, breaking down the stovepipes and ruts that prevent better sharing must become a high priority. Congress should pass legislation that changes the clearance and security granting authority to a single agency of government so that clearances are valid throughout government, not just in individual agencies, as one way of breaking down these barriers.

The simplistic yet obvious conclusion of the need for better human intelligence and better understanding of the nature of the threat and the potential enemy can never be in dispute. The issue here again is operational: How can this be made to happen? The idea of moving from a national defense mentality in training, educating, and recruiting individuals must be replaced by a broader national security basis. This includes better legal education of both intelligence and law enforcement personnel.

It is equally apparent that government requires far more translators as well as specific experts in narrow areas of importance. To achieve this, private-public partnerships must be expanded and funded. The problem is that given deficits and debt, money is in short supply. That means far more attention to cutting programs with limited or no real value added is essential. This requires discipline, courage, and close cooperation between Congress and the executive branch, characteristics that are in shorter supply than funding.

At the same time, safeguards and better protection of constitutional rights and civil liberties must be put in place. Future Patriot Acts can protect the public from terror, but what will protect the public from greater government intrusion and an erosion of freedom in the name of public safety?

Senator Diane Feinstein's proposed Privacy Act of 2003 established greater protections for personal identification information, such as social security numbers, driver's license information, and other key data. As government surveillance powers extend into the Internet and mobile phone systems without safeguards, it is apparent that the public will increasingly turn to encryption and other means to make these communications more secure. Such means, already a matter of keen importance and a great deal of effort, almost certainly will lead to greater difficulty for the government in conducting appropriate surveillance and investigation. Hence, the need for legal safeguards is vital.

Congress would be well advised to mandate full consultation with the Department of Justice before guideline changes can be made. Congress has this power in Article I and it must assert it. Administrations will complain on excessive intrusion by the legislative branch; after all, no attorney general wants to complicate the assignment. However, changes to regulations and guidelines that affect basic liberties and can intrude on constitutional guarantees cannot be left to a single agency or branch of government to determine. A Security and Freedom Commission could be very helpful in this regard. As the president is required to present to Congress a document on the nation's national security strategy, a document on the balance between steps in the war on terror and ensuring basic freedoms should be legislated and required.

As part of greater transparency, to prevent further excesses and abuses in allowing the war on terror to intrude upon daily life beyond justifiable and legitimate reason, specific checks might include:

1. Grant resources and authority to the General Accounting Office (GAO) and Department of Justice Inspector General to monitor implementation of antiterror guidelines
2. Mandate more consistent, timely, and open disclosure of information on the Patriot Act and other war on terror legislation and actions to Congress and the public
3. Ensure greater judicial oversight of search orders so courts are not effectively granting "blank warrants" and wiretaps
4. Require that agencies provide to Congress specific names and numbers of people being monitored for FISA searches
5. Require executive branch officials to certify that suspects are actually using the device to be tapped with roving wiretaps
6. Prevent abuses of pen register/trap and tracing of content by defining more precisely terms such as "routing", "addressing", and "content" to clarify what information may and may not be accessed through these means
7. Ensure closer congressional monitoring of the use of surveillance techniques, such as Carnivore, so that content of communication is not seized illegally or without authorization
8. Strictly define the meaning of international and domestic terrorists and terrorism to conform with the political and strategic boundaries of the threat rather than use broad and vague dangers through issuing legal equivalents of military "rules of engagement"
9. Require law enforcement and intelligence agencies to provide comprehensive reports to Congress about use of Patriot Act powers

THE RISKS

The global war on terror is open ended. Unlike World Wars I and II, there will be no discrete and clear armistice on the eleventh hour of the eleventh day of the eleventh month or a document of unconditional surrender signed on the teak deck of a great battleship in Tokyo Harbor. Nor are there any metrics to define success and failure and victory and defeat.

America is also a nation that can be stampeded to overreact. September 11 provoked, as it should, the strongest reaction and feeling of national violation. However, reflection is equally important. The war on terror has produced huge increases in spending for homeland security, law enforcement, intelligence, and military forces. The issue is whether this has made America safer and more secure. In many ways that answer is yes. In others it is no. And in still other ways, the jury is out. In one area however, the tentative findings are serious and suggest that the nation is neither safer nor securer. These relate to the clash between security and freedom.

From raising warning alerts announcing increased risks of terrorist attack—none of which fortunately have transpired—to impingement on individual freedoms, Americans must be concerned. It is disconcerting that American citizens can be labeled enemy combatants and be deprived of their constitutional rights on that basis. If charged with heinous acts, including treason or killing their fellow citizens in acts of treason, they should be prosecuted and punished, if convicted, to the limits of the law. However, that prosecution should take place in open court and not in a secret tribunal.

The risk is, where does one draw the line? Another is, what authority allows the president and Congress to deprive citizens of basic rights of due process and habeas corpus outside the most extraordinary circumstances? If the war on terror requires these intrusive actions, then war must be declared to provide the legitimacy for disregarding or negating parts of the Constitution. If war cannot be declared because Congress will not do so or the public will not support a declaration, then one conclusion is clear.

Constitutionally guaranteed rights cannot be ignored. That applies, of course, only to American citizens. The decision should be made that Americans accused of terrorist acts or supporting terrorism should be tried in open U.S. courts as was Oklahoma City bomber Timothy McVeigh. That right need not and should not automatically be extended to non-U.S. citizens.

A further consideration is the political consequence of the next attack. No president can easily tolerate such an attack politically. While a future September 11 could motivate strong public support, it is as likely that accountability will be placed on the White House. On that basis any president will be judged by his fellow citizens. Investigations and inquiries will demand to know why America slept and why another attack could have happened, given all of the resources and attention devoted to prevention.

Hence, administrations will tend to favor actions that make attack less likely even at some expense, certainly perceived as acceptable, to civil liberties and public freedoms. That is natural. It will take enormous courage to restrain this understandable bias. That courage can only be made effective if Congress puts in place measures such as a Freedom and Security Commission and mandates that the executive branch more fully disclose how it is waging this war on terror. Otherwise the risks to this republic and democracy are as severe or more severe than the terrorism that the White House intends to prevent. Islamic extremists who are bright and cunning will understand this weakness. They will choose to exploit it as Ho Chi Minh exploited American humanity and the ultimate rejection of tolerating the deaths of more of its citizens in a distant war.

The contradiction of Islam is one means for this assault to continue. As long as some believers of the Islamic faith regard women and followers of other religions in a fundamentalist sense as second-class citizens and seek the right to practice their beliefs as protected by the Constitution, one set of challenges will be provoked. As extremists recognize that the threat of terrorism may force the United States to deny its citizens certain rights in order to defend the entire nation, this realization will be exploited.

Common sense and transparency are the best antidotes. Whether either can be mandated into the process is a vital step in this fight against extremism. Sadly, as the slogan "war on terror" has distorted the real nature of the struggle and allowed the United States to concentrate on symptoms and not causes, impingement on civil liberties, too, will continue. Under those circumstances the United States could win the battle against terror and lose the war to maintain freedom and democracy. Those are the real stakes and the real risks.

Note: The excesses in the treatment of Iraqi prisoners under U.S. custody in al Ghraib prison were a shocking and horrific example of how human rights, individual dignity, and respect for the law can be trampled in an overly zealous pursuit of the war on terror. These tragic revelations were exposed as this book was in production and can only be covered in a footnote.

8
People Are More Important
Than Guns in the Rating of a Ship

The United States will not be any more successful in winning the global war on terror than it has been in winning wars on drugs, crime, poverty, inequality, and a plethora of other issues if it does not change course. In fact, the United States could lose this war as currently being waged. One set of reasons relates to mistaking symptoms for causes, underestimating the real dangers, and believing that overwhelming military strength can indeed bring fundamental and positive change to the strategic landscape of the greater Middle East. A second set relates to the difficulty in resolving the profound contradictions that impede progress in making the nation safer and securer.

First, the war should not be directed solely against terror. Terror is a tool and a tactic. It can never be eliminated by itself and without addressing its causes. Second, that America is at the peak of not only its power and strength but also its vulnerability to disruption must be understood. Traditional policies and tools that worked during the Cold War to contain, deter, and ultimately defeat the Soviet Union have far less relevance today.

The greater danger is not necessarily different from Lenin and the Communist Party of a century ago or Hitler and the Nazis two decades later. The threat is jihadist extremism and its political agenda cloaked in theological disguise. Terror is a weapon. One major target is the vulnerability of society and the profound ease with which it can be disrupted.

Extremism has broad agendas. Establishing some form of fundamentalist Islamic regime in keeping with the strictest interpretations of the Koran and with or without borders is certainly one goal. Ensuring survival of this regime with Saudi money and access to Pakistani nuclear weapons is another. As a means to these ends, overthrowing regimes in both of those strategic bookend countries in the crescent of crisis cannot be dismissed. For those who ignore these warnings, do not forget Lenin and Hitler.

Osama bin Laden is neither a Lenin nor a Hitler. But surely, within the ranks of the believers and the converts, a potential leader must exist. As recruits to bin Laden's and other Islamic extremist groups grow, a competent leader or leaders will emerge. Given the political aspirations of these groups and the inherent vulnerability of all societies to disruption through terror and other means, the dangers are clear. Unfortunately the current boundaries of the global war on terror do not fully cover these larger dangers.

INTELLECTUAL CHALLENGES

The battle is political, ideological, theological, social, and cultural and, of course, is joined with violence and death. The bulk of the battleground is not global and entails the greater Middle East, Europe, and North America. While not technically a world war, future global stability is at stake. The fight against jihadist extremism and its ambitions can be won over time only by using all of the instruments of policy, coercion, and persuasion. In that regard, to return to words of the author of this chapter's title, John Paul Jones, the United States and its allies have "not yet begun to fight" in this broader context.

The American political and national security systems are not currently organized or intellectually prepared for the tasks that lie ahead. Business as usual will not work even if that brings a more sophisticated understanding of the competing forces and interests that threaten the nation's safety and security. Iraq, Iran, Pakistan, and North Korea make this case. The administration went to war in Iraq to destroy weapons of mass destruction that do not appear to have been there. With Pakistan, because of the need to maintain a strong alliance and friendship to wage the war on terror, the United States tolerated probably the most egregious case of nuclear proliferation in history.

While the Bush administration admits diplomacy is the tool of choice in dealing with Iran and North Korea, it has not sought to create new mechanisms and relationships to aid in removing nuclear weapons and stabilizing either region. New and different relationships and, yes, alliances are vital. This is an intellectual rather than an operational shortcoming.

CONSTITUTIONAL CHALLENGES

Furthermore, beyond the nightmare scenarios of future September 11s in which biological and nuclear agents may find use, Islamic extremists pose direct threats to America's democracy, its Constitution, and its legal system. Two of the most significant were addressed. The first relates to Islam and religious freedom. The second relates to the tension between freedom and security, favoring the latter and doing irreversible damage to the former.

Islam is a diverse religion. It is also a religion that has never embraced profound reform as Christianity and Judaism have. There is a segment of Islam that is fundamentalist in outlook but not so radical that it eschews violence and terror. Central tenets regarding women and other religions do not conform to Western values or often to Western laws. But how will this play out under assurances of freedom of religion and speech, not only in the United States but also in other democracies?

In France, for example, the Chirac government has imposed an edict that proscribes the wearing of ostentatious religious apparel including head scarves, burqas, oversized crucifixes, and stars of David in state schools. The government argued that because French law and tradition mandated the separation of church and state, dress must respect this division. The backlash was substantial.

These examples contrasted the potential collision between the general proposition regarding freedom of religion and the tenets of individual religions that challenge those values and traditions. Many Muslim women will argue that it is not contradictory to respect the role of women in that religion and still profoundly support women's rights. But that view does not always conform to the values and views of mainstream America. So the issue is how these divergent positions can or will be reconciled. This could become a major constitutional conflict if and when members of the Islamic faith use the legal process to advance their right of religious freedom.

The second inherent danger is allowing the quest for security to damage individual liberties permanently. Air travel is a small example. Understandably fearful another air hijacking over American skies could be politically terminal, the White House has directed massive funding into the Transportation Security Administration for airport security. Passengers will be disrobing at security checkpoints forever, while much of what goes by airfreight is not searched. Further, terrorists could commandeer a large plane in Canada, Mexico, or the Caribbean.

The only solutions are for the public to understand better the enormity of the stakes that are involved and for Congress to play a far more intrusive oversight role. Establishing the Freedom and Security Commission is one way to make permanent some of the oversight mechanisms and checks and balances needed to keep this balance between freedom and security. As recommended, the incorporation of a Sarbanes-Oxley-like law to regulate oversight and conduct of government is another means of ensuring that both freedom and security are protected.

FINDING THE PROPER NORTH STAR

On its current course the United States government cannot assure its public that the country will be made safer or securer in the future. Obviously, great strides have been made in recognizing the new dangers. But that understanding has not been as incisive and penetrating as warranted if the aim is to protect the country. The main enemy is not terror and terrorists. The enemy is political-theological doctrine that has distorted and hijacked parts of Islam as the ideological basis for creating a fundamentalist regime in the greater Middle East. The countervailing strategy has international and domestic components.

The strategic center of gravity for protecting America and its allies is not geographic although the Greater Middle East is a region of major significance.

The focus must be political-ideological even though many of the actions will be geographic. Defeating jihadist extremism is akin to defeating Communism and Nazism. The difference is that jihadist extremism does not have regional boundaries or a specific state bonded with a virulent ideology. At the same time other potential hot spots, such as the Korean peninsula and Central Asia, cannot be neglected and must be made part of this broader strategy.

First and foremost, this countervailing strategy must deal with the causes of extremism and not just the symptoms. The geographic center is the crescent of crisis. Iraq is not and never was the fulcrum. Egypt, Saudi Arabia, Iran, Pakistan, and the Arab-Israeli-Palestinian conflict are. The notion of a strategic trifecta advanced in Chapter 3 becomes the basis for this strategy.

If the Arab-Israeli-Palestinian conflict can be redressed and mitigated, major advances in making many people safer and securer will be gained. That conflict is a principal cause of terror, terrorism, and instability. Relieving it will and must have enormous and positive consequence. The questions are how and whether this can ever be achieved and what the costs of failure and success will be.

The Arab world in general and Saudi Arabia in particular must recognize publicly and in writing Israel's right to exist and the sovereignty and integrity of its borders and also renounce any ambitions of driving Israel and Israelis from the region. In turn, Israel must recognize the rights of Palestinians and a Palestinian state. But incentives and other agreements are imperative.

To engage Syria to recognize Israel and sign a peace treaty, the Golan Heights must be returned. To oblige legitimate Israeli security needs, the transfer would be over a period of time and would lead to a demilitarizing of that crucial piece of strategic real estate and stationing outside forces, most likely American, as the guarantors of peace. Both Israel and Syria would have access, and protection to both sides would be guaranteed by the presence of neutral military forces with enough capability to blunt and defeat any attempt to establish complete control of the Heights and threaten Israel.

Military forces, possibly NATO, could be assigned first to the Gaza Strip as peacekeepers and enforcers and as part of an incremental process leading to an independent Palestinian state. Perhaps a five-year transition period could be established with outside forces assuming increasing geographic responsibilities predicated on success in the Gaza Strip that would reduce and end terror and lead to Palestinian autonomy. Meanwhile substantial financial aid to both Israelis and Palestinians would have to increase. Here the Arab states would have the responsibility. Some of the funds could be shifted to Israel from the substantial amounts that go to buying weapons of war as, presumably, there would be less need as peace becomes more likely.

Regarding Egypt and Saudi Arabia in particular, substantial progress in opening the political process and moving toward a more pluralistic system under the rule of law must be made. Because the likely risk of revolution and political coups in both states could easily lead to more—not less—autocratic governance, persuasion and reason must outweigh coercion and threat as the mechanisms for change. Both countries have religious fundamentalists who hold great sway and authority. Yet unless these powerful political forces are neutralized or convinced, no positive action will follow.

Although Egypt and Israel have signed a peace treaty, Saudi recognition of Israel will go a long way in alleviating a root cause of contention among Arabs and fundamentalists. Such recognition will also energize opposing and even enemy factions refusing to tolerate Israel's existence. Yet this is the single most important action that can catalyze peace and lead to a more stable region. The result will be a blow, perhaps mortal, to extremism and to those seeking to use that theology to overthrow local governments and to establish a fundamentalist regime in the region.

Second, India and Pakistan constitute perhaps the most dangerous flashpoint in the world. Signs of progress in late 2003 and 2004, the meetings between leaders of both states and cricket matches won by India—perhaps the twenty-first century equivalent of "ping-pong diplomacy" that broke the chill between China and the United States—offer glimmers of hope, but these steps must continue to grow. The public admission by Pakistan's revered inventor of its nuclear bomb, Dr. A. Q. Khan, that he had illegally transferred nuclear information and materials to states such as North Korea, Iran, and Libya in return for significant payments underlines how complicated and difficult this process is.

Pakistani President Musharraf immediately pardoned Khan. Public sentiment was strongly in support of Pakistan's most famous and admired figure, even though he had been perhaps the single greatest proliferator of nuclear technology in history. The United States and other countries expressed no criticism. The situation in Pakistan was that delicate. However, American actions in Iraq to disarm Saddam of weapons he did not possess and American attempts to stem the flow of WMD technologies were not helped by Khan's confession that a strong American ally in the war on terror, without whom we could not have so easily ended Taliban rule in Afghanistan, was a far worse violator than many of the states to whom this material and information were sent.

Here, given these highly complicated and often crosscutting interests, U.S. diplomacy must be able to help privately and publicly. One public way to help reduce the chances of conflict and of nuclear war is to convene an international conference on preventing the use and spread of nuclear weapons. This conference would include all nuclear powers and invite those suspected of or with nuclear ambitions such as North Korea, Israel, and Iran.

Drawing on the parallels with the Organization for Cooperation and Security in Europe (OSCE), this conference would include the United States, Britain, France, Russia, China, India, and Pakistan. North and South Korea, Iran, and

Israel would be invited to attend as either full members or as observers. The purposes of this conference would be to determine formal means of preventing using nuclear weapons, eliminating their proliferation, and reducing the number that currently exist. In this case, the United States and Russia would be extending their nuclear reduction treaties to this format and would presumably agree on decreasing these numbers further.

A useful way to invite full participation is for the Bush administration or its successor to abandon the label "axis of evil", but at a price. As Libya surprised much of the world in announcing it would eliminate its mass weapons programs, Iran and North Korea would be drawn back into the sphere of diplomacy by showing good faith in participating in this conference and by actions that demonstrate adherence to the spirit and the aims meant to lead to no use, no proliferation, and reduction of inventories.

THE VITAL ROLE OF NATO

A critical part of this approach is through NATO. NATO can play a fundamentally important role not only a force for security in Afghanistan and probably Iraq but also as a powerful force for stability with a worldwide focus. Using it in the Middle East and in the Arab-Israeli conflict is one approach. NATO and its NATO Response Force (NRF) have been given responsibility for security in the Olympics to be held in Athens, Greece, in the summer of 2004. Here are the arguments for a new NATO and why it can help build stability for decades.

For NATO to be as effective in the twenty-first century as it was in the last, the role, mission, and capability of the alliance must change. That change must be accompanied by sufficient political commitment to deal with matters of balancing sovereignty and consensus with some ability to conduct early use of force without the cumbersome decision process that otherwise would make such deployment impossible. Also, states must commit to providing the political and financial capital to changing force levels, structure, and capability to conduct these new missions.

These are enormous tasks. As defense ministers and chiefs of defense staffs learned at the ministerial meetings in October in Colorado Springs, during deployment of the very high readiness component of the NRF to evacuate noncombatants from an explosive situation, the situation escalated quickly and the force had to be reinforced. NATO was then faced with escalating further to defeat insurgents who had driven out the legitimate government or to complete the evacuation and withdraw. As these decisions were being debated, weapons of mass destruction stolen by the terrorists and placed on hijacked ships in the Mediterranean had fired at NATO's southern flank.

What is interesting about this scenario is that no NATO official doubted its authenticity or challenged whether or not such a crisis was possible. All agreed that it was. For the United States armed with that knowledge, the issue is carrying out the Prague commitment. America must do all in its power to facilitate that outcome.

The reality, however, is that publics and politicians in every NATO state are largely unfamiliar with the stakes and consequences. The NRF is so far an unintentionally well-kept secret. Unless or until politicians and publics understand the value and benefit of what this new NATO brings to bear, the necessary changes in political and decision-making authority are unlikely to be made and obstacles will not be removed.

Competition for bandwidth in the public debate is keen. Consider the competition for air and print space. As this book was literally being finished, the presidential campaign and the Democratic primaries were dominating the news. The Super Bowl and the tawdry half-time show in January with a "wardrobe malfunction" proved that bad taste does not detract from public exposure, in this case in the press. Revelations about Iraqi weapons of mass destruction, allegations of intelligence failure, the wars in Iraq and Afghanistan, prosecution of the war on terror, the Academy Awards and Golden Globe Awards, and March madness and the college basketball championships all won airtime. However important NATO and national security are for the nation, they will be obscured by the realities of what people wish to see and hear.

The only alternative is a literal full-court press by NATO officials. NATO needs a powerful and penetrating public information image, which it has never had to be concerned about before. Of course NATO never was deployed to Afghanistan in the first fifty-four years of existence and may actually end up as an alliance serving in Iraq.

ON THE HOME FRONT: CONGRESS AND THE PRESIDENT

Despite the creation of the Homeland Security Department and the realignment of the FBI that made counterterrorism the top priority, the national security organization is still largely a creature of the Cold War. Stovepipes and ruts tend to dominate structure. Argued before, the only way that permanent and positive change can be made is by changing the law and by changing Congress. The National Security Act of 1947 as amended is the basis. The NSC system, unification of the Department of Defense, and establishment of the CIA were principal achievements of the law.

Change is required in at least two ways. First, Title X must expand the responsibilities of the individual services beyond preparation for the conduct of prompt operations incident to combat. Services must also have greater authority and direction in dealing with aspects of the war on terror, stability, peacekeeping, support, and related operations in keeping with missions that are currently being carried out. Removing the air, sea, or land responsibilities for the individual services and directing preparation for joint and combined operations incident to operations and irrespective of medium, integration will advance.

Second, joint operations cannot work unless they become part of the interagency process. Defense can be entirely "joint." But unless other departments share this goal, then the stovepipes and ruts will never disappear. As long as military force, intelligence, law enforcement, and counterterror and stability operations in failed or failing states are required for success, the ability to accomplish this requires interagency joint operations.

One step Congress can take now is to transform the educational and training structure for national security and defense. The senior educational organization for national defense is the National Defense University (NDU), located at Fort McNair in the nation's capital. The National Defense University includes the National War College, the Industrial College of the Armed Forces, the service senior and junior war colleges, and other colleges and schools put under its jurisdiction.

The National Defense University should become the National Security University. The mission should shift to national security, of which defense is a critical part. Enrollment should expand from the current relatively small percent of non-DoD, State, and CIA students to provide education for the increasingly larger number of personnel actively engaged in national security.

This shift from NDU to NSU should extend down to service academies and ROTC units and could be expanded in student bodies and focused on national security. A certain number would enter the military services and tailor their programs accordingly. However, other students who work in national security from intelligence to law enforcement to homeland security to Treasury and even potential congressional staffers and civilian employees would be graduates. Perhaps each would get a reserve military commission and be required to spend time in the reserves, thereby broadening the base of Americans with military experience, a qualification that increasingly seems to gain approval across the nation.

The point is that national security is going to require a far larger segment of able and qualified citizens to serve. An NSU approach would be an excellent means of helping this transformation and beginning the education across the many lines and professions that will be critical to ensuring the nation's future safety and security. Further, to give NSU clout, consideration should be given to putting the president of the NSU on the NSC.

Third, and this can occur inside or outside the law, Congress must reorganize. There are good reasons why Congress is still organized around the thirteen appropriation bills as it has been for decades. However, as is the case with Homeland Security where there is so much oversight involving nearly every member, that simply cannot work.

Because national security is so important Congress should establish a National Security and Homeland Defense Joint Committee. This committee would have the responsibility of direct coordination and interaction with the NSC to reach preapproval on key policy decisions and resource priorities. However, because of partisanship Congress has moved to approving spending through gigantic omnibus bills that contain many provisions. Security and defense are too important to be subject to the same vagaries.

Toward the end of 2004, as this book comes off the press, Congress will be in for a rude awakening; the Department of Defense will have run out of money for operations in Iraq; the one hundred billion dollars that was appropriated for that purpose will have long been spent; and its budget request of $407 billion for fiscal year 2005 was increased by $10 billion. However, because of the cost of operations in Iraq and Afghanistan, the services will still be billions of dollars underfunded for the year. The range of underfunding could be anywhere from $20 to $60 billion depending on how events unfold. But the impact of this unexpected bill will be stunning.

Left to the current way of doing business, in the midst of a presidential election and an annual budget deficit approaching or exceeding six hundred billion, finding a sound way out of this predicament will not be easy. Reorganization of Congress will encourage closer interaction between the branches of government. However, the magnitude of this funding problem will almost certainly have a major, long-term disruptive impact on the Defense Department, military capability, and the private companies who supply these goods and services.

How can more rationality be imposed on a political system designed to be inefficient as the ultimate safeguard for individual freedom? One recommendation would be to write a Sarbanes-Oxley Law for government. Sarbanes-Oxley was meant to impose greater transparency on publicly traded companies and greater responsibility on chief executives to certify the accuracy of all financial, profit and loss, and other official statements. Congress and the president should be treated in similar fashion.

First, to get around the excesses of lumping all programs in single omnibus bills, members of Congress must be required to certify reading and understanding all pieces of legislation on which they vote. Failure to comply would disqualify or negate their vote.

Second, the appropriate official in the executive branch would certify that each budget for his department is to the best of his knowledge accurate. The same applies to laws. Any law that specifies certain spending and funding levels and, in due course, those thresholds are broken by certain percentages, say 25 percent or more, the legislation would come up for automatic review or recession. For example, the Medicare Prescription Drug Bill that projected original total costs of some three hundred fifty billion dollars and soon after being signed into law jumped in cost by about one hundred fifty billion dollars would fit this category. This requirement for fiscal responsibility would help in gaining control of fiscal deficits and accounting and would add missing discipline.

The interface of law enforcement and intelligence is an area that will require several major actions. The fundamental issue that can transform the nation's ability to deal with countering terror and waging this battle is sharing both information and intelligence. The United States has robust intelligence capability beyond the federal level. State, city, and local law enforcement also have put in place substantial related intelligence activities.

Beyond the federal government, state and local governments have substantial intelligence resources, most but not of all which are law enforcement. After September 11 many of these law enforcement capabilities were refocused on counterterrorism. Most states have well-developed counterterror squads and resources. Because state, city, and local law enforcement have long histories of joint operations, in the main, communications tend to work. In most states, police on local beats understand terror threats and know how to ensure proper units are notified.

In New York City, for example, the deputy mayor for counterterrorism is a retired army special forces colonel and ambassador in the Clinton administration with counterterror responsibilities in the State Department. New York City clearly has a more vivid and personal appreciation of the effects of terror and has done well in mobilizing facilities. Other states have employed individuals highly experienced in counterterror. A main complaint, about which more will be said, is the widespread perception of failure of the federal government to share necessary information and intelligence with state, city, and local law enforcement and counterterror officials. Too often in evaluating intelligence, state, city, and local capabilities are ignored. If the war on terror is to be won, and if the nation is to be made safer and securer, this is one area that must be rectified.

Another area that has to be rectified is how and who issues security clearances. The fact is that each department has its own process. A Top Secret clearance issued by one department will not lead to permanent and automatic clearance at other departments. Therefore, someone with Top Secret code word clearances transferring between departments must go through a complete security check. When he was national security advisor for President Reagan, Frank Carlucci made a universal security clearance program a high priority. It failed. Congress should pass a law to redress this failing. Not only would considerable time and money be saved but also information sharing would be assisted and, while there could be potential problems, the benefits seem to outweigh the costs.

Finally, the contradiction between protecting the nation and ensuring civil liberties cannot be neglected. Earlier, a Freedom and Security Commission was recommended. Congress should establish such a commission for oversight and review of those laws and regulations put in place to protect the nation to ensure an ultimate check and balance. With subpoena power and the authority to investigate, this commission would emulate the Securities and Exchange Commission in ensuring proper balance between government's responsibility to protect the nation and citizens' constitutional guarantees.

DEFENSE

The Defense Department has clearly had the leading role in the war on terror, as well as on the wars and peace that were waged in Afghanistan and Iraq. While engaged at an extraordinary level of operational activity, the department is still in the process of transformation. That process must be institutionalized. Moving toward a National Security University system and bringing joint operations and transformation to the broader interagency process can be useful in making these permanent.

The fact is that the all-volunteer force designed to prevent future Vietnams by making full-scale deployment of the active component dependent upon mobilizing substantial numbers of reserves, thereby requiring public support, probably cannot survive in present form. The Defense Department is beginning to examine alternatives. However, because many domestic constituencies are involved, as with base closing, this process will be highly political and not necessarily correctable in the short term.

The Pentagon should consider several of these recommendations. First, force sizing should be based on the ability to fight two contingencies, each requiring about 150,000–175,000 personnel for a total war fighting force of 325,000–350,000, with two more in training or reserve, for a total of 700,000 troops. Then 300,000–500,000 troops could be assigned for stability and in postconflict and related types of operations, leading to a total force of 1–1.2 million active duty personnel.

At a time when the Defense Department rightly claims insufficient land forces, moving to a smaller force may seem unworkable and infeasible. But the design of this force, in concert with the strategic redeployment plan and the far greater combat power available, will enable fewer numbers. As Rumsfeld noted, this would be done at "eighty miles an hour" and could not be done overnight. However, this is the general direction in which the nation must go if it is to be safer and securer.

Two other related points are important. In the war on terror and in Iraq, suicide bombers are a—or are *the*—weapon of choice. For some reason suicide bombers seem beyond the comprehension of many Americans and Europeans. Yet considerable experience with suicide bombers has been part of American history.

During World War II the Japanese practiced suicide as part of Bushido, or the warrior code. Hari Kiri, or suicide by either a ceremonial knife or Samurai sword, was preferable in many cases to surrender. Even Japanese civilians committed suicide rather than surrender.

But the truly frightening suicide attacks were Banzai charges by infantry and Kamikazes or divine wind pilots who attempted to crash their aircraft into allied ships. During the Battle for Okinawa thousands of Kamikaze strikes were launched against the allied naval force. As Fleet Admiral Nimitz remarked after the war, in prewar planning the only item the Navy had not anticipated was Japanese suicide attacks. About 5 percent of all of the Kamikazes hit their targets and managed to sink about 100 allied warships—remarkable losses in any case. Over a third did not reach their targets. The rest were shot down or simply missed.

Suicide bombers in Iraq and elsewhere are unlikely to reach the scope and potential threat that Japanese Kamikazes posed. But suicide was dealt with in an earlier war and came to be an accepted hazard of war. Similar thinking might happen here.

Last, for all the controversy over illegal billing and outright theft by major civilian contractors in Iraq, the fact is that the United States and the coalition allies could not operate without them. U.S. forces are dependent for food, shelter, and other amenities on civilian contractors. This has been one object of outsourcing. Indeed, in terms of reconstruction, only civilian contractors have the capability, and only civilian contractors have access to the world's largest air lifter, Russia's AN-124.

Retired Adm. Joe Lopez, a senior executive at Kellogg, Brown and Root (KBR), a subsidiary of Halliburton (a private company much maligned for allegedly committing wrongdoings), notes that of some fifteen thousand employees currently in theater, their killed and wounded proportionately are about half the U.S. military killed and wounded since hostilities ended. There may be wrongdoing. If there is, it must be stopped. If it can be proven, then offenders must be prosecuted and punished. However, congressional suggestions to bar these firms, and there are only a few American firms doing this important work in Iraq, would be a major error.

The reality is that no one else would be able to do the work, and the U.S. effort would fail. The blood shed by civilian employees working on behalf of the United States would have been wasted. Hence, a careful investigation and evaluation of what actually were criminal or unlawful acts and what were not is vital. A rush to justice would be disastrous.

A NATIONAL SECURITY POSTSCRIPT

One case casts a harsh and penetrating light on the global war on terror and why there must be fundamental changes in waging this fight. Much of this arose after the first draft of this book was completed, but these events reinforced the conclusion that U.S. strategy and tactics must be recast to attack causes and not only symptoms of the dangers that threaten the nation. While there may have been failures in the intelligence process over veracity and accuracy regarding Iraq, a larger failure is the fundamental difficulty in sharing information with appropriate offices and people across federal, state, and local boundaries.

The failure to find Iraqi weapons of mass destruction so far has precipitated a firestorm over whether intelligence failed or was ignored or manipulated by the White House. In fact the issue should not be whether or not the intelligence community failed. The important issue is the judgment that led to the decision to go to war and extends to judgments about what the peace in Iraq would entail. A corollary is determining how intelligence is shared, particularly with nonfederal authorities, a major point of the second case.

FAILURE OF AMERICAN INTELLIGENCE OR JUDGMENT

The revelations of late January and early February 2004 by David Kay, former head of the Iraqi Survey Group charged to locate Iraqi weapons of mass destruction (WMD), and CIA director George Tenet opened the Bush administration to massive criticism and controversy. The two central pillars of the administration's argument for war to remove Saddam—possession of WMD and imminence and urgency in eliminating that threat—were demolished. As noted, Kay told Congress and the public that it was unlikely WMD would be found, most likely because Iraq had in fact destroyed those weapons or did not have them in the first place.

Tenet gave a passionate defense of the intelligence community. Declaring that no one had ever told the president that the threat was imminent, the tone and content of his speech was in the starkest contrast to the presentation Secretary of State Colin Powell had made one day short of a year earlier to the UN in advancing the case for war. On that day, sitting directly behind Powell alongside U.S. ambassador to the UN John Negroponte was George Tenet. Powell, equipped with a sound and light PowerPoint slide show, told the UN Security Council that the evidence proving Saddam's possession of WMD was "irrefutable and unarguable." Part of Powell's briefing included chilling tapes of radio and telephone conversations between Iraqi officers presumably caught in the act as they exchanged orders over deploying and relocating Iraqi chemical and biological weapons.

The conclusion Powell drew left little question. Iraq had WMD and was moving them either across borders to Syria or other states or to tactical military positions in advance of using them should war ensue. In separate testimony to Congress, Defense Intelligence Agency head Vice Adm. J. Jacobi stated,

> . . . he will continue to defy international will and refuse to relinquish his WMD and related programs. Should military action become necessary to disarm Saddam, he will likely employ a host of desperate measures. We should expect him to use WMD on his own people, to exacerbate humanitarian conditions, complicate allied operations, and shift world opinion away from his own transgressions by blaming us.

Indeed, the majority view across government and among civilian experts was that Saddam had and would use WMD.[1]

Parallel commissions have been established in Washington by the president and Congress and in London by the prime minister to assess intelligence in how it related to September 11, the war in Iraq, and necessary steps to be taken to reinforce what is good and correct what is not. The official intelligence community of the United States government consists of a dozen and a half agencies that spread across most cabinet departments. The U.S. spends about $40–50 billion a year on the intelligence community, the bulk of it spent by the Department of Defense to buy technical systems such as satellites, communications intercept capabilities, and a range of other electronic surveillance and analytical equipment.

Director Tenet also revealed in his speech that the CIA's Human Intelligence or HUMINT capability was being rebuilt, a process that would take about five more years to complete. HUMINT has been a source of controversy for a long time. The argument over what HUMINT really can achieve and the degree that it has been overvalued has never been fully settled.

Following Vietnam and the hearings under Idaho Sen. Frank Church in the late 1970s, many excesses were alleged against the CIA. Testimony by former Director of Central Intelligence (DCI) William Colby gave further credence to these charges. As a result HUMINT resources were cut. Because the threat was the Soviet Union, common wisdom believed that sufficient intelligence could be gleaned through national technical means, i.e., satellites and electronics eavesdropping. President Jimmy Carter's administration and his DCI, retired Adm. Stansfield Turner, had the responsibility for imposing these changes, which have been long criticized for degrading HUMINT.

HUMINT obviously is an essential collection tool. The acronym crudely means spies. However, the usual modus operandi for the CIA was not to conduct James Bond–like covert spying missions by breaking and entering Soviet headquarters, although presumably a bit of that was done. Instead CIA agents operating under the cover of diplomatic immunity as second secretaries, press officers, or other embassy assignments had the duty of recruiting foreign sources who, in essence, would do the spying. Some of this was done by turning, i.e., convincing, bribing, blackmailing, or coercing foreign nationals to work for the CIA.

The Soviet KGB and other intelligence services routinely did the same with some notable successes. Kim Philby and other senior British MI-6 agents had been turned by the KGB, providing Russia with treasure troves of information in

1. This writer was one of the few who did not support that view. Based on interviews with senior military officials in this and at least one other country, with operational commanders who had been responsible for no-fly zone strikes, and with UN and IAEA documents, the conclusion I reached was that it was unlikely Saddam possessed weapons, although, clearly, he had strong ambitions and that, left unconstrained, he would obtain them.

the 1960s. Other CIA agents operating outside diplomatic channels at great personal risk were known as NOCs for not under official cover.

It cannot be proven to a certainty. However, this process of recruiting and turning foreign nationals probably achieved less success than the effort going into it. Most of the classic breakthroughs were through voluntary defections and Soviets who were walk-ins, secretly approaching the CIA to turn against their country. In the Cold War, with largely Anglo-Saxon and Caucasian individuals on both sides, this method of ferreting out information could work. But consider the war on terror.

As Clinton's first CIA director R. James Woolsey pointed out, a white male CIA operative who graduated from a first-rate American university would have some difficulty fitting into the culture of the locales the war on terror require. Terrorist networks are highly compartmentalized. Many members have known each other for years or have close family ties. These organizations were not, as Woolsey succinctly put it, American Kiwanis or 4-H Clubs.

Penetrating these organizations and dealing with these individuals required people of similar ethnicity or race and unsavory backgrounds to establish any credibility. Further, the laws and rules that bound the agency restricted use of these clandestine types and placed limits on how unsavory they could be. The result was akin to penetrating the Mafia with Ivy League types who spoke no Italian and had no common background.

The key issue is balance. Good analysis requires good analysts. HUMINT can be enormously useful. However, it is often overrated and is no substitute for judgment. Merely by enhancing HUMINT it should be assumed that intelligence will be made better. Alternatively, by failing to recognize that collection and analysis are at the heart of good intelligence, there will not be improvements.

The intelligence community relies on intense processes of analysis, review, and coordination in drafting a final product. National intelligence estimates (NIEs) are the best known. They are highly classified to protect not just the assessments but the sources and methods for obtaining the intelligence. Generally, national intelligence estimates have a certain nuance, with many footnotes to connote differences of opinion, caveats, and occasionally opposite minority positions. As George Tenet reminded everyone in his Georgetown speech on February 4, intelligence is not ever all wrong or all right. Shades of gray always exist.

Regarding the processing of the NIE on Iraq that was presented to the White House and Congress in the fall of 2002, the various commissions will examine in detail what happened and why. One point is unarguable. The president, by his own public statements, believed the NIE provided sufficient rationale on Iraqi WMD to justify war. Further, a vast majority of members of Congress, some who have since opposed the war, voted for it on the basis of the NIE.

As the presidential election grows closer and absorbs the energy and attention of the nation, very likely debate will focus on the narrow issue of intelligence and whether it failed or succeeded. That is a useful but secondary matter.

The future security and safety of the nation will rest on many factors, principally the judgment of its leaders about the decisions they make to achieve those aims. Making those judgments on the basis of any single input including intelligence would seem inadequate. Far more than intelligence is important.

The current political system makes judgment a commodity that is not only rare but also increasingly difficult to reach given how the process operates. That both the president and many members of Congress took the NIE on Iraq at face value and accepted it raises some interesting questions. Why were there no other sources inside the government to challenge the assumptions and provide alternative insights?

During the Cold War this absence of curiosity and opposing views did little damage, because the threat had so many inhibitions and internal contradictions that victory was likely almost irrespective of our actions outside going to war. If readers accept the possibility that the dangers could be as great as argued in this book, then it follows that greater judgment and understanding are essential.

Ultimately business never can be finished. It can be resolved. To do that, judgment will count. The challenge for Americans is to demand the best judgment from their leaders. On that basis, the answer to the question of whether the United States is safer and securer can have the merit of at least reflecting the truth, not merely political rhetoric and slogan. Absent those criteria, the United States will never be fully safe and secure again.

Epilogue

I n the two months between completing the manuscript in February and editing in April, both the war on terror and the reconstruction effort in Iraq received grievous setbacks. March 11, 2004, exactly two and a half years after the destruction of the Twin Towers in New York City, ten bombs exploded during rush hour in Madrid. Nearly 200 innocent civilians died; around 1,500 were injured. The bombers were Algerian terrorists with the longer term explicit aim of returning the "caliphate" or Islamic control to the Iberian peninsula. The expectation is that more of these attacks will occur, possibly in Athens during the Olympics and, with the fall of the Aznar government in Spain over its pre-election handling of the attacks, to coincide with November elections in the United States.

By late March the violence and chaos in Iraq spread. Shias, loyal to a young cleric named Moqtaba al Sadr, began an active campaign of resistance, attacking both coalition forces and civilians. Through April the violence continued. Meanwhile coalition forces were actively engaged in putting down Sunni insurgents in Fallujah and other cities. The fighting was as fierce as any during the brief war in 2003, and many senior officials in the United States were fearful of civil war breaking out in Iraq.

At home the Commission on Preventing Terrorist Attacks against the United States (known as the 9/11 Commission) held two and a half days of open hearings in Washington. The star witnesses were former White House counterterror czar Richard A. Clarke and, only after the White House was forced by public opinion to permit her testimony, national security advisor Dr. Condoleezza Rice. Clarke's testimony corresponded with the release of his new book, *Against All Enemies*, in which the former NSC official charged the Bush administration with not taking the threat of terrorism seriously enough before September 11 and then doing great harm to the war on terror afterward by going to war in Iraq. Mr. Clarke had spent ten years in the White House working for four presidents on counterterrorism. The White House vigorously struck back to counter the allegations and, with political allies in Congress and the media, accused Mr. Clarke of all manner of distortions and "profiteering" from his privileged position in government.

The White House at first refused to allow Rice to go before the commission. After an uproar and the ubiquitous appearance of Clarke across the American media, it consented. Rice's testimony went a long way to defuse Clarke's allegations. But observers did not understand why the White House had been so obstinate and politically short sighted not to put Rice on the public stand initially. The recommendations of this commission are due late July 2004.

The tragedy is that several more crucial elements are missing so far in assessing September 11, charges of intelligence or judgmental incompetence in failing to find the weapons of mass destruction that justified going to war in Iraq, the war on terror and the process of bringing democracy to Iraq. Rather like DoD's policy toward homosexual behavior—"don't ask, don't tell"—there has been a reluctance to ask the toughest questions. If that reluctance continues, the battle against terror cannot be successfully won nor can the nation be made safer. In simplest terms, what other questions should the nation be asking regarding the events before and after September 11?

First, on September 12, 2001, the United States had garnered an unprecedented amount of international good will. The NATO alliance, for the first time in history, invoked "Article V," declaring that the attack against America was an attack against NATO. Since then that good will has been squandered. And worse, it has been replaced with profoundly negative views among friends and allies abroad about America's policies in the war on terror and Iraq. How this came about and how, if at all, this damage can be repaired are questions that must be answered.

Second, the Bush administration's strategy rested on the assumption that the best means to bring peace and stability to the greater Middle East and to win the war on terror was to occupy Iraq, democratize it, and use that lesson as the basis for favorably transforming the strategic landscape of the region. But is that a valid, viable, and attainable aim? Or is that goal as far-fetched and explosive as the assumptions that produced the quagmire in Vietnam and other foreign policy disasters? This is perhaps the more important question, even if it comes second.

Third, on what basis did the administration assume that the postwar reconstruction and democratization would proceed smoothly, quickly, and with relatively low numbers of forces on the ground? Why was no one put in charge, and why did the administration fail to anticipate many of the issues and obstacles that seemed obvious to a wide range of commentators outside government and to members of Congress inside it?

Fourth, loudly and clearly, the presidential transition and confirmation processes are badly broken. Irrespective of the contested election that limited the new Bush team's preparations for assuming power and filling vital administration positions, it simply took too long to select, vet, and confirm officials. Cabinet secretaries are usually speedily confirmed. However, Secretary of Defense Donald Rumsfeld was "home alone" in the Pentagon for weeks until his deputy Paul

Wolfowitz came aboard in May. Depending upon second- and third-level echelon appointees from previous administrations is no substitute for having a functioning team in place early.

Clearance forms take days to fill out and require considerable expense for legal opinion. It is ironic that mistakes or errors in filling those forms could lead to criminal charges. Revealing the most personal matters of family and finances, available to the whole world, deters many who would otherwise serve.

For those lacking a security clearance, background checks also take time, and now that the FBI is dedicated to countering terrorism, the time lags can only increase. Surely there must be a better way to field senior officials to serve in government. "Why is this so?" is a question that the commission must address.

Fifth, as if we did not know, our process of government poses the greatest obstacle to taking decisive action absent an event as horrific as September 11 or Pearl Harbor. One lesson from Mr. Clarke's book is that while the Clinton administration fully understood the threat of al Qaeda, by his account it was not capable of responding in kind. And if the Bush administration did underestimate the danger of terrorism, how did the professionals in government, including Congress, permit that to happen?

My own personal quarrel with Mr. Clarke is not that he is right or wrong but that he may be underestimating both the dangers of the terrorist threat and the strategic consequences of occupying Iraq. Clearly any White House will go into a protective stance and erect strong defenses against such allegations. Have we forgotten Vietnam so soon? And a presidential campaign is perhaps the worse yet only way the nation can get to the bottom of such controversies. However, as with people, if there are symptoms of illness, not consulting a qualified physician is foolish.

Let us hope that this bipartisan 9/11 Commission can become that physician, along with other commissions that are making parallel examinations. Regardless of what these examinations conclude for this and earlier administrations, the toughest questions must be addressed. We cannot delude ourselves with a policy of "don't ask, don't tell."

Those questions must return answers. In that regard this writer's answers to what needs to be done are repeated below in Ten Steps to Defeat Global Terror:

1. *Americans must recognize that the term "global war on terror" implies an aim of winning that is simply not achievable.* There is no way that the "global war on terror," like wars against crime, drugs, poverty, and disease, can ever bring total victory. Instead we must understand that the battle is against "Jihadist extremism" and particularly those individuals who have captured and perverted a respected religion for political and revolutionary purposes and who use terror as a tool and a tactic to achieve political ends.

2. *Americans must realize the extent of the real danger posed by jihadist extremism is political; terror is not an end in itself* and the broader aims of these organizations and individuals are not significantly different from those of Lenin and the Bolsheviks a hundred years ago or Hitler and the National Socialist Party eighty years ago. The aim is to establish some form of regime or regimes steeped in the teachings of radical Islam with access to Saudi money and Pakistani nuclear weapons and with the broader intent of spreading their religion globally.

3. *And Americans must realize the danger posed by jihadist extremism is not the massive destruction of society through thermonuclear war. The new danger is one of massive disruption through real or threatened terrorist attacks* aimed at dislocating and disrupting our lives, doing great harm to our economies and our perceptions of safety and security, and causing us to overreact in ways that advance the enemies' agenda by imposing penalties on our freedom and individual liberties.

4. *In its current state, American governance is not up to the task of keeping the nation safe.* With an excessive fixation on campaigning for, winning, and keeping office rather than providing good governance as the sad outcome and with the profoundly negative partisan nature of politics today, we will fail in the task of keeping America safe, secure, and prosperous unless our government radically changes its priorities, policies, and organization.

5. *To prevail we must overhaul both our attitudes and machinery for securing the safety of the nation.* To that end the White House and the Congress must be made to work more closely through major reform in organization and in the law that moves national security from its orientation in the Cold War and the last century to the challenges and demands of this century.

6. *To remove some of the dysfunctional aspects of government, disciplines for Congress and the executive branch must be instituted to ensure the governing process is improved.* A proposed "Sarbanes-Oxley" law, passed in the wake of the corporate scandals to hold corporations, corporate leaders, and their accountants responsible, must be adopted for government.

7. *Fundamental changes in law enforcement and intelligence and in safeguards to protect individual liberties must be implemented at a time when security requires greater government imposition and intrusion.*

8. *America does not need a system for defense in the narrow sense but, more broadly, a system for ensuring security.* That means defense is a subset of security with obvious implications for how we organize, train, equip, prepare, and educate our people for this task.

9. *To prevail, we must adopt comprehensive, not narrow, solutions to the major problems facing us.* That means we must strive more to resolve the profoundly difficult conflicts between the Israelis and the Palestinians and between Indians and Pakistanis. This will require a global solution, with Arab recognition of Israel, and Israeli recognition and acceptance of a legitimate and viable Palestinian state. A modified Marshall Plan for the region, with full international support, is essential abroad as well.

10. *We must expand regional security arrangements more broadly. NATO is our first and most important relationship.* It must be transformed in keeping with the commitments made at the Prague Summit in November 2002. New relationships must be created. To that end, a conference such as the Conference on Security and Cooperation in Europe (CSCE) of the 1970s about nuclear proliferation and elimination of nuclear weapons, along with the possibility of use, will be created among all known and suspected nuclear powers. Korea will be the first test case in showing how the nuclear genie can be returned to its bottle permanently.

Afterword

here is much wisdom in what Harlan Ullman has prescribed here. The Bush Administration's approach to the Global War on Terrorism is clearly off the mark: a halfhearted strike against Afghanistan that eliminated the Taliban regime but failed to nab al Qaeda high command; a mistaken lunge into Iraq, which has overextended the armed forces and provided an opportunity for Al Qaeda to whack us on the cheap; an over reliance on the military at the expense of the other elements of national power; damaged relationships with allies and long-time friends; a disastrously deteriorating image in the Islamic world; a flawed effort to strengthen homeland security; and a fundamentally mistaken notion that the way to win is to kill terrorists.

Harlan is also right when he says the next Administration must take a new approach and move forward. As he notes, we must think more in terms of national security, not just national defense. And this means that the military role in the effort must be relegated to its appropriate priority: as a last resort and in self-defense. But even here, its possible use must be weighed against the consequences and costs, for it is difficult to change people's minds in the Islamic world by killing their relatives. Harlan has done a good job of sketching out some of the concepts and approaches that will be necessary. But let's start with the fundamentals.

Our opponent is a global religious ideology that extols men and women for sacrificing themselves in order to transform the world order. This is not just a religion but a religious ideology. That is, radical Islam interprets the world and claims to prescribe actions far beyond most religions. It has detail, depth, and denial—details of the prophets' writings, depth in almost any area (subject, of course, to the interpretations of the texts), and denial of other truths or interpretations. It is so powerful in its grip on the minds of its believers that it should be classed as an ideology. And it is this ideology of radical Islam that no Western thinker has as of yet given us the code to crack. While the United States has been hard at work to kill or detain terrorists, it will be even more important in the long term to dissuade them. The difficulty with the current Administration's tactics is precisely this: in dealing with fanatics, death is not deterrence, it is merely the martyrdom to which they aspire. The way to end the movement is to take away the ideology (not the religion itself, but just the faith in the most extreme interpretations) that motivates and justifies martyrdom.

So the place to start is with the concept of challenging an ideology itself. Consider the challenge the West faced with Communism. We have had long experience with the Marxist-Leninist approach to the world. It was written in books, taught in colleges and universities, and ceaselessly propagandized for seven decades from the Soviet Union and its satellite states. Like radical Islam, it also called for sacrifice, but the wellsprings of its motivations were of course different. Marxism-Leninism was materialist, denying the idealist vision of the world. It claimed to be scientific, purporting to find real-world causes for the evolution of societies and states. It was also optimistic, promising a far better future for mankind, and even the emergence of a far better human being. Through the teachings of Marxism-Leninism it was possible to understand and explain most of what happened in the world and to determine how one should take action in response.

Except there was a problem with Marxism-Leninism: its scientific base was not only flawed but also over time demonstrably unworkable as a prescription for policy and action. Attempting to implement Marxism-Leninism led to "contradictions," numerous contradictions including the failure of the Soviet system of economic growth to provide the basis for the material prosperity and the transformation of human beings and ultimately the failure to transform society as the ideology predicted. As history played out, the Soviet system and its Marxist-Leninist ideology were doomed by their own internal contradictions as their own citizens and leaders lost faith in what they were saying.

Now consider Islam. It has never been a unitary faith. The majority of those within Islam have practiced a strict religious code but not one which is incompatible with other cultures or even the secular societies of the West. Historically, Islamic culture led in scientific and mathematical innovation. Islam, as it evolved in the centuries after Mohammed, more a religion and less a complete ideology. Not so with radical Islam, the fundamentalist Wahabi and Shia sects—they are far more universalistic in their aspirations, dominant in their control, and exclusivist in their prescriptions.

It has become commonplace to recognize that the war on terror is actually a civil war within Islam—it is a struggle for dominance over those who follow the prophet Mohammed. But because of the universalistic pretensions of radical Islam, it is susceptible over time to the vulnerabilities of any ideology—namely, internal contradictions. Because radical Islam is inherently non-materialist, the contradictions have been easy thus far to evade. After all, there are no warriors returning to cast doubt on the prospect of the seventy-two virgins awaiting the martyr's arrival into Heaven. And there are no states yet having been returned to the posture of seventh-century Saudi Arabia struggling to live totally according to the prescriptions of radical Islam. Thus far the radicals have achieved control only in Iran—and here the religious leaders in power behind the parliament are struggling to cope with profound popular alienation. For the radical Sunni, only the warriors are thus far living their code, and here they are drawing from young people alienated from secular societies by material inequalities, cultural isolationism, or homesickness. Already contradictions are at work.

The *madrassas* in Pakistan provide one kind of contradiction. Imagine the graduates of these indoctrination and training camps in the modern world: they are taught to use a rifle whose working they cannot understand, communicate with radios whose principles are foreign, and consume food produced by methods that would be impossible to maintain with the limited education they are receiving. If this were to be the model for education under Islam, the society of which it is part would quickly decay back to the pretechnological age. The sad state of Afghanistan foreshadowed the problems that will confront radical Islam if it ever controls a state.

Of course, there are sophisticated software engineers and communicators who have rallied to the call of radical Islam. But the very Western education that gave them their skills also leaves them vulnerable to the doubts and concerns of a materialist, secular view of the world. And this is before the radicals have taken over even a single state. Their ideology has served well thus far to motivate acts of destruction, but it will hardly be sustainable if required to be engaged in practical problems of economic and political development.

The challenge for the West, therefore, is to recognize the ideological nature of the threat we are confronting and work to force it to face up to its inherent contradictions. In the near term, this should be a theme promoted by our friends in the Islamic world and by implications in our own communications with them. And in this effort our best advocates will be those among the radicals who can be "deprogrammed" and swung back over to the side of moderate, pragmatic Islam. Working with the Saudis and others, we should be encouraging the emergence of a school of the "deprogrammed" and promoting their presence within mosques and across the Islamic world. The value of captured terrorists may be less in the information they have to share and more in the disruption they can sow back inside the terrorist organizations if they are deprogrammed and then sent forward on a new mission for moderate Islam.

By the way, handling the ideological challenge is going to be very difficult for Westerners. But it is natural for the Saudis and other "believers." This is precisely the value that our Islamic friends and allies could bring into the efforts to deal with terrorists. While they may lack the forces, they are rich in the ability to use their faith. WE are desperately in need of their help.

Dealing with radical Islam as an ideology is the foundation for long-term success, but it will not be sufficient. As Harlan Ullman suggests, following through on the theme of national security and not just national defense, major changes are required in the priorities and institutional support to promote balanced growth and development around the world. Providing meaningful opportunities for personal advancement and family prosperity can become major factors in winning the struggle against radical ideologues, for easing the sting of historical humiliations and injustices will help dry up recruiting.

We are at the earliest stages of understanding and promoting worldwide economic development. There are major academic and political issues, the barest outlines of which are visible in the contentious issues of free trade and agricultural subsidies that bedevil trade negotiations. Despite the efforts of the United Nations Development program, we are far short of the skills, knowledge, and institutional assistance and leadership required to promote development.

One of the most important institutions should be NATO, dealing with counterterrorism, non-proliferation, and even development as security issues, rather than simply focusing on reaction forces and military activities. Of course this will be a major stretch beyond current thinking. For over five years the United States has continued to dog the Europeans to increase investments in their military forces. And, as Harlan Ullman describes, we are finally getting traction with the idea of NATO reaction force, to replace the Cold War vestiges that we held until the late 1990s. But programs like Partnership for Peace already demonstrate NATO's potential for adaptation and proclivity for changes. We should be pushing hard, above the military level, for these changes within NATO.

The changes should include a far deeper integration of the intelligence systems of the member states, a commitment to work non-proliferation and counterproliferation issues through NATO rather than unilaterally or bilaterally, a capability to conduct multinational counterterrorist operations (as last resort), and a commitment to pursue common and collective policies promoting development in the Middle East and Africa. While there are current U.S. efforts in these directions, they lack the coherence and priority necessary to successfully transform the Alliance. NATO should become the primary mechanism for trans-Atlantic security cooperation, but this can only occur with a stronger, more comprehensive vision for our needs in the struggle against Islamic extremism.

A broadened NATO can also be useful in dealing with problems of diplomacy in the Middle East and in providing diplomatic backstopping in resolving the dispute over Kashmir as well—work which, as Ullman points out, will help reduce the lure of radical Islam.

Still, there remains the problem of the current extremists and those who cannot be dissuaded from their resort to violence. Soon after 9/11, Secretary of Defense Rumsfeld pronounced that the best defense is a good offense. It was a statement not only factually incorrect but also institutionally self-serving, for it has become clear that the lack of effective protections at home encouraged highly risky military operations abroad.

This brings us to the issue of Homeland Security. As Ullman points out, if there was one key failure of the Bush administration, it was reluctance to embrace the true scale of needs for Homeland Security, which range from effective intelligence integration to more effective programs for port security, cyber security, immigration and tourism, and bioweapon defenses. Much of this requires new technology and new understandings about the use of data within society. These are major challenges requiring not only additional resources but also new laws and new protections for the rights of our citizens. Not much of this is glamorous; little makes good TV coverage, and much of it must remain highly classified. But what is critical now is to recognize the need for renewed attention to this area. The nation is at risk, but its defense can be strengthened considerably, and should be.

Overall, Harlan Ullman has given us a comprehensive and insightful assessment of the state of our campaign to protect ourselves against Islamic extremists. His ideas are worth the most serious consideration by policy makers and opinion leaders. It is not too late to turn the ship of state in the right direction, but we need a more accurate compass. This book helps provide it.

Wesley Clark

White House Summary of the Global War on Terror[1]

ATTACKING TERRORIST NETWORKS AT HOME AND ABROAD

The United States and its partners are attacking the leadership and infrastructure of terrorist networks at home and abroad. We are on the offensive, denying access to safe havens, funding, material support, and freedom of movement. Our efforts, and those of our allies, have disrupted terrorist plots and incapacitated terrorist leadership.

Defeating Terrorist Leadership and Personnel. Terrorist leaders provide overall direction for their campaigns of terror. While the loss of leadership forces some groups to collapse, others promote new leadership, while still others decentralize, making our challenge even greater.

- Of the senior al-Qaida leaders, operational managers, and key facilitators the U.S. government has been tracking, nearly two-thirds have been taken into custody or killed. Counterterrorist activities against al-Qaida leaders have weakened that leadership and diminished the group's ability to plan and carry out attacks.
- These efforts against senior al-Qaida leaders, including Khalid Shaykh Muhammad, the 9/11 mastermind, and Muhammad Atef, Osama Bin Ladin's second in command until his death in late 2001, have left gaping holes that the organization has yet to fill. Just as significant, with the help of allied nations, we have been able to disrupt terrorism facilitators—movers of money, people, messages, and supplies—who have acted as the glue binding the global al-Qaida network together.

International Operations, Arrests, and Investigations

- Pakistan has taken into custody more than 500 extremists, including al-Qaida and Taliban members. These include senior al-Qaida operational leader Khalid Shaykh Muhammad, September 11 conspirator Ramzi bin al Shibh, and USS *Cole* plotter Khallad Ba'Attash.
- Our counterterrorism cooperation with Saudi Arabia has significantly increased. Joint counterterrorist components have been established, information is being shared more broadly than before, and Saudi security forces have put several al-Qaida ring leaders and facilitators out of action,

Source: www.whitehouse.gov/homeland/progress/summary.html. 26 January 2004.

many of whom were involved in the May attacks in Riyadh, and arrested scores of other terrorists. Two of the most prominent terrorists include Yusif Saleh Fahd Allyari, who was killed on June 1, and Abu Bakr al-Azdi who was taken into custody on June 26.

- In Asia, the August 2003 capture of terrorist chief Hambali (aka Riduan bin Isomuddin)—a known killer who was a close associate of Khalid Shaykh Muhammad—has further disrupted terrorist leadership. Hambali is a lethal terrorist who is suspected of backing major operations, including the attack in Bali, Indonesia, and other recent attacks.
- Jordan continues its strong counterterrorism efforts, arresting two individuals with links to al-Qaida who admitted responsibility for the October 2002 murder of USAID Foreign Service Officer Lawrence Foley in Amman. They are very active against our terrorist foes.
- In June 2002, Morocco took into custody al-Qaida operatives plotting to attack U.S. and NATO ships in the Strait of Gibraltar. They, too, are making great efforts against this common enemy.
- The United States and Southeast Asian allies have made significant advances against the regional terrorist organization Jemaah Islamiyah (JI), which was responsible for the Bali attack last October that killed more than 200 people. In early August 2003, an Indonesian court convicted and sentenced to death a key JI figure in that bombing. Cambodian authorities shut down an organization whose employees were providing support to JI. Early this year Singapore passed a general law outlawing support to terrorists; this law was partially aimed at JI, but applies to any organization wishing to use Singapore as a base to plot acts of terror.
- Singapore, Indonesia, the Philippines, Thailand, and others in Southeast Asia took into custody terrorist leaders and operatives from local al-Qaida–affiliated terrorist groups or al-Qaida members traveling through their countries.
- France, Germany, the United Kingdom, Italy, Spain, and other European nations disrupted al-Qaida cells and are vigorously pursuing other terrorist leads.

Domestic Operations, Arrests, and Investigations

- Using authorities provided by the USA Patriot Act, the Department of Justice, working with other departments and agencies, has conducted its largest investigation in history, thwarting potential terrorist activity throughout the United States.
- Since September 11, 2001, the Department of Justice has charged over 260 individuals uncovered in the course of terrorist investigations, and convicted or secured guilty pleas from over 140 individuals, including

"shoe bomber" Richard Reid, who was sentenced to life imprisonment for attempting to destroy American Airlines Flight 63.
- The U.S. government has disrupted terrorist cells in Buffalo, Seattle, Detroit, and North Carolina, and alleged terrorist cells in Portland and Tampa.
  - In Buffalo, six U.S. citizens recently pled guilty to providing material support to al-Qaida and admitted to training in al-Qaida–run camps in Afghanistan.
  - In Seattle, Earnest James Ujaama pleaded guilty to providing material support to the Taliban.
  - In Portland, seven individuals were charged with engaging in a conspiracy to join al-Qaida and Taliban forces fighting against the coalition in Afghanistan.
  - Two individuals in Detroit were convicted of conspiring to support Islamic extremists plotting attacks in the United States, Jordan, and Turkey.
  - In North Carolina, members of a cell who provided material support to Hizballah were convicted, with the lead defendant sentenced to 155 years in prison.
  - In Tampa, Florida, eight individuals were indicted for their alleged support of the Palestinian Islamic Jihad (PIJ).
  - In Northern Virginia, 11 men were indicted for conspiring to violate the Neutrality Act and firearm laws based on their participation in military-style training in the United States and travel by several of the defendants to Lashkar-e-Taiba (LET) camps in Pakistan in preparation for conducting violent jihad in Kashmir and elsewhere.
  - In two narcoterrorism cases in San Diego and Houston, a number of individuals have been charged in connection with plots to trade weapons for drugs.

Denying Terrorist Haven and Sponsorship. We are working to deny terrorists the support and sanctuary that enable them to exist, gain strength, and plan and prepare for operations.
- During Operation ENDURING FREEDOM, the United States built a worldwide coalition of 70 countries that dismantled the repressive Taliban regime and denied al-Qaida a safe haven in Afghanistan.
  - In July 2003, our forces began Operation WARRIOR SWEEP along with elements of the Afghan National Army. We detained around 100 enemy fighters and captured a cache of some 25 tons of explosives.

In August and September 2003, our forces combined with Afghan militia forces to conduct Operation MOUNTAIN VIPER, which drove Taliban forces out of their remote mountain hideaways and out of Afghanistan, killing upwards of 200.

- Iraq is now the central front for the war on terror. Through Operation IRAQI FREEDOM, the United States and its coalition partners defeated Saddam Hussein's regime, effectively eliminating a state sponsor of terrorism and a regime that possessed and had used weapons of mass destruction (WMD). While members of the old regime and foreign terrorists are trying to reclaim Iraq for tyranny, we are taking offensive action against enemies of freedom in the Iraqi theater. Specific counterterrorism successes include:
  - Eliminating Iraq as a sanctuary for the Abu Musab al-Zarqawi network, which helped to establish a poison and explosives training camp in northeastern Iraq. Associates in the al-Zarqawi network also used Baghdad as a base of operations to coordinate the movement of people, money and supplies. Al-Zarqawi has a longstanding relationship with senior al-Qaida leaders and appears to hold a position of trust with al-Qaida.
  - Shutting down the Salman Pak training camp where members of many terrorist groups trained.
  - Killing or capturing to date 42 of the 55 most wanted criminals of the Saddam regime, including Saddam's sons Uday and Qusay.

Eradicating Sources of Terrorist Financing. The United States continues to work with friends and allies to disrupt the financing of terrorism by identifying and blocking the sources of funding, freezing the assets of terrorists and those who support them, denying terrorists access to the international financial system, protecting legitimate charities from being abused by terrorists, and preventing the movement of assets through alternative financial networks.

- On September 23, 2001, President Bush signed Executive Order 13224, freezing the U.S.–based assets of individuals and organizations involved with terrorism, and authorizing the Secretaries of State and Treasury to identify, designate, and freeze the U.S.–based assets of terrorists and their supporters.
- Since September 11, 2001, 209 of the 212 countries and jurisdictions in the world have expressed their support for the financial war on terror; 173 countries have issued orders to freeze the assets of terrorists; terror networks have lost access to nearly $200 million, which have been frozen or seized in more than 1,400 terrorist-related accounts around the world; of that total, over $73 million has been seized or frozen due to the efforts of the United States. Over 100 countries have introduced new

terrorist-related legislation, and 84 countries have established Financial Intelligence Units.

- U.S. authorities have issued blocking orders on the assets of more than 300 terrorist organizations and terrorist supporters, effectively denying them access to the U.S. financial system. The arrests of key financial facilitators and fundraisers have resulted in a significant decline in monetary contributions to terrorist organizations.
- The United States welcomes the September 6, 2003, political decision of European Union Foreign Ministers to designate the leadership and institutions of HAMAS as a terrorist organization and to freeze their financial assets.
- Since September 28, 2001, all 191 UN Member States have submitted first-round reports to the United Nations Security Council Counterterrorism Committee on actions they have taken to suppress international terrorism, including blocking terrorist finances as required under United Nations Security Council Resolution 1373.
- On November 7, 2002, the Treasury Department issued voluntary best practices guidelines for all U.S.–based charities to address concerns that charitable distribution of funds abroad might reach terrorist-related entities and thereby trigger a blocking action on the part of the Treasury Department.
- The FBI has aggressively pursued groups, individuals, and networks that provide financing for terrorism worldwide. The FBI uncovered facts showing that the Benevolence International Foundation (BIF) and Global Relief Foundation (GRF), Islamic charities holding themselves out to be conduits for directing aid to the poor and needy of the Islamic world, were actually conduits for funding Islamic fighters engaged in battle throughout the world, including Chechnya. BIF and GRF have been designated as global terrorist entities, and their international organizations have been successfully disrupted and dismantled.

SECURING THE HOMELAND

While the United States and our allies continue direct actions against terrorists and their infrastructures abroad, we are simultaneously strengthening the security of the homeland. The President signed significant new legislation that has advanced the war on terror, expanded our intelligence and law enforcement capabilities, bolstered transportation security, stockpiled vaccines, provided equipment and training for first responders, and reorganized the Federal government to address today's security challenges.

Since September 11, 2001, the President has signed numerous critical pieces of legislation into law including:

- Homeland Security Act of 2002
- USA PATRIOT Act of 2001
- Aviation and Transportation Security Act of 2001
- Public Health Security and Bioterrorism Preparedness and Response Act of 2002
- Enhanced Border Security and Visa Entry Reform Act of 2002
- Maritime Transportation Security Act of 2002

These laws, combined with the redirection of the Federal Bureau of Investigation (FBI) into an agency focused on preventing terrorism and the redoubling of efforts at the Department of Health and Human Services (HHS) to improve the nation's preparedness for identifying and responding to bioterrorism, have reorganized the institutions of the Federal government and provided significant resources in our arsenal to fight terrorism. To continue meeting the new threats of the 21st Century, the 2004 budget includes $41 billion to continue homeland efforts—more than doubling 2002 funding.

REORGANIZING THE FEDERAL GOVERNMENT

The Department of Homeland Security

- On November 25, 2002, the President signed the Homeland Security Act of 2002. The Act established a cabinet-level Department of Homeland Security (DHS) and transferred to it 22 existing Federal entities dedicated to preventing, mitigating, and responding to terrorist attacks on the United States. To execute the Act, the Administration undertook the most extensive reorganization of the government in the past 50 years to ensure that the United States would have one Department with the primary mission of protecting the American homeland.
- The Department is securing our borders, transportation systems, ports, and critical infrastructure; analyzing intelligence; augmenting the response capabilities of states and local governments; and conducting research to develop the next generation of terrorism countermeasures.

Intelligence and Information Sharing

- At the President's direction, the Director of Central Intelligence, the Director of the FBI, and the Secretaries of Defense and Homeland Security, working with the Attorney General and the Secretary of State, established the Terrorist Threat Integration Center (TTIC) to integrate and analyze terrorism threat–related information collected domestically and abroad. TTIC focuses on "connecting-the-dots," and since becoming operational on May 1, 2003, has issued hundreds of

terrorist threat-related products. TTIC has over 100 officers drawn
from partner agencies, a number expected to grow to several hundred by
this time next year. Also at the President's direction, key elements of the
CIA's Counter-terrorist Center (CTC) and the FBI's Counterterrorism
Division (CTD) will co-locate with TTIC in 2004 to enable still greater
coordination.

- To ensure that the Department of Homeland Security and other organizations needing information related to threats to the United States
promptly receive all such information, Attorney General John Ashcroft,
Secretary of Homeland Security Tom Ridge and Director of Central
Intelligence George Tenet signed a Memorandum of Understanding
(MOU) in March 2003. Actions being taken under this MOU, as well
as other interagency agreements and processes, are implementing a new
systematic approach to interagency information sharing.
- The CIA doubled the size of its Counterterrorist Center (CTC) and
quadrupled the number of counterterrorism analysts in the wake of September 11. In particular, CTC enhanced the number of analysts dedicated to chemical, biological, radiological, and nuclear issues, and
significantly increased the volume and scope of strategic and tactical
analytic reports delivered to senior Administration officials on such top-
ics as terrorist infrastructure and capabilities, network analysis, and terrorist profiles. CTC's cooperation with foreign intelligence services on
counterterrorism issues also has risen sharply.

Law Enforcement

- One of the most significant law enforcement tools in the war on terrorism is the USA Patriot Act. Passed in Congress by an overwhelming
majority, the Act has strengthened our ability to prevent, investigate,
and prosecute acts of terror by providing enhanced tools to detect and
disrupt terrorist cells. The Act removed major legal barriers that had
hampered coordination between the law enforcement, intelligence, and
national defense communities in their efforts to protect the American
people. Now police officers, FBI agents, Federal prosecutors and intelligence officials, while working within the safeguards of our Constitution,
can better protect our communities by uncovering terrorist plots before
they are carried out. The Act also updated the law to accommodate new
technology and new threats, allowing us to fight a digital-age battle with
modern tools. Many of the tools the Act provides to law enforcement to
fight terrorism have been used for decades to fight organized crime and
drug dealers, and have been reviewed and approved repeatedly by our
courts.

- Under the leadership of the Attorney General, the FBI is being transformed into an agency dedicated to the prevention of terrorism, while remaining committed to other important national security and law enforcement responsibilities.
    - Under the revised Attorney General's Investigative Guidelines and other reforms, the FBI has increased its analytic capabilities, improved law enforcement coordination, increased information sharing, and overhauled its information technology systems.
    - The Attorney General established the National Joint Terrorism Task Force at FBI Headquarters and expanded to 66 fully operational Joint Terrorism Task Forces. There is a JTTF in each of the 56 field offices, as well as a growing number in FBI's smaller Resident Agencies. These interagency organizations focus exclusively on terrorism, bringing together personnel, intelligence, and capabilities from Federal, state, and local law enforcement, DHS, the Intelligence Community, and other Federal agencies.
    - The FBI has centralized its own activities for intelligence gathering and analysis and, for the first time, created a 24-hour counterterrorism watch office to serve as the focal point for all incoming terrorist threat information. The watch office quickly distributes information to appropriate elements in law enforcement and the Intelligence Community.
    - The FBI's Legal Attache (Legat) Program, with over 45 offices around the world, greatly enhances the capability of the United States to wage the war against terrorism and addresses the full range of criminal threats to the United States in an increasingly globalized world. In the aftermath of the September 11 attacks and throughout the following year, FBI Legats facilitated the rapid deployment of approximately 700 FBI personnel overseas to investigate terrorist attacks against the United States and allied interests.
    - At the President's direction, the Department of Justice (DOJ) established the Foreign Terrorist Tracking Task Force (FTTTF), as one step in Federal agencies' efforts to identify potential terrorists attempting to enter or remain in the United States. Managed by the FBI with participation from DHS, DoD, and other government agencies, analysis conducted by the FTTTF has resulted in over 300 referrals made to law enforcement or Intelligence Community agencies.
    - Under the direction of the Attorney General, the U.S. Attorneys have constituted and led Anti-Terrorism Task Forces (ATTF) in each of their respective districts, coordinating numerous

anti-terrorism initiatives, information sharing programs and training sessions, and forging unprecedented levels of outreach and cooperation with state and local law enforcement.

Analysis and Warning

- The Department of Homeland Security disseminates information regarding the risk of terrorist attacks to Federal, state, and local authorities, to include the public and private sectors. Further, information regarding the risk of terrorist attacks, including such information prepared by DHS, is distributed to all FBI Joint Terrorism Task Forces through the FBI's National Joint Terrorism Task Force.
- The Information Analysis (IA) division of the Information Analysis and Infrastructure Protection (IAIP) directorate of DHS is doing unprecedented work in assessing the nature and scope of terrorist threats to the homeland. Some of the Department's work in this area is carried out in part by IA analysts who are full partners and participants in the President's Terrorist Threat Integration Center (TTIC) initiative, and physically located at TTIC. Other threat analysis is carried out by IAIP analysts located at Headquarters, in close coordination with TTIC. IAIP also will provide full intelligence support to all elements of DHS, including conducting its own independent analysis of threats to the homeland, and "red teaming," in which DHS analysts try to anticipate potential attacks by thinking like the terrorists. DHS relies upon the analysis produced by IA to help determine priorities for protective and support measures and provide information to Federal, state, and local government agencies and authorities, and private sector entities.
- The multi-agency partners in TTIC integrate and analyze terrorist threat-related information, collected domestically and abroad, to form a comprehensive threat picture, and disseminate such information to recipients who take preventive action.
- Since September 11, 2001, the FBI has received and assessed the credibility of approximately 3,600 threats to the United States. The National Threats Warning System has issued 62 threat warnings, 55 Be On the Lookout (BOLO) alerts, and 82 Intelligence Bulletins. These warnings are disseminated to more than 18,000 state and local law enforcement agencies in the United States, over 60 Federal agencies and subcomponents, and all U.S. Attorneys.

Military

- To strengthen the effectiveness of U.S. military forces engaged in homeland security, the President authorized the establishment of U.S. Northern

Command (USNORTHCOM). It began operations on October 1, 2002, and will be fully operational by October 2003. USNORTHCOM eliminates gaps among the different military organizations that currently have homeland defense responsibilities and strengthens military support to civilian agencies.

Reducing America's Vulnerability to Terrorism. DHS is maintaining America's open land, sea and air borders, facilitating the legitimate flow of commerce and people, while at the same time detecting and interdicting terrorists and their weapons before they enter the United States. The Administration is also strengthening our critical infrastructure protection efforts by coordinating the activities of Federal agencies responsible for infrastructure protection and combining information from the Intelligence Community, Federal, state, and local law enforcement, and the private sector to map threats to critical infrastructure against known vulnerabilities.

Operation Liberty Shield

- The Department of Homeland Security, in conjunction with numerous departments and agencies of the Federal government, implemented "Operation LIBERTY SHIELD" to increase protective measures during a period of heightened alert in March 2003. This comprehensive national plan to protect the homeland increased security at our borders, strengthened transportation sector protections, enhanced security at critical infrastructure, increased public health preparedness and ensured that all Federal response assets could be rapidly deployed. It built the foundation for our country's critical infrastructure protection programs.

BORDER SECURITY

Document Security

- The Department of State has developed new tamper-resistant visas, extended the application review process, enhanced the visa lookout system, and improved information sharing among U.S. law enforcement agencies and the Intelligence Community. In 2003, visa screening requirements were tightened, requiring face-to-face interviews for almost all applicants.
- The Department of State has developed the Terrorist Interdiction Program (TIP) to assist nations at high risk of terrorist transit by providing them with a computer database system that enables border control officials to quickly identify people attempting to enter or leave the country. TIP is now in 12 nations and will expand to 18 by the end of 2003.

Tracking, Monitoring, and Interdiction

- In December 2001, the United States and Canada signed the Smart Border Declaration, which included 30 action items for increasing security, enhancing joint law enforcement, improving physical and technological infrastructure, and facilitating the trade and movement of people between the two countries. The U.S.–Mexican Border Partnership, signed in March 2002, contains a similar 22-point action plan.
- Strong cooperation between the United States, Canada, and Mexico has resulted in several programs that will enable the Department of Homeland Security to focus its security efforts and inspections on high-risk commerce and travelers: Free and Secure Trade Initiative (FAST), the U.S.–Canada NEXUS program, and the Secure Electronic Network for Traveler Rapid Inspection (SENTRI).
- DHS is operating the Student and Exchange Visitor Information System (SEVIS), which tracks foreign students who come to the United States, ensuring they are actually enrolled and attending classes, while facilitating the entry of legitimate students.
- The U.S. Visitor and Immigrant Status Indication Technology system (U.S. VISIT) is designed to make entering the United States easier for legitimate tourists, students, and business travelers, while making it more difficult to enter the United States illegally through the implementation of biometrically authenticated documents. The system will utilize biometric identifiers—a photograph and fingerprints—to build an electronic check-in/check-out system for people coming to the United States to work, study, or visit. The U.S. VISIT system will replace the current NSEERS program, integrate the SEVIS program, and accomplish the requirements for an automated entry/exit system. The system will scan travel documents to enable inspectors to check against databases to determine whether the individual should be detained or questioned further. U.S. VISIT will begin its first phase of operation at international air and sea ports of entry by the end of 2003.
- Approximately 10,000 Border Patrol Agents are now patrolling our borders. By January 2004, some 1,000 will be assigned to the Canadian border, an increase of more than 50 percent over the past 12 months.

Port Security

- Enhancing our security measures abroad, the DHS Bureau of Customs and Border Protection (BCBP) launched the Container Security Initiative (CSI), establishing tough new procedures to target high-risk cargo before it is loaded on containers headed for U.S. ports. As of August 2003, 19 of the world's major ports, handling two-thirds of cargo containers destined for the United States, have agreed to participate in CSI. There are plans to expand the initiative to 27 additional high volume-ports in strategic locations throughout the world.

- Operation Safe Commerce (OSC) is a public-private partnership to fund new initiatives designed to enhance tracking and security for container cargo moving through the international transportation system to the United States. OSC helps facilitate the efficient movement of legitimate commerce.
- DHS now requires electronic advance cargo manifests from sea carriers 24 hours prior to loading in a foreign port to give officials more time to check for potentially dangerous cargo.
- Non-Intrusive Inspection (NII) technology inspects shipping containers determined to be high risk by the U.S. Automated Targeting System (ATS). Sophisticated large-scale radiation detection portals and hand-held technologies substantially increase the likelihood that nuclear or radiological materials and weapons will be detected.
- Since September 11, the Coast Guard has made the largest commitment to port security operations since World War II, including over 124,000 port security patrols and 13,300 air patrols. The Coast Guard boarded more than 92,000 high interest vessels, interdicted over 9,473 individuals attempting to enter the United States illegally, and created and maintained more than 94 Maritime Security Zones.
- In implementing the Maritime Transportation Security Act of 2002, the Coast Guard will require ports, vessels, and facilities to perform security assessments, develop plans, and address security deficiencies. Both domestic regulations and international requirements oblige all nations to develop and implement port and ship security plans by July 1, 2004.

Aviation Security

- There are some 48,000 newly trained Federal screeners deployed at our nation's airports, where new baggage inspection equipment helped the Transportation Security Administration (TSA) institute 100 percent checked baggage screening. All airport personnel must now undergo background checks.
- DHS and the Department of State suspended the Transit without Visa program (TWOV) and the International-to-International transit program (ITI), eliminating terrorists' ability to exploit these programs to gain access to U.S.–bound aircraft or the United States.
- The Federal Air Marshal program was expanded so that thousands of protective air marshals are now flying on commercial aircraft.
- All large commercial passenger aircraft flying within or to the United

States now have hardened cockpit doors to help prevent their hostile takeover. Armed pilots who have received Federal training can also defend their aircraft.

- DHS and other agencies are working with foreign countries, airports, and local and Federal law enforcement agencies to prevent the proliferation of shoulder-launched missiles that can be used against commercial aircraft. DHS is conducting vulnerability assessments at key U.S. airports.

Critical Infrastructure Protection

- "Critical infrastructure protection" refers to efforts to enhance the security of physical and cyber-based systems and assets that are essential to national security, national economic security, or public health and safety. Protective actions include a wide range of activities designed to reduce the vulnerability of critical infrastructures in order to deter, neutralize, or mitigate terrorist attacks.
- DHS meets with industry on a regular basis to share information, lessons learned, and best practices. DHS has been working with the economic and industrial sectors to develop a range of vulnerability assessment tools to meet their unique security challenges and needs. The security plans factor in the identified vulnerabilities to create a community-based approach to enhancing the security of critical infrastructure. Recent efforts include the following:
    - DHS has recently begun a comprehensive training program that involves chemical facility operators, site security managers, and local law enforcement personnel. The training takes those who would be involved in the prevention of a terrorist attack at a facility and ensures everyone understands its vulnerabilities, risks, and protective measures. The training uses realistic terrorist threat information, and has resulted in a public/private team better equipped to prevent terrorists from using our chemical facilities as a tool to attack Americans.
    - The U.S. chemical industry has worked in partnership with the Department of Homeland Security and others to evaluate vulnerabilities and put enhanced measures in place to ensure the safety of its facilities and neighboring communities.
    - DHS has developed reports on common vulnerabilities to critical infrastructures, reports on indicators of terrorist activities in or around facilities, and security plan templates for use by local and state law enforcement personnel, as well as the private sector. The Department is beginning a national effort to provide technical

assistance with the implementation of tailored security plans based on these documents.

- The Department recently created a Soft Targets Unit with the Protective Security Division to assist state and local law enforcement in reducing vulnerabilities to attack in shopping malls, entertainment venues, sports stadiums, and other public gathering areas.
- Passage of the Safe Explosives Act of 2002 strengthened the ability of the Bureau of Alcohol, Tobacco, Firearms and Explosives' (ATF) to prevent the acquisition of explosive materials by terrorists and others who would misuse them. Among other things, it expanded the Federal explosives permitting requirement to ensure that all persons who acquire explosives have been subjected to a background check and issued an ATF permit.
- The Information Analysis and Infrastructure Protection (IAIP) division of DHS established a Critical Infrastructure Information Program Office to handle voluntarily submitted information about threats and vulnerabilities. IAIP released draft regulations for implementing the Critical Infrastructure Information Act this spring and is now developing the final guidelines.

Cyberspace Security

- In June 2003, DHS created the National Cyber Security Division (NCSD) as a focal point for the Federal government's interaction with state and local government, the private sector, and the international community concerning cyberspace vulnerability reduction efforts.
- A central element of the NCSD is the Cyber Security Tracking Analysis and Response Center, which examines cyber security incidents and coordinates efforts to mitigate damage.
- During the recent rash of internet worms and viruses, the NCSD played a central role in coordinating national response efforts. NCSD rapidly convened technical experts from government, industry, and academia to analyze and develop guidance that they promptly shared with Federal, state and local governments, infrastructure operators, and individual computer users.
- Through the FedCIRC (Federal Computer Incident Response Center) program, NCSD also provided extensive guidance and assistance to Federal agencies during these virus and worm events. This aid significantly reduced the impact of these events on government systems.

Enhancing Detection, Response, and Recovery from Biological and Chemical Terrorism

- The Administration has bolstered the nation's defense against an attack with a biological or chemical weapon through several parallel and complementary efforts. DHS, the Department of Health and Human Services (HHS), and other agencies are focused on detection, response, and research and development.
- The Administration has directed approximately $2.5 billion to state and local public health agencies, hospitals, and other health care entities since September 11, 2001, to improve planning, implement rapid secure communications, increase laboratory capacity, and upgrade the capacity to detect, diagnose, investigate and respond to a terrorist attack with a biological agent, and provide clinical care and treatments for those affected.
- As part of his proposed Project BioShield, the President has requested $5.6 billion to accelerate the development and acquisition of next-generation vaccines and other products to counter bioterror threats. Project BioShield will accelerate the National Institutes of Health's (NIH) research and development of countermeasures, permit the FDA to make promising treatments quickly available during emergencies, and allow the U.S. Government to purchase needed countermeasures as soon as they become available.
- The National Institutes of Health's (NIH) civilian biodefense research budget has been increased from around $100 million prior to September 11, 2001, to $1.5 billion in 2003. The President has proposed an additional $1.6 billion for 2004. The NIH's investment focuses on new drugs and vaccines, and diagnostics for high-threat agents such as anthrax, smallpox, Ebola, and others.
- DHS's BioWatch program has placed detectors in over 30 cities, providing the capability to detect a variety of biological agents of concern. Samples from these detectors are tested in federally supported local laboratories and provide results within 12 to 36 hours.
- The Strategic National Stockpile was enlarged to 12 pre-positioned 50-ton packages of drugs, vaccines, medical supplies, and equipment that stand ready for immediate deployment to anywhere in the United States within 12 hours. In the last year, the stockpile has been expanded to treat 12 million persons exposed to anthrax and to treat injuries following a chemical attack.
- The Department of Defense has immunized over 490,000 soldiers and support personnel against smallpox. Though the Administration does not currently recommend smallpox vaccinations for the general public, HHS has acquired enough smallpox vaccine to immunize every person

in the United States, if needed, following a smallpox attack and has begun immunizing health care personnel who would administer the vaccine.

Agriculture and Food Security

- The Food and Drug Administration (FDA) increased the number of food safety inspectors by 655, doubling its capacity to conduct safety inspections of our food systems.
- The U.S. Department of Agriculture (USDA) increased personnel at borders by 50 percent over FY 2000 levels to enhance efforts to keep foreign agricultural pests and diseases from entering the United States. The number of ports of entry with FDA staffing has increased from 40 to 90.
- The USDA and HHS issued complementary regulations establishing new safeguards for the control of select agents that could pose a threat, in accordance with the Public Health Security and Bioterrorism Preparedness and Response Act of 2002.
- The National Animal Health Laboratory Network and the National Plant Diagnostic Laboratory Network were developed with land-grant universities and state veterinary diagnostic laboratories around the country to create plant and animal health laboratory networks that have increased our capability to respond in an emergency.
- The food regulatory agencies, Food Safety and Inspection Service (FSIS) and the Food and Drug Administration (FDA), have evaluated over 35 different domestic and imported food and product categories for vulnerabilities to terrorist attack. The Administration is evaluating and implementing plans and new technologies to protect against potential attacks to the food supply.

Enhancing Emergency Preparedness and Response Capabilities. Despite our best efforts at preventing future attacks, terrorism will continue to be a threat, and we must always be prepared to respond to an attack. We are better prepared to minimize the damage and recover from any future terrorist attacks by equipping and training our first responders and public health personnel.

First Responders

- The U.S. government provided $7.9 billion in grants between 2002 and 2003 to help state and local responders, public health agencies, and emergency managers prepare for terrorist attacks. The President's 2004 Budget request included an additional $5.2 billion to ensure first responders and public health and medical personnel are properly trained and equipped Progress Report on the Global War on Terrorism 16 to respond to terrorism. This includes funds to purchase protective gear for working in hazardous environments and devices for detecting and disarming explosives and other dangerous materials.

- Departments and agencies throughout the government have taken actions to increase preparedness by providing first responders with training and exercise opportunities. Since September 2001, approximately 346,000 responders have been certified on basic preparedness concepts.

- At the Federal level, a recent weapons of mass destruction exercise entitled TOPOFF2, involved two major U.S. cities (Chicago and Seattle), as well as major response elements within the U.S. government up to the cabinet level, and portions of the Canadian government. This exercise provided an opportunity for analysis of the abilities of Federal, state, and local response mechanisms to respond to a complex terrorist attack. In August 2003, the Department of Defense conducted a multi-level exercise to test USNORTHCOM's ability to respond to multiple, simultaneous homeland security and Federal relief events.

- During FY 2003, DHS provided assistance to upgrade the number of Urban Search and Rescue teams capable of addressing weapons of mass destruction (WMD) from 6 to 28.

- More than 700 Citizen Corps Councils have been formed in communities, states, and territories to better prepare communities to meet the threats of terrorism, crime, public health issues, and other disasters. Community Emergency Response Team (CERT) training is now available in 417 localities in 46 states and one U.S. territory.

National Response Plan

- The Department of Homeland Security is creating a fully integrated national emergency response system that can adapt to any terrorist attack or natural disaster. They are also consolidating Federal response plans and building a national system for incident management.

- The National Response Plan is being developed, under the direction of the Secretary of Homeland Security, to coordinate and integrate all Federal domestic incident prevention, preparedness, response, and recovery plans.

- The President directed the development of a National Incident Management System (NIMS) to make Federal, state, and local entities interoperable during incidents. Development of the NIMS will involve consultation with state and local organizations, the private sector, and other Federal agencies.

STRENGHTENING AND SUSTAINING THE INTERNATIONAL FIGHT AGAINST TERRORISM

Success in the global war against terrorism depends on the actions of a powerful coalition of nations maintaining a united front against terror. Over 170 nations continue to participate in the war on terrorism by taking terrorists into custody, freezing terrorist assets, and providing military forces and other support. International organizations are becoming more agile, adapting their structures to meet changing threats. We support the actions of our partners as they facilitate international, regional, and local solutions to the challenge of terrorism.

Global Efforts to Fight Terrorism

- On September 11, 2001, only two nations had adhered to all 12 international anti-terrorism conventions and protocols. Now more than 30 nations belong to all 12, and many more have become parties to most of the conventions and protocols and have passed implementing legislation to put them into effect.
- The United Nations Security Council, through its Counterterrorism Committee (CTC), has taken on a new, important role under Resolution 1373 as the coordinator of UN member states in efforts to raise the global level of counterterrorism capability, cooperation and effectiveness.
- On June 26, 2002, President Bush secured agreement on a U.S.–sponsored plan for G-8 action on transport security. The G-8 committed to accelerated action on pre-screening people and cargo, increasing security on ships, planes and trucks, and enhancing security in airports and seaports. The G-8 initiative also enhances transport security through better intelligence, coordinated national efforts, and international cooperation against terrorist threats.
- At the 2003 G-8 Summit in Evian, leaders established a Counterterrorism Action Group (CTAG) of donor countries to expand and coordinate training and assistance for countries with the will, but not the capacity, to combat terror, focusing on critical areas such as terrorist financing, customs and immigration controls, illegal arms trafficking, and police and law enforcement.
- On June 2, 2003, President Bush agreed with other G-8 Leaders at the Evian Summit to a series of controls on Man-Portable Air Defense Systems (MANPADS), surface-to-air missile systems designed to be carried and fired by individuals, which are a major threat to civil aviation. Additionally, the Department of State is working to strengthen the 2000 Wassenaar Arrangement guidelines on these shoulder-launched missile systems and is providing bilateral assistance to help eliminate at-risk stockpiles and improve security of national inventories of these weapons.

- The G-8 Leaders took significant steps to expand international cooperation on projects to prevent the proliferation of weapons of mass destruction in the first year of the Global Partnership Against the Spread of Weapons and Materials of Mass Destruction launched by leaders in June 2002. The Partnership has been broadened to include Finland, the Netherlands, Norway, Poland, Sweden, and Switzerland. The G-8 also launched an initiative to improve the security of radioactive sources and prevent their use by terrorists in so-called "dirty bombs."
- On May 31, 2003, the President announced the Proliferation Security Initiative (PSI), designed to combat the trade in weapons of mass destruction, their delivery systems, and related materials to and from states and non-state actors of proliferation concern. This proliferation, together with terrorism, constitutes the greatest threat to international security. On September 4, 2003, Australia, France, Germany, Italy, Japan, the Netherlands, Poland, Portugal, Spain, and the United Kingdom joined the United States in announcing the PSI Statement of Interdiction Principles, consistent with national legal authorities and international law and frameworks.
- The International Atomic Energy Agency's (IAEA) Nuclear Security Action Plan provides advice, training, and equipment to its 136 Member States to combat nuclear terrorism. The United States has contributed $15.9 million since the Action Plan's inception in March 2002. The IAEA coordinates its nuclear security activities with the United States and other donor states to mutually reinforce our nuclear security goals.
- International arms export control regimes—Australia Group for chemical/biological weapons, Wassenaar Arrangement, Missile Technology Control Regime and Nuclear Suppliers Group—have added to their guidelines the need to prevent acquisition of controlled items by terrorists, and are in the process of adopting other measures to achieve this goal.
- The Radiological Threat Reduction program identifies and pursues actions that can be taken to reduce the threat of a radiological attack against the United States. Working with the International Atomic Energy Agency, this program aims to assist countries that are technically or financially unable to secure high-risk orphan or surplus sources.
- The Department of Defense established the Regional Defense Counterterrorism Fellowship Program, funded at $20 million per year, to provide coalition counterparts with the training and education necessary to establish and maintain effective counterterrorism programs in their home countries.
- The Department of State's Foreign Military Financing (FMF) program, which focuses on military professionalism and the equipping of often

beleaguered armed forces throughout the world, is providing a direct infusion of badly needed resources used to combat terrorism.

Regional Efforts to Fight Terrorism

- On June 26, 2003, the President announced a $100 million Eastern Africa Counterterrorism Initiative to expand and accelerate counterterrorism efforts with Kenya, Ethiopia, Djibouti, Uganda, Tanzania, and other countries, as appropriate.
- On October 26, 2002, President Bush obtained agreement for an Asia-Pacific Economic Cooperation (APEC) Leaders plan on Fighting Terrorism and Promoting Growth that contains specific commitments to secure key Pacific Rim infrastructure B transport, finance, and communications B from exploitation or attack by terrorists.
- The North Atlantic Treaty Organization (NATO) has endorsed an ambitious transformation agenda designed to enhance its capabilities by increasing deployment speed and agility to address new threats of terrorism. Other organizations, including the Organization of American States (OAS), the European Union (EU), the Organization for Security and Cooperation in Europe (OSCE), the Association of South East Asian Nations (ASEAN), the Australia, New Zealand, and United States (ANZUS) Treaty members, the APEC forum and others, took concrete steps to combat terrorism more effectively and to cooperate with each other in the fight.
- The Department of State initiated a Counterterrorism and Law Enforcement Joint Working Group with Pakistan and greatly enhanced counterterrorism cooperation with India, Japan, and China. It has also launched an intensive training program for Pakistan counterterrorism units in Crisis Response Team and investigation techniques.
- Colombia has developed a democratic security strategy as a blueprint for waging an aggressive campaign against designated foreign terrorist organizations (FTO) such as FARC, ELN, AUC, and other illegal armed groups. U.S. Congressional passage of new authorities for Colombia, in July 2002, enhanced the flexibility of U.S. security assistance against illicit drugs and terrorism. We are now noting an elevated rate of desertion from Colombian FTO ranks, and the AUC declared a ceasefire in December 2002. In July, the AUC and Government of Colombia agreed to formal peace talks.
- Last year Argentina, Brazil, Paraguay, and the United States established a regional counterterrorism mechanism to focus on practical steps to strengthen financial and border controls and legislation and enhance law enforcement and intelligence sharing. The mechanism is built on the

framework of the "Tripartite Commission of the Triple Frontier," creating the "3+1" format.

- The Department of State has strengthened its counterterrorism cooperation with Russia through the bilateral Counterterrorism Working Group, which has held regular sessions in the United States and Russia, dealing with terrorism issues over most of the world.
- Using a combination of diplomatic encouragement and operational support (including our Georgia Train and Equip military assistance program), the United States supported Georgia's successful efforts against terrorists in the Pankisi Gorge. These efforts led to arrests of suspects wanted for terrorist actions in Russia and Western Europe.

Diminishing the Underlying Conditions that Terrorists Exploit. Many terrorist organizations exploit to their advantage conditions of poverty, social disenfranchisement, unresolved political and regional disputes, and weak state structures. The United States has embarked on a number of initiatives designed to foster broadbased economic growth and development, open societies to global trade and investment, and promote the health and education of people worldwide. As more countries become active participants in the global economy and offer their people the benefits of good governance, economic opportunities, and health and education, terrorists will be denied both recruits and safe havens.

Global and Regional

- Based on Presidential direction, the United States developed and began implementation of the Middle East Roadmap to encourage progress towards a long-term resolution to the Arab-Israeli dispute.
- This spring, the President launched the Middle East Initiative, which contains a number of economic and trade actions, including a proposed Middle East Free Trade Agreement, to reduce economic disparities that fuel discontent, anti-American violence and terrorism.
- In February 2002, and again in September 2002, President Bush committed additional U.S. assistance to Pakistani President Musharraf. This included $2 million in democracy assistance for technical support, including training of election commissioners, observers, and political party monitors for the October 2002 Legislative Elections; a multi-year $100 million educational support program; Department of Labor grants to combat child labor and provide vocational training; initiation of discussions on expanded cooperation in science and technology; and creation of a Joint Economic Forum to expand cooperation. During President Musharraf's June 2003 Camp David meeting, President Bush announced the Administration would work with Congress to provide Pakistan with

a comprehensive $3 billion five-year assistance package to bolster Pakistan's counterterrorism capabilities and alleviate poverty conditions on which terrorists strive.

- In March 2002, the President launched the Millennium Challenge Account (MCA) initiative, a 50 percent increase in official U.S. development assistance over three years, and a challenge to donors worldwide to increase the effectiveness of their foreign aid. The MCA will channel its funds only to developing countries that demonstrate a strong commitment to ruling justly, investing in their people, and encouraging economic freedom. The focus of this assistance is to significantly increase the sustained long-term growth rates of recipient countries and create models of stability and progress throughout the developing world.

- In December 2002, the Secretary of State inaugurated the Middle East Partnership Initiative (MEPI), which is comprised of programs to encourage democratic growth in societies that have been denied it, economic freedom to foster growth and reduce hopelessness and despair, and high quality, inclusive education to train youth for a global economy.

- In 2002, the United States launched the Trade for African Development and Enterprise (TRADE) initiative, a multi-year capacity building initiative that will promote regional integration and cooperation, as well as the Africa Education Initiative to increase access to quality basic education opportunities on the continent.

- United States continues to provide assistance to the countries of the Andes through the Andean Regional Initiative, which focuses on building stability and democracy in the region and providing economic alternatives to illegal drug trafficking and narcoterrorism.

Afghanistan

- The United States led the world in providing humanitarian assistance and reconstruction efforts in Afghanistan. In FY 2002 and 2003, the United States provided over $900 million annually in aid to Afghanistan. The U.S. Congress passed the Afghanistan Freedom Support Act, which authorizes $3.47 billion for Afghanistan over fiscal years 2003–2006. In conjunction with U.S. combat operations to root out remnants of al-Qaida and Taliban terrorists, the President has announced a doubling of U.S. assistance to Afghanistan to over $2 billion this year. The Afghans are in the final stages of producing that country's first constitution in nearly 40 years. We are working hard with the government of Afghanistan to raise additional funds from friendly countries and to provide conditions supportive of national elections in 2004.

- More than 403,000 metric tons of food have been delivered since operations in Afghanistan began. The United States is assisting in the repair of more than 4,000 km of roads, reconstruction of 28 bridges, and rehabilitation of over 6,000 water wells, canals, dams and water systems. We rebuilt 72 clinics and hospitals as part of a 3-year $133 million health program and rehabilitated 200 schools. In 2002, over three million students went back to school (33 percent girls), double the number previously enrolled. The U.S. government has provided $10 million to rebuild the national radio network.

- The United States is the lead nation for establishing, training, and equipping the new Afghan National Army, committing over $400 million to this endeavor, and will provide similar amounts over the next several years. The United States is funding a facility to train police, judges and prosecutors in modern criminal justice principles and human rights.

Iraq

In addition to destroying terrorists, our strategy in Iraq—the central front for the war on terror—includes helping Iraqis assume responsibility for their own defense and future.

- In the short period of time since April 9, the day the Governing Council of Iraq declared to be their new independence day, the Coalition Provisional Authority (CPA) has made progress in the areas of security and political development.
- Judicial systems are beginning to function, recruiting for the New Iraqi Army has begun, and uncensored radio, TV, and print media are proliferating for the first time in decades.
- Currently, one police academy is operating in Baghdad and two others are being repaired and staffed. Approximately 46,000 Iraqi police are being rehired nationally, and 250 have completed the Transition and Integration Program. In addition, a civil defense force, facilities protection service, and Iraqi border guards will be involved in defending the security of their own nation.
- Universities and primary schools have reopened. CPA is creating a program to employ 300,000 Iraqis in public sector jobs. Local political infrastructures are beginning to emerge and some small businesses are bustling.
- Over 2,500 tons of pharmaceuticals have been delivered since May 1, 2003, with distribution throughout the country. Thousands of tons of food are flowing into Iraq weekly, and extensive projects are underway to increase water supplies and improve sewer systems.

CONCLUSION

The Administration is aggressively implementing the objectives of the President's *National Strategy for Homeland Security and National Strategy for Combating Terrorism,* rooting out terrorism abroad, forming international coalitions, equipping first responders with additional tools, enhancing intelligence capabilities, cutting off terrorist financing, securing our borders and transportation systems, enhancing response capabilities, developing medical countermeasures, and adding protective measures for critical infrastructure. All Federal agencies are integrating their efforts better than ever before and coordinating with state, local, and private entities to prevent future terrorist attacks on American soil.

International and domestic efforts have led to the removal of terrorist leaders and personnel and the disruption of numerous plots. Iraq and Afghanistan no longer provide state-sponsored or government-supported sanctuary and training grounds for terrorist groups. Initiatives by the United States have provided good governance, health and education, and given more countries the opportunity to be active participants in the global economy, strengthening states that terrorists might otherwise seek to exploit.

The United States is working aggressively with its regional and international partners to combat terrorism. The threat is global, and the United States is coordinating its response by building alliances, increasing capacity, and reducing vulnerabilities.

The United States and its allies have made great progress in the Global War on Terrorism, but we must maintain our dedication and vigilance. While many terrorists have been brought to justice, others are plotting to attack us. We will remain on the offensive, preemptively stopping terrorists seeking to do harm against the United States, its citizens and partners, and creating an international environment that is inhospitable to terrorists and all those who support them. Victory against terrorism will occur through the sustained efforts of a global coalition dedicated to ridding the world of those who seek to destroy our freedom and way of life.

Index

United States Department of Treasury, 147, 153, 209

United States Immigration and Naturalization Service, 161

United States Marine Corps, 60, 61, 151–52

United States Navy, 142n2, 145

United States Supreme Court, 160–61, 168, 169

unity of command, 151–52

unlawful combatants, 168–69

U.S. Automated Targeting System (ATS), 216

U.S.-Canada NEXUS program, 215

U.S.-Mexican Border Partnership, 215

U.S. Northern Command (USNORTHCOM), 139, 142, 214, 221

U.S. Visitor and Immigrant Status Indication Technology system (U.S. VISIT), 215

Vajpayee, Atal Bihari, 117

Vieira de Mello, Sergio, 73–74

Vietnam, 20

Vietnam War, 13, 18, 23–27, 33, 82

Villepin, Dominique, 41–42

Virginia, 207

visas, 214

Wahabis, 69, 73, 113, 117, 200

Walker, Sir Michael, 64

war, 59, 68, 143–46, 186

War of Atonement, 140–41

Washington Times, 52, 59

Washington Treaty, 41, 77, 88, 99, 194

Wassenaar Arrangement, 222, 223

Wassom, Herbert, 124

weapons of mass destruction, 9, 11, 17, 28, 42–44, 46–53, 94, 97, 187–90, 208, 221, 223. *See also* nuclear weapons

West Bank, 120–21

West, F. J. "Bing," 59

White, Thomas, 48, 138n1

wireless base stations, 128

wiretapping, 162, 164–65

Wolfowitz, Paul, 45, 63, 149, 194–95

women, 4–5, 71, 177, 178

Woolsey, R. James, 190

World Bank, 90, 122

A World Transformed (Bush and Scrowcroft), 99

World War II, 58, 160

Wye Plantation talks, 118

Wynne, Greville, 20

Ya'alon, Moshe, 119

Yugoslavia, 49, 99, 125

Zarqawi, Abu Musab al-, 208

Zia, President, 124

Zinni, Anthony C., 48

About the Author

A columnist for the *Washington Times*, Harlan Ullman is a contributor for Fox News, BBC, and Japan's NHK, the largest public station in the world. Widely published with a half dozen books to his credit, his last book, *Unfinished Business: Afghanistan, The Middle East and Beyond: Defusing the Dangers to America's Security*, won critical praise. He is also the principal author of the term "shock and awe."

After graduating with honors from the Naval Academy, Ullman served twenty years in the Navy, including over 150 combat missions and patrols in and off the coast of Vietnam in command of a Swift Boat and five tours on destroyers, the last tour in command. He also spent nearly two years in the Royal Navy, much of it at sea as ship's company in a frigate. He was later on the staff of the Royal Britannia Naval College at Dartmouth.

Ashore the Navy sent him to the Fletcher School of Law and Diplomacy where he was awarded a master's degree, a master's in law and diplomacy, and a PhD with emphasis on international affairs, finance, and economics. A former professor at the National War College, he directed the course of instruction in Military Strategy.

After leaving the service he joined the Center for Strategic and International Studies as Senior Fellow and director of the political-military and strategy programs. Currently he is a Senior Advisor at CSIS and a senior fellow at the Center for Naval Analyses, both in Washington, D.C.

He has served as a senior partner and vice chairman of two companies in the high technology area, and he currently serves as Chairman of a three-dimensional radar and electromagnetic inductive imaging company and advises a number of companies as well as senior officals in government. A distinguished visiting scholar at the Stevens Institute of Technology in New Jersey, he is part of a study on homeland security with particular reference to port security and assists the prestigious Royal United Service Institute in London in establishing a U.S. presence.

Harlan Ullman is married to the Hon. Julian M. Ullman. They reside in Georgetown with their welsh corgi.

The Naval Institute Press is the book-publishing arm of the U.S. Naval Institute, a private, nonprofit, membership society for sea service professionals and others who share an interest in naval and maritime affairs. Established in 1873 at the U.S. Naval Academy in Annapolis, Maryland, where its offices remain today, the Naval Institute has members worldwide.

Members of the Naval Institute support the education programs of the society and receive the influential monthly magazine *Proceedings* and discounts on fine nautical prints and on ship and aircraft photos. They also have access to the transcripts of the Institute's Oral History Program and get discounted admission to any of the Institute-sponsored seminars offered around the country.

The Naval Institute also publishes *Naval History* magazine. This colorful bimonthly is filled with entertaining and thought-provoking articles, first-person reminiscences, and dramatic art and photography. Members receive a discount on *Naval History* subscriptions.

The Naval Institute's book-publishing program, begun in 1898 with basic guides to naval practices, has broadened its scope to include books of more general interest. Now the Naval Institute Press publishes about one hundred titles each year, ranging from how-to books on boating and navigation to battle histories, biographies, ship and aircraft guides, and novels. Institute members receive significant discounts on the Press's more than eight hundred books in print.

Full-time students are eligible for special half-price membership rates. Life memberships are also available.

For a free catalog describing Naval Institute Press books currently available, and for further information about subscribing to *Naval History* magazine or about joining the U.S. Naval Institute, please write to:

Membership Department
U.S. Naval Institute
291 Wood Road
Annapolis, MD 21402-5034
Telephone: (800) 233-8764
Fax: (410) 269-7940
Web address: www.navalinstitute.org